The Idea of the Humanities

A Publication of the 75th Anniversary
of the University of Chicago

THE
Idea of the Humanities
AND OTHER ESSAYS
Critical and Historical

-»»-«««-

R. S. Crane

-»»-«««-

VOLUME TWO

THE UNIVERSITY OF CHICAGO PRESS
Chicago and London

Library of Congress Catalog Card Number: 66-30214

THE UNIVERSITY OF CHICAGO PRESS, CHICAGO & LONDON
The University of Toronto Press, Toronto 5, Canada

To Richard McKeon

Contents

III

Literary Criticism and Literary History

History versus Criticism in the Study of Literature

To the old question of what should be the principal aim of those departments in a university which are concerned with the art of literature two recent essays by two distinguished American professors of English have given sharply contrasting answers. The primary purpose of the literary scholar, argues Howard Mumford Jones in a vigorous paper in the *English Journal,* ought to be "historical, not aesthetic." He should be "in the broadest sense the historian of literature," the interpreter of its shifting fortunes in a world of time and change, the chronicler of its evolving ideas and forms; and he can properly leave to others, better equipped in point of temperament or training, the perplexing and uncertain task of passing critical judgments and settling values.[1] With no less vigor, on the other hand, John Livingston Lowes, in his presidential address before the Modern Language Association in December, 1933, declares himself the champion of criticism as the goal and only justification of literary study. "For the ultimate end of our research," he writes, "is *criticism,* in the fullest sense of an often misused word." And although, as a "fundamental prerequisite" to this end, he approves

Published in the *English Journal* (College Edition), Vol. 24 (1935); reprinted by permission of the National Council of Teachers of English. Several of the other papers in this volume, especially the two that immediately follow, are attempts to resolve the opposition between history and criticism on which this essay turns and should be read as enlargements or qualifications of its argument.

[1] "Literary Scholarship and Contemporary Criticism," *English Journal* (College Edition), 23 (1934): 740–58.

heartily of the contemporary devotion of literary scholars to the accumulation of "exhaustive and exact" historical learning, he hopes that we may in the future, without sacrificing any of our zeal for knowledge, recapture something of the humaner spirit of those older scholars who were also, and primarily, critics of the literature whose history they studied.[2]

The issue raised by these two essays is plainly one we ought to face. Are we to look upon ourselves as mainly historians of literature or as mainly critics? The answer we give to this question will determine not only the view we take of the proper place and function of our departments in the university, but also, to a greater or lesser extent, the policy we pursue with respect to courses and appointments, examinations and dissertations, and ultimately perhaps the orientation of research. It is one of the most important questions we can consider; and the only satisfactory way I know of approaching it is through a careful and, as far as can be, impartial analysis of the two programs of literary study between which we are asked to choose.

1

There should be no difficulty in discovering what is involved in a study of the art of literature which is primarily historical in its aims. We have only to ask ourselves what is involved in the writing of history in general and then to apply our conclusions in the light of what we know about the nature of literature considered as an art.

A history of anything, it goes without saying, must rest upon research among the documents of the past. From the documents, by processes of inference which need not concern us here, the historian derives elementary propositions of fact the subjects of which are persons living at some earlier time and the predicates characterizations of these persons with respect to what they did or suffered or to their habits or other traits of one kind or another. These propositions are the materials of history, but they are insufficient by themselves to make a history. Nor does a history yet exist when to these primary characterizing propositions the historian, by further research and demonstration, adds others which in conjunction with them state the "causes" of the characteristics or the actions. The essential condition of the existence of a history in the proper sense

2 *PMLA*, 48 (1933): 1399–1408.

of the word is the possibility of so organizing the characterizing and causal propositions given by research that a narrative results—a narrative the theme of which is a particular sequence or several connected sequences of change in human affairs, effected between such and such dates through the agency of such and such causes. The development of such a narrative gives us a history, and its unity, if it has unity, is always statable in a single narrative proposition the subject of which represents an entity capable of undergoing the kind of change expressed by the predicate. History, in short, is a discipline which has as its ultimate purpose the discovery and verification of intelligible narrative propositions about the past.[3]

That a fine art can profitably be made the object of historical research and interpretation is an assumption which, whether sound or not, has seldom been questioned in academic circles in recent times. I think that, properly qualified, the assumption is sound. But it is important that we should see exactly wherein the profit lies and what in general the nature and limitations of a history concerned with works of art must be.

Let us suppose that the art is literature, and let us begin at the bottom with the establishment of particular propositions of fact about the actions and habits of writers and the characteristics of individual writings. The range of possibilities is great; indeed, we are limited in what we can do at this level only by the availability of documents, the extent of our command of the requisite techniques of bibliography, paleography, philology, and the like, and the neces-

---

[3] The whole argument about literary history which follows rests upon two main assumptions concerning history in general: (1) that the proper subject matter of history is change in human affairs, and (2) that a good history should contain only propositions which, in addition to being in themselves both intelligible and demonstrable from the documents, are clearly relevant to the central narrative theme of the history. I am aware that many works which should perhaps be called histories have been constructed on principles very different from these and that, especially in Germany at the present time, a type of historical interpretation has come into wide vogue which aims at the development, not of narrative propositions about causally related sequences of events, but of characterizing propositions concerning the "spirit" or "structure" of epochs, and in which the criterion for the inclusion of statements about the acts or habits or productions of individual persons is not any kind of causal or narrative relevance but merely the possibility of construing them analogically as exemplifications of the particular *Geist* which the historian has discovered in the age. An extreme specimen of this kind of history is Paul Meissner's recent *Die geistesgeschichtlichen Grundlagen des englischen Literaturbarocks* (cf. the *Philological Quarterly*, 14 [1935]: 152–54). I have refrained, however, from introducing this distinction into the text: to have done so would have complicated the argument without altering in any fundamental way its conclusions.

sities of proof in issues of fact. We can explore, sometimes in minutest detail, the biographies of authors; we can settle the dates and the circumstances of composition of their works; we can restore the texts of these works to the form they were originally intended to have; we can interpret their language and clarify their thought; we can trace the sources of their quotations or allusions, we can enumerate their editions and translations; in a word, we can do all the things that learned editors and commentators have for generations done for the classics—and many of the non-classics—of the ancient and modern world.

At a somewhat higher level of historical complication than this are the researches which have as their object the establishment of causal propositions about the acts of writers or the characteristics of their works. Here again the field is wide. Authors of all ages, even those who have made the loudest boasts of originality, have had their "sources"; they have all written, at the very least, under the influence of some tradition of structure or style or thought; they have all been molded by the circumstances of their personal careers and by the political, economic, and social conditions in the midst of which they have lived. And it is frequently possible, by methods familiar to all scholars, to discover and prove genetic relationships of one or another of these various kinds.

By themselves, however, these researches, even those of the second type, do not constitute literary history. Their results are merely the materials out of which literary histories may be written, and the relevance of any of them to any history we may wish to construct can be determined only when the theme of that history—a narrative proposition—has been discovered. Like the historian of any other form of human activity, the historian of literature is the chronicler and interpreter of change; he is fulfilling his function only when the knowledge he has of the literary past is integrated into an explanatory narrative of the transformations undergone, during some determinate period, by some writer or some group of writers or some body of readers with respect to some literary problem or ideal.

It is, then, with the nature of the narrative propositions that may be formed about literature that we must concern ourselves if we wish to understand the possibilities and limitations of literary history. Now in a sense these propositions are not about literature at all.

Their subjects, when the propositions are stated in a primary form, are not works or the properties of works but persons—writers or readers as the case may be. "During the later years of his life Dryden made increasing use of alexandrine lines and triplets in order to vary the rhythm of his couplets." "Between about 1650 and 1690 English writers of prose gradually abandoned the Senecan model of prose style for a more purely Augustan ideal." "After 1830 French readers rapidly lost their enthusiasm for the poems of Ossian." "During the later years of the eighteenth century the managers of London theaters became increasingly interested in developing landscape scenery in the 'picturesque' style." It is true that propositions like these—and they are typical of the narrative propositions of literary history—may be stated in such a way as to suggest that the change taking place is a change undergone by some specifically literary entity. For example: "English prose style evolved between about 1650 and 1690 from a Senecan to a more purely Augustan model." But it requires only a simple analysis to see that this transformation is merely a grammatical one and that it is only in a derived sense that the change in question can be predicated of "English prose style" instead of "English writers of prose." A literary history, like any other history, is a narrative of the changing habits, beliefs, attitudes, tastes, and purposes of individual persons and groups or organizations of persons living in particular times and places; it is not a history of literature but of literary men. It ought, to be sure, to have unity; and unity in a narrative history is impossible except in terms of some characteristic which remains constant through the predicates of the constituent propositions; so that in one sense a literary history can be said to be about (say) the rise of a literary form or the development of a style. But this should not blind us to the fact that its real subject is the changing behavior, during a particular period, of a particular writer or group of writers interested in a particular literary problem and influenced by a particular complex of conditions.[4]

---

[4] In stating this point I have avoided calling attention to the ambiguity involved in the word "change" when used to characterize the two histories represented by the propositions about Dryden and the seventeenth-century English prose writers, respectively. As a matter of fact, whereas the change described in the first of these propositions is an actual alteration in the habits of an individual author who himself retains his identity during the process, the change predicated of English writers of prose between 1650 and 1690 is change only in the sense in which a statistical curve of unemployment for a given section of the American population between (say) 1927 and 1935 may be

A further point: If we examine typical narrative propositions of literary history, we see that such knowledge as they give us of the art of literature is exclusively—and necessarily—information about its accidental characteristics. It is impossible that there should be, for example, a history of tragedy as such, or of lyric poetry, or of the epic. These terms are universals; they represent natures which do not change, however differently at different times they may be defined by critics or embodied by artists in particular works; as essences they lend themselves only to general and scientific, not to historical, statement. We can, it is true, construct narrative propositions in which certain authors interested in writing tragedies (let us say French authors of the seventeenth century) are said to have undergone such and such a change either in their conception of what tragedies should be or in their use of a particular device (for example, the unity of time or place) for realizing this conception in their works. But these propositions tell us nothing about the nature of tragedy as a form of art; they presuppose, indeed, that we already have such knowledge, and confine themselves, as historical propositions must, to pointing out, and possibly also explaining, a particular sequence of changes in the *conventions* of the art effected by particular writers in a particular period. Their subject matter, in other words, is not what must be in the given form of literature but what for various accidental motives a particular group of literary men have agreed should be.

For this reason, and also for another reason which will appear presently, the narratives of literary history must remain indifferent to questions of literary values. Values, to be sure, may enter, but they can be only the values held and propagated by the actors in the

---

said to represent change. That is to say, what remains fixed is not the group, "English writers of prose," since that is in a constant flux as writers die or cease to write and other writers make their appearance, but simply the fact that during the years in question there were always writers interested in the problem of English prose style. What changes, moreover, is not necessarily the stylistic habits of any of the individual writers belonging to the group—though there may, of course, be instances of such change—but merely the numerical proportions existing at different times during the period 1650–90 between the writers who solved the problem of style by imitating Seneca and those who solved it by adopting Augustan models. The distinction is of considerable importance for the general theory of history, but it obviously does not affect the point made in the text that at bottom literary histories, whether of the one type or the other, are about, not literature itself (which as a body of created objects can undergo no change), but the habits and tastes of particular literary men.

history; they cannot be the values of the historian. To violate this principle is not merely to risk turning the history into propaganda for a special esthetic creed; it is also to introduce into the selection of the constituent propositions hopelessly conflicting criteria. Let us take one of the narrative propositions cited in illustration of an earlier point: "Between about 1650 and 1690 English writers of prose gradually abandoned the Senecan model of prose style for a more purely Augustan ideal." Let us assume that we know what is meant by the two end terms contained in the predicate of this proposition and let us ask ourselves how we should be guided in selecting the numerous propositions about individual authors and works which would be necessary to a fully developed historical treatment of the theme. Clearly, in the first place, any propositions would be relevant of which the subjects were English prose writers of the period named and the predicates characteristics of their writings which could be brought under one or another of the two terms between which the change in question is asserted to have taken place —and this irrespective of whether these writers, as writers, were good, bad, or indifferent. Clearly also, in the second place, any propositions would be relevant, no matter what their subjects, the assertion of which in conjunction with propositions of the first group could be supposed to afford some kind of causal explanation of the change from the one fashion in prose style to the other. That is all. In other words, there are only two properly historical grounds on which the propositions of a narrative history can be selected—narrative grounds and causal grounds. Now it is conceivable that the authors and works selected by these criteria might be the same as the authors and works selected by criteria of a purely literary sort such as are appropriate to an anthology of the best prose (in the judgment of the compiler) written in England during the seventeenth century; and the importance given to them in the two books might also conceivably coincide. But such a harmony between historical and esthetic standards of relevance would be entirely accidental. The criteria proper to a history and to a critical anthology are essentially different, and it is not in the interest of excellence in either form that they should be mixed. That the distinction has not always been clearly recognized is shown by the many attacks on modern historians of literature for what is said to be their excessive attention to undistinguished and minor works. These attacks, insofar as they rest on esthetic grounds, are beside the point when it is a question of publications professing to be histories and not works of criticism, for it is clear that in a history propositions about minor and undistinguished works may be quite as relevant, narratively or causally, as anything that may be said about the major and distinguished works which alone, properly, interest the critical anthologist. It is one of the conditions of adequacy in a literary history, in short, that the historian should not be too insistent on his literary standards.[5]

Finally, it is well to observe how far the writer of a literary history who conceives of his task as a historian should is limited in what he can appropriately say of particular literary works. In one respect, indeed, his case is no worse than that of the esthetic critic: neither the one nor the other has any means at his disposal whereby to express in words the unique combination of form and matter which constitutes the individuality of a poem. That is something forever inaccessible either to statement or to explanation: for critic no less than historian *individuum est ineffabile*. There is, however, an important difference. For whereas the critic, as we shall see later, can center his attention solely, if he wishes, on particular masterpieces considered as organic wholes and utilize all the resources of esthetic analysis in an attempt to seize as much as possible of their distinguishing structures and styles, the historian, if he is to remain truly a historian, must restrict his characterizations of individual literary works to the traits, whatever they may be, which serve to link these works one with another in the particular causal sequence he is trying to exhibit. A series of critical portraits, even when it is a series unified by such a proposition as "Between 1740 and 1770 English writers produced in rapid succession at least a dozen masterpieces of prose fiction," is not a history. Many so-called histories, it is true, have been built on formulas precisely like this; but, however valuable they may be as collections of literary essays chronologically arranged,

[5] To say this is not of course to deny that the historian of literature must be also a critic in the sense that he must possess an analytical understanding of the art with which he deals: the better the analysis, indeed, the better the history, other things being equal. Nor is it to imply that the literary historian should not be guided, in his choice of problems for investigation, by judgments of relative literary value or importance. The point is merely that he cannot, without sacrificing the virtues proper to a history, allow his esthetic preferences to control his selection of facts or to color his interpretation of the changes he is engaged in tracing. Historical exposition is one thing, criticism is another.

they are not really histories since they lack an essential element of all narrative constructions, namely, continuity. They can be made into histories only through the discovery of some characteristic common to the writers (other than merely their capacity for writing masterpieces of a certain kind) which persists through the period in question and is the subject of change—for example, an interest in a particular technical problem or an attachment to a particular model of style. And when this constant element is found it will invariably be seen that an adequate development of the resulting narrative proposition requires by no means all the statements which a critic would consider appropriate to an esthetic analysis of the same body of works. For the historian as historian is interested in individual literary productions only insofar as they can be treated (1) as manifestations of the special characteristic which is undergoing change or (2) as "events" or sources of influence helping to account for the change. And in either case he is less concerned with exhibiting those combinations of traits which define, however far from exhaustively, the individuality of a work than with tracing in it the reflection of a common technique or tradition of thought.

What, then, is the profit to be derived from the writing and teaching of literary history? A simple answer can be given. It is the same kind of profit that is to be derived from the historical study of changing fashions in ideas or beliefs or manners or anything else—namely, the satisfaction of one's desire to know and to understand the significant transformations in human affairs, and, though this does not always follow, the cultivation of a less dogmatic attachment to the conventions and prejudices of one's own age. These are both important goods: whether they are sufficient to justify us in making of the pursuit of literary history, with all its limitations on the esthetic side, the principal object of literary study in a university can be determined only after we have seen what is involved in an alternative program of criticism.

2

We shall understand here by literary criticism any reasoned discourse concerning works of imaginative literature the statements in which are primarily statements about the works themselves and appropriate to their character as productions of art. To describe criticism in this way is to differentiate it, in the first place, from literary appreciation, although it is not to say that appreciation—by which I mean the direct sensory and imaginative intuition of literary works with whatever emotion may accompany such intuitions—is not a most important end, as it is certainly a necessary condition, of any criticism that we may undertake. Good criticism, indeed, will always spring from appreciation in the critic and it ought to lead to appreciation in his readers; but in itself, as reasoned discourse, it is bound to be at once something less than appreciation and something more. Something less because, as we have seen, no body of statements about a work of art can ever hope to communicate with any adequacy that immediate knowledge of the unity and individuality of the work which is ours as we read it; something more because that immediate knowledge, however rich and vivid it may be, still falls short of the kind of *understanding* of literary productions which criticism, whatever else it may attempt to do, seeks first of all to attain. And this brings us to a second point, also implied in our description. The essential thing about the understanding to which the literary critic aspires is that it is understanding of literary works in their character as works of art. It is not criticism but psychology when we treat poems or novels as case books and attempt to discover in them not the art but the personality of their authors. It is not criticism but history or sociology when we read imaginative writings for what they may tell us about the manners or thought or "spirit" of the age which produced them. It is not criticism but ethical culture when we use them primarily as means of enlarging and enriching our experience of life or of inculcating moral ideals. It is not criticism but autobiography when we content ourselves with stating our personal preferences with regard to them or the adventures of our souls in their presence. Criticism as we shall understand it is not any of these things; it is simply the disciplined consideration, at once analytical and evaluative, of literary works as works of art.

As such it has, to borrow Lowes's phrase, a number of fundamental prerequisites. In the first place, if it is indeed to be reasoned discourse and not merely an irresponsible recording of impressions, it must obviously rest upon some kind of theoretical comprehension of literature itself. It is only in terms of general propositions about metaphors, for example, that we can deal intelligently with the imagery of a given poem; it is only in the light of what we know about the general nature of tragedy that we can comment to any purpose on the peculiar structure of the tragedy before us. There would be no need to reiterate these truisms were it not that, under the influence of the prevalent anti-intellectualism, they have frequently been denied by critics who have professed to see in the process of criticism only an exercise of sensibility or at most of sensibility guided by historical facts. It is one of the weaknesses of the program of literary studies suggested by Lowes that he gives no place, among the prerequisites of criticism, to the theory of the art with which it is concerned. Yet theory, however much it may be denied or neglected, is inescapable: if we examine the writings of even the most impressionistic of critics, we are certain to find, lurking behind the particular characterizations and judgments, a more or less consistent set of general propositions. It is not a question, then, whether principles are essential to criticism or not, but merely what body of principles should be selected and how far it is desirable that they should be explicitly recognized by the critic himself. On the first of these questions there is no need to be dogmatic; so long as the theory adopted is really a theory of the art of literature and not of something else—for example, not a theory of ethics as with the New Humanists or of politics as with the Marxians—and so long as the analytical devices it provides are reasonably exhaustive and consistent among themselves, it is indifferent for the purposes of this discussion what its philosophical affinities may be.[6] Not so, however, with the second question; here a more positive answer is required if the problem is, as we have been assuming, the orientation of literary studies toward a reasoned and disciplined consideration of particular works of art. Theory we must have in any case; but surely much will be gained, especially in the way of securing a common ground of agreement within the limits of our philosophical approach, if the principles with which we operate are given explicit statement and subjected to rational examination before being used in the criticism of individual works.

But principles, even the most adequate and clearly formulated principles, are not enough. The study of particular writings in the light of a general theory of literature is, indeed, the critic's central

6 See on this point a suggestive essay by Paul Goodman, "Neo-Classicism, Platonism, and Romanticism," in the *Journal of Philosophy*, 31 (1934): 148–63.

task. But it is not a task which can be trusted to perform itself, and it will always be a task badly performed if the critic, however sound his principles, is unable to distinguish between those which are appropriate to the composition before him and those which are not. There have been many critics with the most admirable theories—Dr. Johnson is occasionally an example—who yet failed egregiously when it was a question of applying them to cases, just as there have also been critics—I. A. Richards may be mentioned—who, in spite of holding inferior theories, have yet written excellent "practical criticism." The moral is not that we should contemn principles on the romantic ground that they are necessarily at odds with taste, but simply that we should recognize the importance—as a second prerequisite of good criticism—of a sensibility in the critic sufficiently subtle and sufficiently disciplined by experience to enable him to see what elements in his general theory are applicable to the circumstances and what are not. The great critics are those who have shown the most tact and feeling in the always delicate process of bringing reason to bear on works of art.

But—and we now come to a third prerequisite—tact and feeling are also sometimes not enough. They are not enough, obviously, if the text is bad and it becomes necessary to restore it or to establish it anew. They are not enough if our understanding of the writer's language is inadequate to a correct grammatical construing of what he has written. They are not enough if there are difficulties of allusion or implication in the work which we cannot conquer without special knowledge such as the author took for granted in the contemporaries for whom he wrote.

That these simple facts and others like them afford a sufficient justification for much textual and philological research and for at least the more intelligent of the explanatory commentaries that have been prepared for many of the great literary classics can hardly be a matter for serious debate. But the problem of the relation of historical learning to criticism has been enormously complicated in recent times as a result of the devotion of university departments of literature to the distinctively modern enterprise of literary biography and historiography. There are not many professors of literature among us, it is true, who would unhesitatingly agree with Jones that their primary purpose should be historical, not esthetic. Most of them wish to be looked upon as at least potential critics, and in the meantime, being engaged in researches on the private lives of authors, the sources and genesis and influence of works, the development of themes and forms, the vicissitudes of the theater and the book trade, they undertake to vindicate their studies against attack by insisting that, since before we can understand or evaluate we must have facts, the more we can learn about the history of literature the better our criticism, when we finally come to write it, is bound to be. Even Lowes, for all the severe things he has to say about the increase of specialization in literary research, seems to be concerned simply with recalling to our minds the proper end—namely, criticism—which our zealous accumulation of historical data should serve, not at all with inquiring whether in the light of that end the accumulation itself can be justified in all its parts. Yet that is precisely the question which, if we would see clearly what is involved in a program of literary studies oriented toward criticism, we must try to answer.

Let us grant—it is, indeed, implied in the theory of criticism already stated—that before a critic can properly apply his principles to a particular work of literature he must endeavor to understand the work itself as a composition of words expressing some kind of thought. But what are we to mean by "understand"? Is it to understand a piece of imaginative writing to know under what circumstances or as the result of what experiences of the author it was conceived, from what earlier writings it drew its materials, to what class of readers it was addressed and how it pleased them, what place it had in the history of the *genre* to which it belonged, of what contemporary movements of thought or taste or of what underlying political or social conflicts it was a manifestation? Clearly, in one sense of the word "understand," to understand a work of literature is to know such things as these about it, and it is to this sense of the word that appeal is always made when questions are raised concerning the value, for criticism, of a historical approach. But the term obviously also has another meaning which, as applied to the study of literary productions, carries a quite different set of implications. We understand a work, in this second sense, when we are able to give to the words and phrases it contains the precise denotation and connotation intended by the author, when we can feel sure that none of its essential allusions have escaped us, when we can be confident that, if it includes ideas, we have apprehended them justly and adequately, when we are no longer perplexed by any of its idiosyncrasies of expression or thought.

It is important that we should distinguish sharply between these two meanings of "understand"—between the meaning in which to understand is equivalent to knowing *why* an author said what he said (in a genetic or historical sense) and that in which it is equivalent to knowing *what* it is that he is saying and his reasons for saying it (in the sense of its artistic rationale). For if criticism is essentially a discipline concerned with the analysis and evaluation of particular literary works in the light of general principles of esthetics, it is evident that the kind of understanding the critic requires is primarily, though not exclusively, understanding of the second type. No literary work is other than it is or better or worse than it is because of any circumstances of its origin or of any personal peculiarities of its author or of any filiation it may have with other works or of any reflection in it of the philosophical doctrines or the economic interests of its age. If information about any of these matters helps the critic to approach his authors more sympathetically or with fewer prejudices, well and good; it has thereby justified itself in a humble and negative way. But the learning which criticism positively needs if it is properly to perform its task is not learning of this genetic sort at all; it is merely the kind of learning—equally necessary of course to the historian—which aims at a recovery[7] of the words and sense of a literary work when these have been lost by reason of the lapse of time. Any erudition which serves the purposes of such recovery is to be welcomed, subject to the law of diminishing returns. Erudition which simply enables the critic to say *why* an author has written in a certain manner may be useful for literary history, but it has little or no relevance to the ends of critical interpretation or appraisal. It is not necessary to know the "sources" of a tragedy or a novel to discuss its formal characteristics, although such knowledge may be useful in sharpening the critic's observations; and there is no way in which propositions about an author's private life can properly influence a judgment on the poetic value of one of his lyric poems.

7 The word is Kenneth Burke's, in an article which contains an admirable brief statement of the point here under consideration. See *The Dial*, 79 (1925): 167.

Were we to apply this distinction in detail to the literary scholarship of the past generation, we should find, no doubt, that a good deal of what has been done, especially on the more important writers, is thoroughly germane to the needs of criticism. There has been much competent and at the same time esthetically useful recovery —of the texts of masterpieces hitherto corrupt, of their meaning in the broader as well as the narrower sense of the term. In particular, the growing disposition on the part of experts in philosophy to apply their special knowledge to the exegesis of literary works has yielded fresh and illuminating interpretations of some of the major classics of medieval and modern times: witness, for example, the brilliant essays of Etienne Gilson on *La Queste del Saint Graal,* on Rabelais, and on the *Nouvelle Héloïse* of Rousseau.[8]

All this is true; but what of the great body of purely genetic and historical investigations which have absorbed the energies of so many professors of literature and the results of which have formed the content of so many courses in colleges and universities? Let us be frank with ourselves: if what we want is literary criticism, very little of all this is to our purpose, except in the incidental and negative way to which I have referred. It is not becoming in this connection to speak of one's colleagues, but one can at least allude to oneself. I have recently printed an article, which I should like to think has some historical value, on the role played by the Latitudinarian wing of the English clergy between about 1660 and 1725 in disseminating the complex of ethical ideas which has come to be known as eighteenth-century "sentimentalism." Now it happens that the influence of this particular current of doctrine can be clearly traced in the writings of one of the greatest literary artists of the middle eighteenth century—Henry Fielding. It was indeed with a view to accounting for certain peculiarities of Fielding's novels, especially the conception of moral goodness which determined the delineation of some of his characters, that my investigations were originally undertaken, and their results, I venture to think, should be of interest to the future literary historian seeking to formulate with greater precision than has been possible hitherto the place of *Tom Jones* or *Amelia* in the evolution of English popular thought. But what of the student who wished to approach these works not as

8 See his *Les Idées et les lettres* (Paris, 1932), and his remarks on Guido Cavalcanti, *Criterion,* 12 (1932–33): 106–12.

historical events but as productions of art? Would he learn anything from my essay that would enable him to analyze their structural and stylistic qualities more completely than earlier critics had been able to do or to assess more justly their excellencies and defects as great imaginative creations? I hardly think he would—certainly not enough to justify all my labors in research! In similar manner I could expose the futility—for criticism—of many other things I have written: essays in biography, in source study, in the development of literary themes, and the like. But I have said enough, perhaps, to indicate how questionable is the assumption, cherished by many professors of literature, that most if not all of their researches in literary history can be defended, not as history merely, but also as a "fundamental prerequisite" of criticism. It cannot be done: if what we want is criticism, we must have principles, we must have sensibility, we must have such learning as is indispensable to the proper reading and interpretation of texts, but that is all: of literary history as such, in its distinctively genetic and narrative aspects, there is seldom need to take account.[9]

It follows, if what has been said so far is sound, that a program of literary studies based on criticism would be a very different program from one directed toward literary history. Its characteristic subject matter would not be writers and the transformations in taste and technique which can be traced among them; it would be imaginative works considered with respect to those qualities which can truly be said to be timeless, not of course in the sense that they have always been apprehended and judged in the same way by different readers, but in the sense that they can be adequately discerned and evaluated in the light of general principles quite apart from any knowledge of their origin or historical filiation. Such a program, moreover, although it would insist on the strictest philological standards of exegesis and textual criticism, would not aim so much at knowledge in the ordinary sense of the word as at discriminating enjoyment

---

[9] For the proper reading and interpretation of texts the kind of learning that goes to the making of literary histories may, indeed, frequently be essential: *The Dunciad* is a case in point. But in general it can be said that the kinds of erudition most important for the critic to acquire are those which are ordered by such disciplines as the history of language, the history of ideas, the history of politics, and the history of society and manners. And what is needed even here is not so much the history itself, in the sense of the narrative interpretation constructed by the historian, as the documents and particular propositions given by research.

and evaluation; and its discipline would lie, not primarily in the establishment and ordering of propositions of fact, but rather in the discovery and application of principles and the cultivation of sensitivity to literary texts. Its products, in short, if it were successful, would be good judges of literature and not merely learned men; and its peculiar value would be measured by the extent to which it helped to conserve, in the midst of a university dominated by science and history, the proper interests of art.

3

It should be evident now what answer I would have us give, as the only departments in the university primarily concerned with literature, to the question posed at the beginning of this essay.

Literary history, I should insist, is a good thing, and it is surely one of our functions to see that its values are safeguarded in the academic world of the future. As a handmaid to criticism its importance is much less than has sometimes been thought, but one can easily go too far in contemning the real services, humble as they may be and in many respects chiefly negative, which it is capable of offering to the interpreter of literary works. It should not be forgotten that if we can now read Dante or Chaucer or Shakespeare in reasonably satisfactory texts and with a greater assurance of grasping their intended meaning than our predecessors could have had, and if we are no longer blind to whole ages of literary production which seemed without merit to the dogmatic critics of the eighteenth century, the credit must be given mainly to the antiquarian and historical zeal of several generations of scholars, comparatively few of whom were critics of any note. It should not be forgotten, either, that in the recent past, at a time when the reigning criticism both within the universities and outside was impressionism of the most irresponsible variety, the growing vogue of historical studies was an important influence in cultivating respect for firsthand knowledge and in providing a much-needed antidote to sentimentality. These are both sound considerations; but the ultimate argument for literary history—the only argument, indeed, that can justify the greater part of what is done in its name—must be, not its value to literary criticism, but the contributions it can make, along with its sister discipline the literary history of ideas, to what everyone will grant is a major concern of any university—the general history of culture. How significant our contributions to this subject can be when compared with those of historians in other fields it its hardly for us to say. Certain it is that as historians—that is, as interpreters of past changes in literary conventions and styles—we have all too frequently merited the criticism that, however expert we may be in documentary research, we have still to master the art of ordering our data in illuminating narrative sequences, and that, chiefly because of this, we tend to dissipate our energy in detailed investigations directed to no visible larger ends. Clearly there is room for much improvement in our techniques of historical narration and in our organization of research; but this is not to say that even now we do not as literary historians play a useful and indeed essential part in the general historical program of the university—and a part, moreover, which only we can play. It is one of the peculiarities of history that although it is entirely concerned with the discovery and organization of particular facts, it nevertheless demands in its practitioners more than a particular or documentary knowledge of the various subject matters with which it deals. The good historian must also be, in the older and broader sense of the word, a scientist; and so if we cannot rely on professional students of "history" to give us technically competent histories of philosophy or of certain types of economic transformations, no more can we trust them to write in a satisfying way of the development of any of the arts. We must do this ourselves, drawing upon what theoretical understanding of the nature of literature we possess; but in doing it we should recognize that what we are doing is history and nothing else, and that consequently our appropriate affiliation, for the time being at least, is with that department in the university the sole function of which is the investigation and interpretation of the human past in terms of change.

When all this is said, however, it cannot be denied that literary history, as one of the two major interests of our departments, has occupied too privileged a place, especially during recent years. However vigorously on occasion we may have professed our allegiance to criticism, it has not been criticism but history to which we have devoted our really serious energy and thought. Research has been our watchword, and with results we need not be ashamed of; but for the most part we have narrowed the meaning of the term until it has come to stand, not broadly for responsible and original inquiries of all sorts, but specifically for inquiries among documents pursued for strictly historical ends. Our teaching meantime has taken a similar course. We have been accustomed to lecture, to undergraduates as well as to graduates, on details of biography, on the genesis and development of "types," on the social backgrounds and the stylistic and intellectual tendencies characteristic of the "periods" of literary growth. We have allowed ourselves to consider, in suggesting subjects for dissertations, only problems for which the historical method provides the appropriate solution. We have tended, in our examinations for higher degrees and in many of our more elementary examinations as well, to subordinate questions about the artistic qualities of texts to questions of a bibliographical or historical nature about writers and the movements of which they were a part. And it is no secret that the scholars in our departments who have attained the highest academic distinctions and who have had the greatest influence in the shaping of our programs have been with few exceptions men whose competence has been chiefly demonstrated by their contributions to historical learning.

The consequences, for the specifically esthetic education of our students, have been—what we all, when we are quite honest with ourselves, know them to be. It is perhaps only indirectly our fault that the majority of the freshmen who come to us from the schools are unable to read a page of poetry or a serious play with any comprehension, I will not say of the subtleties of its form, but even of its plainest literal sense. But it is our fault that of the seniors who have had the advantage of majoring in our departments and of taking and passing our courses, an almost equally large proportion show themselves, when put to the test, to be in little better case—more widely read, no doubt, and historically much better informed, but similarly incapable of intelligently discussing an imaginative work in terms appropriate to its nature. And it is our unforgivable fault that we go on assuming, year in and year out, that the masters of arts and doctors of philosophy whom we send into the world as qualified teachers and scholars in literature are really competent to do anything more adequate to the needs of their profession than the kind of historical investigation which has been their principal exercise in the graduate school. Some of them are, it is true; but we can take little credit to ourselves when such exceptions appear; for the most part we have not taught them—they have been self-taught; and of the greater number of their contemporaries in our graduate courses we know all too well how naive and inarticulate they can be when we ask them to comment on any peculiarly literary aspect of a text—any aspect, indeed, except its external history and, within limits, its thought. It is surely no reason for complacency to realize, as we are often enough forced to do, that in comparison with students of the better sort trained in the schools and universities of England and France, our students, even our most capable ones, tend to be esthetic barbarians.

The remedy I propose is nothing less than a thoroughgoing revision, in our departments of literature, of the policy which has dominated them—or most of them—during the past generation. Ample provision should still be made, especially on the graduate level, for courses and seminars in literary history and the history of ideas. But there should be fewer of these, at least of lecture courses, even on the graduate level, than are now given; and in undergraduate teaching the work offered in the history of literature should be frankly recognized as significant chiefly for what contributions it can make to the general historical culture of the student rather than for any peculiar value it may have in itself as a part of his literary education; it should, in fact, be given, whenever possible, in close connection with courses in political history, social history, and the history of thought. For the parts of our present program thus displaced I would substitute, and this at all levels from the college through the Ph.D., studies of two distinct though closely related sorts. The first of these would comprise systematic work in the theory, generally of all the fine arts, and specifically of the art of literature; it would be of great advantage if this work could be organized and conducted, not by particular departments of literature separately, but by the division of the humanities as a whole. In order to give it substance in the beginning and also to guarantee a sufficiently catholic point of view, it might be desirable to base it definitely on a reading and critical discussion of the principal classics of esthetic theory, in poetry, music, and the plastic arts, from the Greeks to our own contemporaries; the material is abundant and much of it is of a character to provide an admirable stimulus to that further development of the theory of the fine arts which ought to be one of the major objects of such a program as we are considering. But the end of theory, for criticism, is application; and so the second of our two groups of studies would consist of exercises in the reading and literary *explication* of literary texts. How excellent a discipline such exercises are capable of becoming in the hands of an expert and sensitive teacher there is no need to say. The essential thing is that they should not be allowed to degenerate into linguistic or historical investigations or into mere occasions for the parading of personal tastes, but should be kept constantly directed toward their proper objective—the text itself considered as a production of art to be read appreciatively for its own sake in the light of relevant knowledge and of the principles of its kind.

Were such a scheme of studies to be introduced as the major part of the program in literature for the bachelor's degree and as an important part of the program for the two higher degrees, several consequences would certainly follow. We should find it necessary to alter completely our present reigning notions of the content and method of our examinations. We should be under strong pressure to discover new types of problems for research. Above all we should be obliged to set up different standards of scholarly competence for the selection of new members of the staff.

I have no illusions about the difficulties we should encounter were we to undertake the reform I have been urging. The personnel we need—where is it to be found? We have many good historical scholars in our profession, but of equally excellent critics, alas, only a few. Men of the type of the older impressionists we could hardly use, and as for the remnants of the Humanists, there is little to be hoped for from the kind of principles—essentially political and ethical rather than esthetic in character—for which they have mainly stood. In the end we should doubtless have to rely chiefly on the younger generation of students and instructors, many of whom show much promise for the kind of literary study I have had in mind and a genuine enthusiasm for its advancement. But the difficulty of finding suitable teachers is not the only problem we should have to face. It would be necessary to have properly prepared students as well, and to give us these there is required something like a renaissance in general education at the level of the high school and junior college.

Perhaps such a renaissance is coming, bringing with it the revived study of the classics in some form or other, bringing with it also the renewed cultivation of those ancient arts of reading and writing upon which any criticism of literature worthy of the name must be firmly based. It may be, though the signs are none too clear. But in any case, and whatever the obstacles, we can at least settle in our minds what a sound program in criticism ought to involve, and having done that we can take such steps as may suggest themselves to insure its realization in the not too distant future.

Criticism as Inquiry;
or, The Perils of the "High Priori Road"

THERE WAS A TIME, in the early and middle thirties, when the problem of criticism, as it imposed itself more and more insistently on American departments of literature, seemed a fairly simple one. The great thing was to make criticism respectable, by winning for it a place in the curriculum, including the graduate curriculum, at least coordinate with linguistics, philology, literary history, and the history of ideas. What is surprising now, when one remembers the dust and heat engendered by that effort, is the relative ease with which the political victory of criticism was brought about. There are many good professors of literature who still look upon the result as a calamity; and painful tensions still exist in many departments between those who claim to be only scholars and those who call themselves primarily critics. But the trend of affairs is unmistakable; I might point to the solemn conclusion which I am told was reached not long ago in a gathering of chairmen of English departments, to the effect that, whatever one might think of it, criticism is here to stay; or to the multiplication in many universities of "critical" courses and even "critical" dissertations; or, most significantly, to the well-nigh universal opening up of the learned journals to papers which, if only by default, must be put in the same category.

It was probably inevitable that the early enthusiasts for this revo-

Based on a lecture at the University of Michigan, 1957; not previously published.

25

lution in the academic study of literature should tend to set criticism in rather sharp antithesis to the established modes of literary scholarship. I did this myself, in 1935, in the essay which immediately precedes this one in the present volume. I should not want, even twenty years later, to repudiate all I said in that paper, certainly not its central thesis of the importance of criticism or the whole of the analysis by which I distinguished criticism from literary history. But I should undoubtedly have framed my argument in somewhat different terms had I been able to foresee all that was to happen in the following two decades.

For it was possible to react against the narrowness of the prevailing philological and historical disciplines in either of two ways—a progressive-conservative way or a root-and-branch way; and what I failed to predict was that the immediate future at least belonged to those radical reformers of literary study—soon to be called, loosely, "new critics"—who were in revolt not merely against the limitations of the older learning but, as it has turned out, against the very conception of intellectual method that give it its status as a learning.

The limitations of the older literary studies were real enough. The great historical scholars of the last age—the age of Gaston Paris, Bédier, Lanson, W. P. Ker, Grierson, Kittredge, Manly, Lowes—were not indeed either hostile or indifferent, as a group, to criticism, nor did they all neglect to study, as we are often told was the case, "the text itself." One can, however, justly say two things of them: first that their criticism was in the main notably inferior in rigor and sophistication to their philology and history; and, second, that the problems which most excited them, and to which their techniques were best suited, were problems that turned rather on the material contents and the historical circumstances of literary works than on their distinctive character as works of art.

It happens that we have become more concerned than these scholars were about questions of the latter sort; that is why we have gone in so generally for criticism. But the burden of proof is surely on those advocates of criticism who would minimize the importance, even for their own studies, of the problems with which the older scholars mainly occupied themselves. It was doubtless necessary, in the middle thirties, to use rhetorical shock tactics to overcome the hostility to criticism of some of their less catholic-minded descendants. But that need have been no more than a passing phase. For there was little reason, once the friends of criticism had got a hearing, why they should not help to reconstruct university literary studies in a spirit of conservative reform: carrying on and reinvigorating the philological and historical tradition, and at the same time, and in this context, developing what that tradition had been relatively weak in—systematic training in the various modes of critical analysis and judgment. So far as I am concerned, that is the only revolution in favor of criticism I have ever been seriously committed to. Anything more subversive of the older order of teaching and research has seemed to me not only bad in itself but bad for criticism; and I have been embarrassed by René Wellek's and Austin Warren's commendation of the Department of English at Chicago for having "boldly reoriented" its whole graduate program "from the historical to the critical." The "critical" is there, assuredly, but so also is the "historical," and in such a relation to the "critical," in intention at least, that neither can be separated from the other.

My first complaint, then, against the persons most actively concerned in the revival of criticism in the universities is that many of them have done criticism, as well as historical scholarship, a bad service by continuing to talk in terms of the antithesis between the two which perhaps had some rhetorical or political justification two decades ago, but surely no other justification then or since. There can be no adequate criticism that is not solidly based on the history of the art with which it is concerned.

But I do not want to dwell any longer on this first aspect of the critical revolt against the older literary learning. For something much more seriously troubling to me than this has been happening at the same time, the effects of which show no signs of disappearing. I mean the emergence within criticism itself of modes of thinking about literature which make not merely for a separation in practice between critical discussion and historical scholarship, but for a sharp and irreconcilable opposition in principle between the two fields. It is about this second, and much more significant consequence of the critical revival, that I want to speak; and I have a special excuse for doing so at the University of Michigan, since it was here, many years ago, that I was first made aware of the basic issue that I think is involved.

It is customary to say that whereas literary scholarship, in its inquiries into texts, sources, conventions, influences, and the like, is concerned with facts simply, the distinctive preoccupation of criticism is with values. And this is of course true. The primary objects of criticism are those characteristics of literary works which are what they are, in a given work, because of the writer's choices between better and worse possibilities of various kinds, material and technical, relative to the task he has set himself and the known possibilities of his art. These choices are all judgments of value, however instinctively they are made. And we ask about these things for the sake ultimately of assessing the artistic rightness and the human significance of the decisions they reflect.

In asking about them, we ought to seek answers that will be commensurate, as far as possible, with the richness, the complexity, the subtlety of implication and suggestion, and the emotional power and moral and intellectual adequacy of what the writer has done. But there is also another requirement, and it is this which sets the problem I want to discuss—namely, that our answers be well-grounded. Our assessment, that is, has to be of the actual decisions of the writer, not of our wishes or preconceptions about these, or our criticism can never be responsible or just. And that means that, although the matters we study in criticism are intrinsically matters of value rather than merely matters of fact, we must view them, in the first instance, as matters of fact. Before we can make proper judgments of a work, we must know what the values are that we are judging and why these particular values, instead of others, happen to be in the work. And in order to ascertain this, we have to ask many questions—for example, about the meanings and implications of the text, its distinctive character as a whole, the artistic problems faced by the writer in composing it, the reasons governing his solutions of these, and his basic moral, social, and intellectual presuppositions—which are just as much factual questions, though they are about values, as any that may be asked concerning the same work by a historical scholar.

But if this is so, it seems reasonable to suppose that our attempts to answer them ought to be conducted in the same spirit of inquiry, and in the light of the same general canons of evidence and reasoning, as are the attempts of the best scholars in other humanistic fields to answer the questions of particular historical fact or causation with which they are specially concerned.

The marks of the good scholar are many, but surely one of the most important is what I would call a habitual distrust of the a priori; that is to say, of all ways of arriving at particular conclusions which assume the relevance and authority, prior to the concrete evidence, of theoretical doctrines or other general propositions concerning the subject matters in question.

The scholar cannot get along, of course, without a body of generalized knowledge, or theory, about the phenomena he may possibly encounter in his studies of particular questions. He can proceed in such studies only by way of working hypotheses, and his ability to frame working hypotheses for a given problem will vary, other things being equal, with the extent of his already acquired understanding of the different sorts of things that may conceivably present themselves in his field of inquiry. The best textual bibliographers, for example, have been those who have brought to the problems raised by individual books (the quartos of *Hamlet,* say) the most complete knowledge available at the moment about the possible practices of compositors and printers and the reasons why these were what they were; they are also those who have taken advantage of every improvement in bibliographical theory to form new hypotheses or to revise old ones for the particular subjects they are studying.

The good scholar is well aware, however, of two other things. One is the inevitable incompleteness of any theory that purports to account for human activities, whether those of printers, politicians, or poets: there is always the chance—perhaps even the likelihood—that there will be in the particular situation he is studying what I shall call an X, that is to say, a hitherto unconsidered possibility of explanation that is more nearly relevant to the problem than any possibility contained in his theory. And the other thing is equally important. The good scholar knows that there is no necessary connection between the grounds on which he has come to entertain a working hypothesis and the grounds on which, if he is able to confirm it at all, it is confirmed; between the plausibility conferred on it by its accord with currently accepted theory and the probability which it may acquire through its capacity, independent of theory, to account completely and uniquely for the facts of a given case. He is therefore bound to look with a skeptical eye on any of the "ruling hypotheses," as they have been aptly called, that tend from time to time to tyrannize over studies in his field; knowing how easy it was, for example, when the "bad quartos" of Shakespeare were generally supposed to represent either sources or first drafts of the plays as we have them in better editions, to bring the textual peculiarities of the first quarto of *Hamlet* into harmony with this dogma, in disregard of such other possibilities as that of "memorial reconstruction," for instance. The ideal is for the scholar to be able to say of any hypothesis he settles on, not merely that it makes sense of the facts—since almost any hypothesis will do this in some fashion—but that *only* if it is true, could the facts, in their totality, be what they are. And he knows that to be able to say this, with even moderate confidence, of any hypothesis, he cannot allow himself to be guided by this hypothesis alone. For he knows that proof in matters of particular fact is always a comparative matter, and that he cannot safely commit himself to a given hypothesis until, with a mind as free as possible from doctrinal prepossessions, he has weighed its probability against the probabilities of all other relevant hypotheses that he can think of. Only thus can the confirmation of a hypothesis of fact be properly independent of theoretical or other general reasons that may have suggested it, and the a priori element in research be reduced to a minimum.

Something like this is what the good scholar aims at; and something like this, I urge, is what the good critic should aim at too, in his approach to the many questions of literary fact he has to deal with. It is a hard ideal to live up to consistently. I know of no historical scholars who have not occasionally or frequently sinned against it; and the temptation to relax is, for various reasons, stronger still in criticism. Here the lure of "the high priori road" continually beckons, as I know all too well myself; I am made very uncomfortable whenever I think of the many times I have given in to it, sometimes in print, sometimes in writings which, by the grace of God or the advice of friends, never got that far.

I am disturbed by these evidences, in myself and others, of laziness and general human corruption. But I am much more disturbed when I see confidence in a priori reasoning and "ruling hypotheses" being erected into a principle of method, or at least an accepted habit of procedure, in studies of particular critical fact. Yet just this has happened, during the past twenty years, as a result in large part of the rise to prominence and widespread academic influence of the criticism still commonly and, vaguely, referred to as "new."

It is sufficient to identify this criticism as merely that variety of present-day critical activity which has concentrated on giving us "readings," "analyses," or "interpretations" of literary works on the basis of what are thought to be improved general theories of literary language or "symbolism" or of literary subject matter or "meaning." This criticism has undoubtedly done a great deal to reinvigorate literary studies by suggesting new guiding ideas, and by forcing us to attend to various species of problems we had too much neglected before; many of its exponents, moreover, are men of intelligence, wide reading, acute perception, and sensitive taste, and all of them have the honor of being serious and zealous friends of literature. All this can be said, however, without affecting my central point, which is that, in relation to the best standards of factual inquiry and proof recognized in other humanistic fields, the general tendency of the movement has been reactionary and obscurantist. This appears both in the kind of theorizing about literature it has encouraged and in its characteristic procedures in practical criticism.

Considered as theorists of literature or poetry, we may say of these critics, as a group, what Lord Bolingbroke said of certain seventeenth- and early eighteenth-century theorists in natural philosophy: "Rather than creep up slowly, *a posteriori*, to a little general knowledge, they soar at once as far, and as high, as imagination can carry them. From thence they descend again armed with systems and arguments *a priori*, and regardless of how these agree, or clash with the phaenomena of Nature, they impose them on mankind."

These critics have certainly not crept up slowly or been content with a little general knowledge. The object of their theorizing is seldom anything much more limited than literature, or at least poetry, as such—all literature, all poetry; present, past, and future. They talk habitually of "poetry" or of "the poem" as if these were names of eternal ideas or of simple homogeneous elements in nature. To parody Whitehead, they seek simplicity but do not distrust it; and so they set down such all-embracing propositions as the following:

that "literature is ultimately metaphorical and symbolic"; that "the language of poetry is the language of paradox" or, in a variant formulation, an "alogical" or "counterlogical" language, based not on "the principle of discreteness" but on a principle of creative interaction diametrically opposed to that. All this is far above what the historical student of literature, even if he is prone to theorizing, can honestly pretend to know. How is it possible, he is bound to ask, so easily to reduce to a single formula the overwhelming variety of aims, subjects, moods, views of life, forms, methods, uses of language he has encountered in past and present writings which have gone under the names of "literature" or "poetry," and how can anyone be so sure of what will be included under these names in the future?

The answer is that these critics have an advantage over the historical scholar in possessing easier and bolder means of arriving at general truths about their subject. They do not need to "creep up, *a posteriori*, to a little general knowledge." They can at once seize upon first principles, purporting to have a universal or approximately universal scope of application, and descend from these, "armed with systems and arguments *a priori*," to the more particular theoretical problems that interest them, such as the special uses of language in poetry or the distinctive nature of the "meanings" which poetry conveys.

The mode of acquiring such first principles differs with different critics. Some of them have merely taken over their primary concepts from other contemporary sciences. There are Freudian critics, for example, who tend to subsume literary works under (say) the theory of dreams, and thus get a ready-made system of symbolic interpretation in terms of manifest and latent content—in spite of the warnings of Freud himself, in his more scientific moments, against just this sort of thing. It is much the same, though the terms differ, with the Jungian critics, or those who combine Jungian principles with secondhand anthropology borrowed from *The Golden Bough;* whence the current dogma that the structure and the emotional appeal of great literary works are functions primarily of the psychological and ritualistic "archetypes" which they necessarily embody and of which the detection in individual works is a simple matter of applying tables of symbolic meanings known in advance: this, again, in spite of repeated statements by Jung that "that which constitutes the essential nature of art must always lie outside the province" of analytical psychology.

I want to emphasize especially, however, the other main way of establishing first principles in this criticism. It is essentially a method of dialectical analysis, in which you begin by laying down some general postulate—as, for example, that "poetry" is the polar opposite of science—and then proceed to work out logically all the implications of this; the nature and attributes of poetry, you assume, will be contained exhaustively in the rational scheme of definitions and distinctions you thus arrive at. There are good examples of this "abstract" method, as David Hume called it, in John Crowe Ransom's discussions of poetry in relation to science in various parts of *The World's Body,* in Cleanth Brooks's proof in *The Well Wrought Urn* that the language of poetry is "the language of paradox," in Charles Feidelson's argument in *Symbolism and American Literature* that metaphor in poetry is something quite distinct from metaphor in prose, and, most recently, in Philip Wheelwright's discussion of "plurisignation" (or multiple verbal meaning) as an essential principle of poetry or "depth language" in *The Burning Fountain.*

The way the method operates can be seen in Feidelson's treatment of metaphor. His conclusion is that, whereas metaphor in prose undoubtedly consists in using words in such a way as to analogize one thing to another, metaphor in poetry, despite most earlier writers on the subject, obeys a wholly different principle, which he calls the principle of creative interaction. In setting forth this doctrine, he discusses, among other texts, Andrew Marvell's phrase "the iron gates of life" in "To His Coy Mistress" ("And tear our pleasures with rough strife / Thorough the iron gates of life"). The phrase does not, he insists, "point out" or "play on" a "preexisting similarity between the logical elements, life and iron gates." What the phrase really does is to establish "the idea of life *under the aspect of* iron gates, and of iron gates under the aspect of life." The tenor of the metaphor "is at once the special kind of life that we can entertain under the aspect of iron gates, and the special kind of iron gates that are capable of being thought under the aspect of life." It is a case, in other words, not of analogy, as it would be in prose, but of "creative interaction."

Now we can, of course, read Marvell's metaphor and all other metaphors we encounter in poems in this way, if we want to; the difficulty is that we can do the same thing, if we want to, for all metaphors in prose. But it is equally possible to continue to read all metaphors, in both poems and prose works, as most people have always read them. Why, then, must we accept Feidelson's revolutionary distinction? The problem, as he states it, is a problem of fact, and his conclusions about both Marvell's metaphor and poetic metaphors in general are advanced as conclusions of fact, with practical implications for literary exegesis. The chain of argument by which he arrives at them, however, is purely a priori and dialectical. What he is saying is that we *must* read Marvell's metaphor and all other metaphors in poetry (but not in prose) in the way he indicates because this follows from the essential nature of poetry. And he knows what the essential nature of poetry must be simply by inferring it from the nature of what he calls "poetic language"; and he knows what the nature of "poetic language" must be because he has begun by dividing all language into two opposing and incommensurable kinds—the language of "logic" and the language of "symbolism"— and has then deduced from this initial assumption that the "symbolic" language of poetry must necessarily possess the contraries of all qualities commonly asserted of "logical discourse." No matter what poets may have done, therefore, or other readers and critics thought, he can be confident that metaphor in poetry cannot possibly involve, as in "logical" prose, a transference of names based on some resemblance between the things they signify. For he knows from his dialectic that the concepts of "transference" and "resemblance," since they are essentially "logical" concepts, are incompatible with the concept of "poetry," not merely, as he explains, "because logic is unpoetic, but even more fundamentally, because poetic structure is not logical." As far as I can see, that is all the warrant he has for saying what he does about metaphor in poetry.

You can perhaps gather from this example what the method is. It is the old method of bipartite division, in which a subject matter is explored, and its elements defined and related to one another, simply by applying to it a more or less elaborate pattern of logically contrary terms unified by a single principle of classification. You start, that is, with a very large concept such as "language" or "discourse" in general; you then move down from this by setting up dialectical oppositions, major and subordinate, within it (as, for instance, poetic discourse versus logical discourse, the symbolic versus the realistic, the ironical versus the simple); and you end by supposing, after the manner of Feidelson on metaphor, that the essential characteristics of poetry are necessarily what this scheme of antithetical distinctions determines them to be.

In order to be quite fair to these critics, I think we must distinguish between what they have been trying to get at in their dialectical theorizing and what they have actually accomplished. There is undoubtedly something in poetic literature—in its peculiar manipulations of language, in its techniques for implying or suggesting more than it explicitly says, in its special preoccupation with concrete experiences rather than with general ideas—to which their speculations point. When Wheelwright, for example, writes a book on what he calls "depth language," he is not talking about nothing; he has his eye on genuine problems well worth exploring. And so too with most of the others. What disturbs me in these theorists is not their lack of real and important problems but their choice of a method for dealing with them, a method which I think is, in the first place, inappropriate to literature and, in the second place, incompatible with inquiry.

It is inappropriate to literature for two reasons (among others). First of all, it disregards the most obvious and fundamental fact about literature—namely, that it is not a natural phenomenon but a product of human invention and art. It is something, therefore, that exists in history and has had its character molded in countless unpredictable ways by it. You can know what its nature is, consequently, only by finding out a posteriori what the men and women who have created it, through the ages, have made that nature to be; and there is no presumption that this can ever be reduced to a single set of logically symmetrical and necessary principles, such as these critics have attempted to formulate. There are indeed necessities in literature, since literature is an art and hence partakes of reason; but these necessities are always relative to the specific tasks which writers set themselves in writing individual works, and they vary according to the widely variant characters of these tasks. If you are writing a lyric poem, for instance, in which the speaker is conceived as being in a very despondent mood, and if you want to elicit the reader's sympathy with his feelings, it is clearly necessary that you show somehow in the poem some humanly significant causes for his state of mind. In this sense of necessity, literature may be said to involve an element of predictability, but only in this sense. For the history of literature shows unmistakably that literature does not have to be, *in general*— as one scholar has put it—"anything determinate at all." To attempt, therefore, to derive its nature a priori from general postulates, to geometrize about it—for that is what these theorists in effect have been doing—is wholly to miss the point.

The other respect in which the method is inappropriate appears when you consider what it does to the concrete natures of particular literary works. A simple example may make clear what I mean. *The Origin of Species* is admittedly a scientific treatise, and *The Ring and the Book* is admittedly a poem; and the two can undoubtedly be contrasted meaningfully with one another in a good many particular respects. But each exists in itself as an individual production, which has come to be what it is as a result of innumerable decisions, by Darwin and Browning respectively, that can be understood sufficiently for each work by itself without reference to the other. It would be absurd, therefore, to base our examination of them on the notion that there is some kind of significant polar opposition between them. They are merely different human productions, which require to be analyzed and judged, accordingly, in different terms; and we only obscure and distort the facts on which our analysis and judgment ought to rest, when we imitate the theorists I have been discussing and reduce the relation between the poem and the treatise to an abstract contrariety between something called "poetry" and something called "science" or "logic." This is to turn poetry and science into hypostatized qualities, with natures determined not by variable human choices and actions—as we know is actually the case—but merely by the logic of the critic's divisions and definitions.

It is futile to try to determine by dialectical analysis of concepts like "language," "discourse," "logic," "science," "symbol," "poetry," etc., any of the actually operative principles of construction, meaning, or value in literature. Literature is just not suited to such a quasi-mathematical treatment.

Furthermore—and this is the second main objection—all theorizing of this kind, insofar as it is taken seriously, is bound to bring inquiry in practical criticism to a stop before it is well begun, or at least to reduce it to a mere application of preestablished dogmas. For you already know from your theory, in some determinate sense, what you ought to look for and what you will be likely to find in literary works before you read them. You know that there will almost certainly be "ambiguity" in the next poem you look at, or that its structure will probably be "some kind of paradoxical tension," or that it will be based on one or another of the currently talked-of ritualistic or mythical "archetypes," or that, if certain objects are mentioned in it, they will necessarily have such and such symbolic meanings, and so on: you put your money into the dialectical machine and, behold, you get the same money back. And there is another and equally serious consequence, following from the fact that theories of this kind are necessarily developed from a single principle by a method of dichotomous division, one thing paired against another at different levels of generality throughout, with nothing left over and no loose ends. You will tend to think about all your problems in practical criticism in simple *either-or* disjunctions: if the work is not "logical discourse," it must be "poetry" and hence have characteristics contrary to those of "logical discourse"; if it is not simple, it must be "ironical"; if it is not realistic, it must be "symbolic"; and so on. You can indeed frame alternative hypotheses for individual works or passages, but only those provided for in the dichotomies of your system. You will know, that is, before you examine a work what all the significantly different possibilities of meaning and structure in literature are; and beyond these you will have no warrant or inducement, in your theory, for venturing to look. There will be, in short, no X's, as I have called them, in your practical criticism that might lead to fresh discoveries, but at best only a narrowed-down choice between *A* and *B*. It is hard to see what research in criticism can amount to under these conditions.

What it actually has amounted to in the dealings of these critics with particular works and writers—under the direct or indirect influence of the fashionable theorizing—I can speak of only briefly. I shall concentrate on a single point; and since it is the style now to talk about "fallacies" in criticism, I shall call what I have in mind the "dialectical fallacy." Let me give an example from my own experience. I once thought for a short time, when I was still more or less a "new critic," that the essential structure of poetic works, as contrasted with prose arguments, consisted in a hierarchy of proportions or metaphors, running upward from lines and stanzas to the poem as a whole. I derived this principle, as my statement of it may suggest, by positing a dialectical opposition between poetry and syllogistic argument, and then merely drawing out one of the logical consequences of this. I took for granted, on the strength of this logic, that the principle was applicable universally; that is, to all poems and indeed to all works of the imagination. And, curiously enough, that proved to be in fact the case. I can take my oath that I never had any trouble, for as long as I clung to my theory, in making any poem, drama, or novel I examined in detail conform most beautifully to its specifications. All I had to do—and this was not hard—was to arrange the words, thoughts, and incidents of the work into proportional relationships with one another. (I did a very neat job of this sort, I recall, on Fielding's *Joseph Andrews* and equally neat ones on the odes of William Collins.) There was no need to trouble myself about biographical or historical probabilities or to raise the question whether the same textual details I had brought into harmony with my hypothesis might not admit of another or simpler explanation. Hypothesis, backed by dialectic, was enough.

I cannot see any difference between this method of mine (of which I now blush to speak) and the procedure by which Wheelwright, in *The Burning Fountain*, establishes the presence of "plurisignation" in Marvell's couplet,

> The grave's a fine and private place,
> But none, I think, do there embrace.

What Marvell is saying in the first of these lines, Wheelwright tells us, is "that in one of its aspects, its privacy, the grave would be a welcome refuge for lovers; that the grave marks an end, in that it deprives lovers of the joy of mutual embrace; and that the grave is very cramping." And he supports this interpretation by attributing multiple meanings to the words "fine" and "private." "On the surface," he says, "the word 'fine' expresses approval of a place so 'private' (also in the most obvious sense) where lovers might embrace without interruption, if only they were any longer capable of embracing at all. But the grave is 'fine' also in marking the *finis*, the end of all earthly joys, the end of all embracing: an attentive reader thus gets a preview of the counteractive idea even before the second line of the couplet makes it explicit. And thirdly, 'fine' carries the added meaning of narrow, constricted: as when we say 'a fine line.' Meanings 2 and 3 of 'fine' stir up a second meaning of 'private,' from the Latin *privatus,* 'deprived.' "

I shall not discuss whether or not this somewhat complex reading of the line is a probable one—that is to say, whether or not we have to apprehend in the line the three meanings of "fine" and the two meanings of "private" which Wheelwright finds there if we want to do justice to the effect Marvell was trying to get. I am concerned merely with the question of proof. What warrant has Wheelwright for asserting that the line means the various things he says it does? His hypothesis clearly states a possibility. We all know that poets do sometimes—and very often in modern poetry—seek effects by means of diction that has to be analyzed much as he analyzes the two words in Marvell. As a recurring device in poetry, "plurisignation" cannot be denied; but why must we conclude that there is actually "plurisignation" here? There is no compelling obviousness in his reading, such as we find in the statement, for instance, that in Hart Crane's line in "Lachrymae Christi," "Thy Nazarene and tinder eyes," the word "tinder" has a double meaning. Wheelwright may be right, but if so, he should have argued the case, and he should have done this by giving some reasons, from the character of the poem as a whole or from Marvell's habits of diction, why it is not just as likely, or more likely, that the poet would have wanted his readers to get from "fine" and "private" only what Wheelwright calls their "obvious" senses, without dwelling on the words too closely, in order that the sudden turn in the second line ("But none, I think, do there embrace") might produce its full effect of witty surprise. It is no argument to say that the multiple meanings attributed to "fine" and "private" here are authorized historically by the *OED,* except on the absurd assumption that particular words in poetry always mean in any given use of them all the different things they *may* mean in the language of the time (this is merely early William Empsonism). The only warrant Wheelwright has, therefore, for asking us to accept his interpretation is that given him by his general theory, in which "plurisignation" is shown to be one of the essential principles of "poetry" merely by logical deduction from the basic antithesis set up in his book between the idea of "poetry" and the idea of "logical discourse."

The "dialectical fallacy," then, is simply the tacit assumption that what is true in your theory as a dialectical consequence must also be, or tend to be, true in actuality—that if you can so read a literary work as to reveal in it the particular kind of meaning or structure that is entailed by your definition of literature, poetry, poetic language, or the like, or by your formula for the author or his age, you have sufficiently demonstrated that it has that kind of meaning or structure. The fallacy lies in the circumstance that, with a little interpretative ingenuity, these conditions can almost always be fulfilled. I have said before how incompatible all this is with the spirit of inquiry. Our theory may tell us, for instance, that poetry is or tends to be symbolic; but there is nothing in this proposition, whatever its dialectical guarantees, that warrants us, as scholars, in saying more than that there may perhaps be symbols in the poem before us. But, by the same token, there also may not be; and so we have no business to conclude that there are unless we are forced so to conclude by the poem itself when we look at it, independent of theory, as the work of a given poet at a given time, and examine it with the other possibility actively in mind. If a non-symbolic interpretation makes adequate sense of the text and, all other things considered, is relatively more probable, then anything we may believe about symbolism and poetry in general is beside the point. And the same would be true of a symbolic interpretation that satisfied the same requirements.

This principle, as I have said, has not always been observed by scholars, even those in the most rigorous philological or bibliographical tradition. But, frankly, I cannot think of any large body of serious writing about literature in our time in which it has been more consistently violated than in the numerous professedly "critical" books and essays, mostly academic in origin, that have been inspired during the last few decades by the vogue of the "new criticism." In these, the "dialectical fallacy" is the almost standard rule of method. You can easily make up a long list of instances, besides those I have mentioned, from the writings of innumerable other critics on classical, medieval, and modern poems, Greek tragedies, the plays of Shakespeare (perhaps above all the plays of Shakespeare), and the novels of Jane Austen, Dickens, Hawthorne, Melville, Henry James, Faulkner, and I know not how many besides.

Not a few of these are the work of men seriously concerned with literary values and intent on bringing home to their readers hitherto unsuspected powers and subtleties of language and meaning in the works they write about; and many of their particular conjectures are illuminating and useful. This, however, only increases one's regret that their effective notions of what constitutes proof in practical criticism—of what makes this kind of criticism well-grounded—are in general so inadequate. They seem unaware, as a group, of the vast difference between interesting and novel speculation presented as fact and fact arrived at by way of perhaps equally interesting and novel speculation but justified as fact independently of speculation.

I do not believe, after extensive reading of their books and essays, that this is an unduly severe verdict on the method which these critics characteristically exhibit. I can only invite you to judge for yourself, but I predict that if you will examine carefully a fair selection of these writings, you will find the typical recipe of their procedure to be something like the following.

The critic's problem is to establish the truth of a particular hypothesis of fact, not hitherto entertained, about the meaning or structure of a given work or passage. He is trying to show, for example, that in Milton's line in "Lycidas," "Bitter constraint and sad occasion dear," the word "dear" has the double meaning of "affecting" and "dire"; or that the real subject of King Lear, expressed more fully through the imagery than the action, is not the tragedy of Lear and his daughters but Lear's final attainment of intellectual salvation; or that the structure of Gray's "Elegy" turns on an "ironical" contrast or "tension" between two modes of burial; or that the essential plot of Jane Austen's *Emma* is the heroine's "awakening to the possibilities of physical love," a "dramatic engagement with experience that moves its protagonist relentlessly through fantasy to reality"; or that Henry James's *The Ambassadors, The Wings of the Dove,* and *The Golden Bowl* constitute an elaborate allegory, in three stages, based on his father's version of Swedenborg's philosophy of religious history.

The proof of the hypothesis, such as it is, rests on premises of two kinds, particular and general. It is commonly assumed, in this criticism, that a hypothesis is confirmed if the details of the work—or, most commonly, a certain selection of them—can be shown to be in harmony with it. This sometimes requires an appeal to history: we are told, for instance, that the word "dear" in Milton's line did have the meaning of "dire" as well as of "affecting" in seventeenth-century English; we are told also that Henry James was in fact interested in his father's Swedenborgian speculations. What is established thus is, of course, only a possibility: the hypothesis *could* be true. Most often, however, the particular premises are internal to the text; and the demonstration—which again yields only a possibility—consists in interpreting what are taken to be "key" expressions, passages, characters, incidents, and so on, in such a way as to match them with the requirements of the hypothesis. The matching is sometimes accomplished by insisting that certain elements of the text are more truly revelatory of the writer's "meaning" than the others; as in the study of *King Lear* just referred to, where the imagery is held to be more significant than the characters and their actions. At other times the matching of text with hypothesis is brought about by finding implications in passages or incidents which fit the hypothesis but are not obviously necessitated or made appropriate by the text, when this is read without the hypothesis in mind; as when it is explained that the real reason why Jane Austen's Emma prefers Mr. Elton to Robert Martin as a possible husband for Harriet Smith is that "physical union with Martin would be unthinkable for Emma" whereas "with Elton it might be grotesque and disagreeable but not impossible." There is nothing of course in the narrative that supports in any way this interpretation of Emma's motives; but the interpretation harmonizes very well with the critic's hypothesis about the plot of the novel; for if that plot is Emma's "awakening to the possibilities of physical love," then it is convenient for the critic to be able to say, as he does, that Emma "actually . . . takes up Harriet in order to enjoy through her an experimental relationship with a man" and that, since Harriet is a puppet through whom she "proposes to enjoy a vicarious love affair, the object of that affair must be at least a possible husband for Emma," which Elton is but Martin is not. At still other times, the matching device is the ascription of symbolic or allegorical meanings, in keeping with the hypothesis, to incidents or characters; as when the son of Maggie

Verver in *The Golden Bowl* is said to represent "the divine-natural man, the redeemed humanity, of the New Church" in the religious argument which this novel is alleged to embody.

That is about all we normally get by way of proof from particular evidence; and it amounts only to asserting that the critic's hypothesis is capable of making some kind of sense out of the text, whether that sense was put there by the author or not. It certainly cannot be said of the hypotheses in my examples that they have any of the marks of obviously true or uniquely relevant explanations: it is much too easy to think of other equally or more plausible ways of accounting for the same facts, which the critic's arguments do nothing to exclude. It is very seldom indeed that a critic in this tradition makes more than a perfunctory gesture toward showing from the facts, internal and external, that *only* if his hypothesis is true, would the work or the passage in all probability have been conceived or written as it is, by the man who wrote it, at the time when it was written.

I think the reason is not hard to give. For behind each of the hypotheses I have cited is a fashionable critical belief, about the validity or general applicability of which the writer raises no questions—the belief that multiple meaning is an essential property of poetry; the belief that the unifying significance of a poetic drama is normally given by its patterns of recurrent imagery; the belief that literary structure is typically a matter of "ironical tension"; the belief that the dominant problem of most novelists—of Jane Austen, for example—is one of sexual adjustment; the belief that serious works of fiction are likely to embody concealed allegories. And it is these general premises of theory rather than particular premises drawn from history or the text or our natural responses to it, that actually do most of the work of demonstration. You have only to consider how little would be left in any of these studies, beyond mere conjecture and particular observation, were the critic suddenly to lose faith in the general postulates he has adopted!

This criticism, in short, is still in an intellectual stage which historical scholarship and the empirical sciences have long since passed through: the stage of "ruling hypotheses" and the "dialectical fallacy." Its characteristic procedure is therefore very much like that of the seventeenth- and eighteenth-century theologians who set out to demonstrate the workings of divine providence in the facts of history or of the physical world. Substitute for divine providence the principle of symbolism or "plurisignation" or "paradoxical tension" or archetypal universality, and see if there is any real difference. It is not too far removed, also, if one attends merely to the logic involved, from the method by which it has been shown that the Earl of Oxford, say, wrote Shakespeare.

It must be granted that the results are often stimulating, but in a sense that recalls Sherlock Holmes's remark on a certain occasion to Dr. Watson: "When I said that you stimulated me, I meant, to be frank, that in noting your fallacies, I was occasionally guided towards the truth."

As I said in the beginning, I was one of those who, in the middle thirties, were urging strongly that criticism be given a better show in our university departments of literature. Since then, observing the course which the dominant academic criticism has taken, I have been tempted very often to think that, if this is what criticism has to be, we might be better off with less of it. But of course criticism does not have to be this sort of thing at all; it *can* be made into a branch of serious learning. It is much easier to take "the high priori road" than it is to leave it, but that can be done. It can be done in various ways: by seeing to it that our students are trained with all possible rigor as scholars before they are encouraged to set up as critics; by forcing them constantly to justify what they say in criticism and to explain how they know, from something other than current theory, that what they say of particular works is true; by subjecting bad method in criticism to as severe rebuke as we give to bad method in bibliography and literary history; by trying to develop gradually a body of general knowledge of literature—a little now, more perhaps tomorrow—that is grounded in literary history and practical experience of writing, instead of in dialectic merely; and by inculcating, finally, in our teaching and practice, an exploratory and inquiring rather than a doctrinaire use of such knowledge in studies of particular works and writers, on the model of the older scholars rather than the newer critics.

Critical and Historical Principles
of Literary History

M Y INTENTION in this essay is to inquire into the principles, both critical and historical, which have most commonly governed the writing of literary history since the origins of that discipline in ancient Greece, and to contrast with these the principles of another mode of interpreting historical differences in literature of which we have had thus far only sporadic and fragmentary examples. And the first question to be considered is naturally that of the materials out of which all varieties of literary history construct their propositions.

1. CRITICAL ELEMENTS

The propositions of any history of literature that is not confined to the external conditions of literary activity necessarily comprise elements of two kinds: terms signifying actions, characters, habits, aims, and circumstances of writers, and terms signifying attributes of literary works; without the latter the history would not be a history of literature and without the former it would not be a history. The elements of the first sort are derived by the techniques of historical research from an examination of available documents, in the light of general knowledge concerning human behavior; their character in any history is relative to the state of the materials and to the histori-

An uncompleted short monograph on varieties of literary history, written in 1950 primarily as a means of clarifying my own ideas on the subject; not previously published.

45

an's intelligence, training, and industry. The elements of the second sort are derived by critical analysis from literary texts, in the light of theoretical assumptions concerning the nature of literary works and the kinds of significant statements that can be made about them; their character in any history is relative to the historian's literary sensitivity but even more decisively to the particular scheme of critical and historical principles which he brings to his task.

It is possible therefore to have as many different schools of literary history as there are schools of literary criticism—or, as we shall see later, schools of historical interpretation. For our purposes only the most far-reaching differences in critical theory need be considered, and we may begin by observing that most literary histories, however great their diversity in other respects, have presupposed a conception of imaginative literature (or poetry) which does not differentiate essentially, but only accidentally, between one of its species and others, or between any of these and writing in general. Differentiations of many kinds, determined by varied criteria, have of course been made, but their warrant has not been found in the principles of construction peculiar to different literary arts but rather in the possibilities of variation inherent generally in human discourse viewed as the joint product of reason and speech. The clearest sign of this is that we have had few literary histories in which the analysis of works, irrespective of kind, does not turn on one simple and ancient distinction—the only one, in fact, basic to a consideration of discourse as such. This has been stated variously as a distinction between things and words, content and form, matter and manner, thought and expression, intention and language, or meaning and symbol. (In addition, arrangement often appears as a third term, necessitated by the fact that, as Quintilian remarked, "not only what we say and how we say it is of importance, but also the circumstances under which we say it.")

There have been many different ways, in this tradition, of viewing the nature of poetic or imaginative discourse—sometimes as expression, sometimes as communication, sometimes as statement, sometimes as resolution of practical problems, and so on—and, correspondingly, many different shifts in the constitution of the two fundamental elements, content and words, and of the relationship between them. From the Hellenistic grammarians and Roman rhetoricians to the "new critics" of the present day, however, some kind of reduction of the various particular forms of poetry, drama, and fiction to modes of discourse has been well-nigh omnipresent in both criticism and literary history; and so seldom has the assumption on which it rests been challenged that some effort is now needed to realize that this assumption is after all not grounded in the nature of things. The reduction itself may or may not be an error in method, but once made it necessarily restricts the historian to such statements about the individual and collective differences exhibited by literary works as can be derived by the permutation and combination, the separation and conjunction, of attributes which any form of poetry may have in common with any other mode of discourse.

There are two ways in which such attributes may be discovered and employed in the characterization and differentiation of works. The first is the way of the philologist or, to give him his ancient name, the grammarian; it consists in the literal exegesis and comparison of texts in terms of the material traits of their content and form in a context of the circumstances of their composition; its essential instruments are textual and historical criticism, grammar (including prosody), the grammatical parts of logic, and bibliography in the traditional sense. With this equipment, and with a common-sense knowledge of human affairs, it is possible to make many precise and verifiable statements about literary texts such as any literary historian, whatever else he may be interested in doing, can neglect only at his scholarly peril. By means of a controlled grammatical reading of any text, its ostensible meanings and intentions can be revealed, its argument disengaged, its language described in linguistic or prosodic terms, and its structure, at least in the more obvious topical aspects of this, made manifest; by means of a comparison of different texts, works can be assigned to their respective genres (either those already defined and named by earlier poets and grammarians or others now first isolated and baptized). Themes, doctrines, images, styles, and other features of content or form can also be identified in terms of the earlier or contemporary traditions they reflect, as when historians point to the conventions of courtly love in Chaucer's *Troilus,* the Franciscan doctrines in Rabelais, the mixture of Newtonian and Shaftesburian ideas in Thomson's *Seasons,* the Dickensian characters in the early Henry James, or the Miltonic traits of verse and imagery in Collins and Gray. The statements thus generated represent knowledge, never of the character of a work as an artistic whole, however, but only of the character of its substantive or "formal" parts; moreover, these are defined in terms of accidents of composition and of the historical affinities of the work with other works having parts that show similar material traits, never in terms of the artistic use of such parts. Most histories depending upon this mode of analysis compare and contrast parts of one work with those of another in terms of differences of kind; but the different kinds tend to be little more than convenient classes derived from obvious differences in the motives and interests of writers, or mere descriptive formulas for the traditions of subject matter or technique which a particular writer or group of writers happened to follow. All the familiar genres are thus reduced to conventions historically determined—tragedy and comedy no less than pastoral, ode, epistle, or sonnet—their distinctions resting upon differences not of constructive principle but merely of opinion and taste, such as are amenable to philological discussion without recourse to any analysis of forms.

The second way of defining the characters and differences of works depends similarly upon the assumption that all kinds of discourse, whether practical or artistic, didactic or mimetic, serious or comic, narrative, dramatic, or lyric, can be discussed significantly in terms of a single set of elements and principles. Unlike the first mode, however, its primary reference is not to the historical origins of works but to their effects upon readers. Its major concern, therefore, is not to describe the material and conventional traits of dramas, novels, and poems, although it may subsume these in its characterizations. Its concern is to discriminate their qualities or "values," not the qualities or values, be it noted, which *Macbeth,* for example, possesses because it is a particular kind of tragedy constructed according to particular principles, which were not all equally operative in the construction of *Othello,* but the qualities or values which any work shares with any other work by partaking in the common causes of all human discourse—language, the mind, society, history, and so on.

Now any element that may enter into a literary work—verse, diction, technique, structure, subject matter, attitude, doctrine, and the like—or any distinguishable complex of these, may have predicates of quality attached to it. And the number of such predicates that may be applied to any work is infinite, since, in the absence of principles differentiating species of work, there is no way, merely by looking at particular poems or dramas, of distinguishing between their essential and their accidental traits. This is why criticism in the qualitative mode has often seemed arbitrary and chaotic to outsiders who have compared the judgments of different critics on the same work. This need not be true for any given critic or school of critics, but if criticism of this sort is to be guaranteed against mere whimsy or irrelevance, the critic must be a philosopher. At least he must be a philosopher to the extent of possessing a general dialectical schematism appropriate to the discussion of any kind of discourse. This alone will enable him to give definition and compendency to his qualitative terms and will guide him in applying them to writers and works. An indefinite number of such schematisms is possible in criticism and literary history, since the structure of terms in any one of them is determined not by inductive investigation into the natures of works as particular kinds of concrete objects but by a logically prior analogizing of poetry to something else. The analogy may be negative, as when poetry is taken as a property of language and is then defined by contrasting it with the language of science or of practical life, or it may be positive, as when poetry is equated with psychological or moral activity, or with the making of myths and symbols, or with scientific or historical inquiry (as in contemporary discussions of prose fiction as "exploration"), and so on. The variety of available analogues for poetry (as for anything else) is without predictable limit, and thus there will always be a "new criticism" with every new generation if not with every new critic. Once the analogue is determined, however, the common necessities of the dialectical method begin to operate. The essence of the procedure, as Plato pointed out, is composition and division—division for the sake of achieving discriminations among particulars and composition for the sake of defining their unity. The consequence, in any writing regulated by the method, is a proliferation of predicate terms paired as contraries or opposites, which in their application to any subject are either separated or joined (sometimes by mere addition, sometimes by the mediation of a third term) to yield propositions and proofs.

In the long period from Greek antiquity to the present nearly all the practical criticism of professed critics (at least outside the technical tradition of Aristotle) and most literary histories concerned with values have been dominated by this preoccupation with the universally predicable qualities of literature as selected and ordered by some scheme of dialectical oppositions and resolutions. The discriminating contraries have been borrowed from many types of discourse—ethical, political, sociological, historical, mechanical, physiological, psychological, psychoanalytical, medical, metaphysical, epistemological, logical, grammatical, rhetorical, semantic—and the unifying devices have ranged from the ethical notion of value as a mean between extremes, characteristic of most criticism through the eighteenth century, to the psychological concept of value as a synthesis of opposite or discordant qualities characteristic of the neo-Coleridgean criticism of our time. There has been much diversity also in other respects: as between those critics and historians who have been clearly aware of the philosophic premises of their schemes (for example, Coleridge and Croce) and those, the great majority, who have not; as between those who, though not philosophers themselves, have conceived of practical criticism as a kind of knowledge (for example, Johnson) and those who have reduced it to a simple rhetoric of praise and blame pursued frequently in a routine spirit (for example, many otherwise distinguished scholars who venture on judgments of quality in their histories); finally, as between those who operate with a comprehensive scheme of qualities deduced from a complex analogue (for example, Johnson and Coleridge) and those who make all their discriminations in terms of one or two very general contrarieties (for example, I. A. Richards, F. R. Leavis, William Empson, Cleanth Brooks).

In spite of all these differences, the tradition of dialectical criticism, as we may call it, has exhibited a remarkable unity of method in its applications of general principles to the analysis of literary works. As with philological criticism, the basis of analysis has been consistently the ancient dichotomy of content and form; but with the absorption of the two terms into a dialectical system their status tends to undergo a striking change. They cease to be merely the distinguishable elements of any grammatically complete utterance and become dialectical opposites, the significance of which is determined by the general oppositions, whatever they may be, of the critic's scheme. Depending upon these, "content" in the sense of the psychological and moral tendencies of the author may be viewed as an internal principle, the soul of the work, in relation to which the "form" is the external body (as in Louis Cazamian); or "form" may be thought of as internal and "content," in the sense of the raw materials of experience, as external (as in Walter Pater). Again, "form" as semantic "structure" may be made the essence of poetry, with "content" as only its paraphrastic statement (as in Cleanth Brooks); or the distinction may be reduced to one between "outer form" and "inner form" (as in Wellek and Warren's *Theory of Literature*); or "form" in poetry may be defined as what distinguishes poetry as synthetic from prose as analytic and "content" identified as social attitude and thus as extraliterary (as in F. W. Bateson); or "form" may be subordinated as concrete "present-ment" to "content" as the moral preoccupations that characterize a writer's "peculiar interest in life" and hence be incapable of judg-ment apart from these (as in F. R. Leavis). There is no need to give more examples, but we may note that much the same thing has hap-pened also, in this mode of criticism, to the originally Aristotelian "parts" of tragedy and epic; thus plot and character are often made dialectical contraries (as in E. M. Forster's book on the novel) and drama is sometimes divided into "drama," comprising plot, character, spectacle, and music, and "poetry," comprising diction and thought (as in some modern discussions of Shakespeare).

The same mode of reasoning has also been used in the derivation and definition of literary kinds. The status and character of these in the many systems of critical dialectic developed since antiquity have varied considerably. Depending upon the premises of the system, dis-tinctions of genre at times have assumed great importance (as in ear-lier neoclassical criticism) and at other times (as in Croce) have been banished from the realm of the esthetic altogether and treated merely as conveniences in the bibliographical description of works. They have represented for some critics (for example, Boileau) dis-tinctions fixed in the nature of things and for others (for example, Johnson) only man-made conventions. In some periods or schools of criticism the list of essentially different genres has been a long one; in others, especially since the eighteenth century, the number has been much reduced. There have been added, moreover, to the traditional genres of the ancient grammarians, many other kinds of differentia-tion, the principles of which depend similarly upon oppositions pe-culiar to the systems in which they appear: differentiations, in which the historical names take on the status of universals, between national or period styles—for example, Attic and Asiatic, French and English (especially for drama), Renaissance and Baroque, Classical and Romantic or Preromantic, Metaphysical and Augustan—or between the styles of individual artists, as when critics oppose the manner of Donne and that of Spenser, or speak of the Horatian, Juvenalian, and Varronian types of satire. Kinds have also been constituted, notably in modern criticism, on the model of dialectic itself; an example being Cleanth Brooks's distinction, following I. A. Richards and, more remotely, Coleridge, between two fundamental kinds of poetic "structure"—that characterized by "wit," that is, the union of naturally opposed impulses or attitudes (thought and emotion, the "poetic" and "non-poetic," the "noble" and "satiric") and that characterized by a "dissociation" of these attributes and a more or less exclusive concentration on one or other of the simple extremes.

The variations in theory have been far more numerous than these few instances will suggest, but the underlying method of definition has remained essentially the same. Distinctions of genre, for all these critics, are distinctions not among species of individual art objects or among historically determined conventions but among general qualities or complexes of qualities which are often identified as peculiarly characteristic of one or another of the recognized forms but not restricted to it. Thus terms like epic, tragedy, comedy, pastoral, lyric, and so on, can be used analogically to designate manifestations of a certain quality no matter in what different literary kinds they may appear; and this is even more obviously the case with such later generic terms as "metaphysical," "Augustan," "romantic," "sublime," "synthetic," and the like. It is inevitable, therefore, that the problem of defining kinds in any dialectical system in which it is important to do this should entail the setting up of general oppositions which will justify, on rational grounds, as distinct from a posteriori inductions, the differentiations the critic wishes to make. Hence the many attempts to discover natural foundations for the basic poetic kinds, sometimes by equating them with fixed differences in society, sometimes by resolving them into temperamental types, sometimes by relating them to elementary distinctions of grammar. Whatever the analogy chosen, the result has uniformly been some scheme of genres, more or less comprehensive, and often, though not always, involving a hierarchical order, in which one kind of writing is set against another as its dialectical opposite (as when comedy is made on all points the contrary of tragedy, or "Spenserian" poetry of "metaphysical") or in which one kind is related to others as the whole of which they are but incomplete contrasting parts (as in the theories, already referred to, of Richards and Brooks).

The same rules of procedure, finally, have governed the selection of predicates for the characterization and discrimination of authors and works. The aim is to discover and formulate distinguishing qualities of mind and art, and given the method, the formulas constructed in any given case must depend quite as much upon the kinds of oppositions furnished by the critic's theory of poetry or literature (even if this is only a more or less coherent set of terminological habits) as upon the data supplied by his texts—what constitutes relevant data, indeed, being determined by the analogy on which the theory rests. This is of course the reason, quite apart from differences of sensibility or taste, why the same poem or poet tends to exhibit so many different characters in the pages of different critics or historians. Thus Johnson, thinking in terms of the general conditions of literary pleasure, finds the distinctive quality of *The Rape of the Lock* in the union by Pope of "the two most engaging powers of an author," that which makes new things familiar and that which makes familiar things new: the crucial aspect of the poem for him, therefore, is its depiction of characters and actions. A more recent critic, however, conceiving of poetry, in opposition to prose, as essentially metaphorical language, locates the peculiar achievement of Pope and the critical problem he presents, "in a very special kind of reconciliation between qualities of poetry and prose, a reconciliation managed even after the maximum concessions have been made": for him the crucial aspects of Pope's poetry lie not so much in its subjects or arguments as in its devices of imagery and expression. Wide as these differences have inevitably been, the method of practical criticism in this tradition has never greatly changed, from the chapters in Quintilian's *Institutes* on the Greek and Roman poets, historians, orators, and philosophers to the essays of T. S. Eliot on the seventeenth-century English poets. Its chief tools, as Eliot remarks, are comparison and analysis, and its operations consist in the joining and separating, by these means, of whatever general literary qualities the critic may think it important to distinguish in a work or, more typically, a writer. An excellent modern example is Eliot's essay on Andrew Marvell. This is too familiar to quote, but one passage, also on Marvell, may be cited from a contemporary historian as an illustration in brief of how the thing is done. Marvell, we are told,

> united in himself, with an independent moderation of his own, a fresh, muscular, agile, and subtle metaphysical wit and the rationality, clarity, economy, and structural sense of a genuine classic, the cultured, negligent grace of a cavalier and something of the religious and ethical seriousness of a Puritan Platonist. To this rare combination of gifts were added, moreover, a feeling for nature at once particular and general, earthly and unearthly, and an individual sensitivity and suppleness of rhythm. In some of these qualities, and in his response to the claims of both contemplative solitude and public affairs, Marvell had a degree of affinity with his friend Milton. . . . He owed of course a prime debt to Donne and Donne's disciples, perhaps a small one to such *libertins* as Saint-Amant, and some other tinctures in his elixir are implied in his praise of Lovelace and of Jonson. These classical and metaphysical, continental and English, epicurean and Puritan, civilized and simple elements are mingled in varying proportions in Marvell's poems and, except in his style, they are not always fused. The Christian and the Platonist are not very close to the passionate lover, nor the poet of gardens to the future political satirist.[1]

And the historian proceeds to manipulate these or other closely equivalent contraries in a series of characterizations of Marvell's principal poems.

It will be recognized, I think, that the critical elements of most literary histories have been constituted by one or the other of the two methods, philological and dialectical, which I have been attempting to describe, or by a combination of them. That they are both legitimate and fruitful methods of solving problems, I should not question. Like all methods in any field, both of them may suffer characteristic corruptions in the hands of incompetent practitioners: the corruption

---

[1] Douglas Bush, *English Literature in the Earlier Seventeenth Century* (vol. 5: "Oxford History of English Literature") (Oxford, 1945), p. 159.

of the first is typically some kind of antiquarian irrelevance; that of the second, random or irresponsible impressionism and the cult of metaphorical statement.

Valid as they are, however, both methods are necessarily limited in the kinds of propositions they permit the historian to make about literary works. Both are concerned with wholes as well as with parts (in different senses of the terms), but in neither is the whole the concrete whole of the individual literary work, determined peculiarly by the choices of the artist. For the philological critic the wholeness of a poem or drama is merely the grammatical completeness of any text; it is, from the point of view of the critic's inquiries, simply a fact which he is given, and his problems consequently center on the parts and entail historical solutions independent of inferences from the whole. For the dialectical critic such inferences are possible, but the primary wholes with which he is concerned are dialectical compositions of qualities inhering in the author as unifying source, with the result that what he is able to discriminate in works are, again, only the characteristics of parts.

And the two methods are limited in still another way. There are three general aspects in terms of which literary productions may be defined: the preconstructional aspect, as I shall call it, comprising the relations of works to their origins and sources, whether these are considered literally or analogically; the postconstructional aspect, comprising the effects of completed works on readers; and the constructional aspect, comprising the artistic principles and judgments operative in their composition. All three of these ought ideally to be taken account of by the historian, but in the two modes of analysis we have so far discussed only the first and the second can be accorded adequate treatment—and that by means of distinctions which inevitably remain general and causally remote from the unique combinations of traits that differentiate individual works.

These limitations can be overcome, doubtless at the expense of other disadvantages, by resort to a third mode of deriving critical predicates for works—that which rests upon what I may call the concept of artistic synthesis.

The ruling assumption of this critical mode is that poetry (as before, in the large sense of imaginative literature) is not distinctively a mode or quality of discourse or a species of knowledge, practical action, expression, communication, entertainment, myth, or the like (although all these things are involved in poetry); it is simply the art (more precisely, the collection of arts) of making individual dramas, lyric poems, novels, short stories, and so on. So considered, a literary work is a concrete whole, or synthesis of parts, of a certain kind, the generic character of which is determined by the fact that it is the product of an artist combining elements of speech, with its various possible rhythms, and elements of humanly interesting experience or thought, by means of devices of technique and arrangement, for the sake of a particular organizing effect or series of effects on our opinions, emotions, or behavior. It is a whole that produces its effect not instantaneously but gradually in order of time; and its parts are consequently of two sorts: sequential parts, from beginning through middle to end, and functional parts that depend on the specific nature of the elements combined in the synthesis and on the mode of their combination. In all works, and in all the temporal parts of any work, we may differentiate effects or problems that derive from the author's choice of medium (as prose or meter of some kind), from his constitution of his subject (as an argument or action or state of character or feeling), and from his selection of a particular manner of representation (as narrative or dramatic). These are the three necessary conditions of the existence of any literary work as a concrete whole and hence the three fundamental criteria by which works of various kinds may be distinguished. In any group of works selected for purposes of comparison, each of these elements may vary in its specific character independently of variation in the others. Thus it is an error of method, in this mode of criticism, to reduce them to any one of the three, as in the doctrine that a literary work is "a system of signs," or even to any two, as in the old dichotomy of content and form. All elements being essential, moreover, no one of them, as it functions in completed works, can be said to be "unliterary" or "esthetically indifferent." The three elements cannot be properly reduced or collapsed, but each of them may be further differentiated in the poetics of a given species of work: Aristotle, for instance, resolves the qualitative parts common to tragedy and epic into plot, character, thought, and diction.

These and similar distinctions have been dismissed as mere "abstractions" by critics more concerned with the responses of readers than with the conditions of success or failure in literary production. For the writer, however, they constitute distinct and real, though related, loci of problems. This can easily be seen if we consider that a playwright, for example, may begin by sketching his plot as a whole, with its constituent incidents and essential determinations of character and thought, in a continuous sequence of speeches, then, in subsequent rewritings, reconsider each of the speeches to see how it would properly go if the characters were specified further in such and such ways, then work through the whole again for the sake of getting a proper maximum of implication in the dialogue, and finally decide that it would be more effective and appropriate to substitute verse for his original prose or prose for his original verse. The critic may therefore take this possibility as the basis of his analysis of works, and his problem then is not merely to identify the peculiar qualities possessed by the parts (in either sense) of any work, but to consider how each part has been made to function in relation to the others and to the artistic whole which the poet has achieved. For the whole in any literary product viewed as a concrete object is, analytically speaking, something over and above the mere combination of its separately determinable elements; it is the form that synthesizes their diverse qualities and local functions in the temporal progression of the words. It is therefore, for the literary artist, a final end or first principle of construction, from which he infers, however instantaneously, what he must do in constituting and ordering the parts. And there must always be, in any well-constructed poem, drama, or novel, some one part (in tragedy, the plot) the form of which determines most completely the form or effect of the whole, whereas the other parts (in tragedy, character, thought, diction, and spectacle) exist in their particular determinations for the sake of it, however "finished" and interesting they may be in themselves.

When literary works are thus conceived, the center of critical attention is appropriately the various problems of object, means, and manner involved in their construction as artistic syntheses of this or that special kind. It is sometimes said that we must abandon the pretence that there are significantly distinguishable literary forms (as distinct from conventions) and consider every poem as presenting a unique set of problems to the poet who makes it and hence to the critic who attempts to say how it is made. It is of course a fact that the composition of each new poem raises questions and poses difficulties for its author which have never had to be faced before. If this were all, however—that is, if no universals were involved and each poem were to be considered completely sui generis—it is hard to see how we could react coherently to any poem or how poets could learn from one another or how any of the literary arts could develop. The truth is that the artistic problems which perplex any author engaged in constructing any new work become problems for him precisely because universals *are* involved. His task is to embody his new materials and insights in words that will be effective in a particular way on the minds of readers, and he cannot do this without being governed, however unconsciously, by what a contemporary novelist has called "rules of construction, mysterious relations in technique, which exist apparently in the nature of art itself, and which oblige the artist to respect them."[2] Some of these, and the problems they raise, are generic to all kinds of writing or to all kinds in which the principal part is (say) a plot (for example, problems of arousing emotion or of intimating character or of achieving suspense and surprise) or to all kinds in which the manner is (say) narrative rather than dramatic. But some of them—and these are the most immediately compelling—are determined for the artist specifically by the principle of construction operative in his work but not unique to it, in the sense that other works having the same principle but a different matter can obviously be written (for example, other novels evoking the same kinds of emotion in the same sequence as *Emma* or *Persuasion*). In the composition of any work aspiring to a high degree of artistic integration there can be no final solutions of the general problems of writing apart from solution of the problems arising from the fact that certain concrete materials are to be given a certain specific form. That is to say, problems of style or the problems of writing, perhaps, a poetic drama cannot be solved independently of the problems the author faces in giving certain materials of his own invention a specific (and hence definable) form, or power—that of a tragedy like *The Duchess of Malfi,* for instance, rather than that of a tragedy like *Othello* or of one like *Venice Preserved.*

2 Joyce Cary, as quoted by Crane, *The Languages of Criticism and the Structure of Poetry* (Toronto, 1953), p. 143.

We can properly continue to talk, therefore, of literary forms, meaning by the term not traditional genres like "epistle," "ode," or "ballad opera," or constructed subject-matter classes like "revenge tragedy" or "graveyard poetry," or any of the many dialectically derived literary types such as "the poetry of synthesis," but species of works, inductively known, and differentiated, more or less sharply, in terms of their peculiar artistic elements and principles of construction. When the term "form" is so taken, distinctions of literary kind may range from the broad distinction between imitative and didactic forms (necessarily implying many subordinate differences in such things as plot, character, thought, and language), through distinctions based on some specific determination of either means, manner, or object (for example, that between recitative, declamatory, and fully mimetic drama), to the most completely formal distinctions, involving specifications of object, means, manner, and effect in some particular causal ordering, of which Aristotle's definition of tragedy in *Poetics* 6, as limited still further by *Poetics* 13 and 14, is the classic example.

From all this two important corollaries follow. In the first place, the principles which differentiate kinds of literary works in this analysis are obviously poetic ends, but their status as such is very different from that of the variously derived ends of poetry or of particular species of poetry in the two other modes of criticism. They are not ends in the sense either of historically known intentions of writers in composing particular works (as when we say, for instance, that Fielding intended *Joseph Andrews* to be a comic romance "in the manner of Cervantes") or of ideal ends dialectically deduced from premises concerning the nature of poetry and its relation to other arts and activities (as in the numerous variations on the *aut prodesse aut delectare* of Horace). Rather, they are ends induced from the history of literature by analysis of the final causes which have actually determined, and therefore can still determine, the production of literary works. We know thus that poems can be written for the sake of inculcating knowledge or of persuading readers to or against some mode of moral or political action, and we also know that writers may go beyond such practical purposes and compose poems of which the ends are the peculiar pleasures afforded by their beautiful and moving representations of different forms of human experience. We know further that when this happens, the imitative ends can subsume, without suppressing, the more general practical aims, so that we can say, with a modern critic, that all art is propaganda though not all propaganda is art. And we know, finally, that after specifically different forms have come into existence and been elaborated in all their parts for imitative purposes, the same forms, or rather the rules and devices they have made available to writers, may again be subordinated to constructive principles of a didactic order (as has happened in our time to many of the highly developed species of fiction, lyric poetry, and drama). For the critic in this mode, consequently, there can be no such thing as "true poetry" or the "ideal" tragedy or novel; his first business, whatever else he may do, is to consider literary works, without prejudice, in the light of the specific ends or principles of construction, whatever they may be, which have in fact, on the best hypothesis he can form, governed their composition and of the theoretically known conditions of maximum excellence peculiar to each.

And the second corollary is a variant of this: it is the all-importance of distinctions of literary species, in the meaning here given that term, to the critic of individual works. For on the assumption, which is basic to criticism of this sort, that no artist, as Eliot has said, "produces great art by a deliberate attempt to express his personality"— he "expresses his personality indirectly through concentrating upon a task which is a task in the same sense as the making of an efficient engine or the turning of a jug or table-leg"—the primary judgments of the critic must clearly be judgments of how well, in terms of its specific requirements, the poet's task has been performed: that is to say, he will make judgments in kind. He will not think of reproaching Milton, in *Lycidas* or *Paradise Lost,* for failing to write like Donne without first asking whether these poems would have been better for the same handling of language and verse as the *Satyres.* In short, he will begin by inquiring, for any work he intends to consider, what its peculiar species is; not for the sake of debating how far it has realized the ideal form of this species, but rather for the sake of knowing what particular criteria are relevant to the analysis or criticism of its parts. Thus he will avoid, for example, the error of judging *The Duchess of Malfi* as if it were a tragedy of the same species as *Othello,* or of discussing the merits and faults of *Murder in the Cathedral* as if it were a drama of a traditional sort rather than a special modern kind of lyric poem, or of treating all great poems, novels, and dramas, whether constructed as imitations or not, as if they were allegories or myths.

It should be easy now to see what must be the critical equipment of the historian who proposes to deal with literary productions, of whatever period, in terms of the concept of artistic synthesis. His first aim must be to achieve a maximum of *artistic* particularity and relevance in his statements about the traits of individual works or historical groupings of works. His procedure is dictated, in its main lines, by the fact that literary works may differ from one another, artistically, both with respect to the character of the whole which the writer has achieved, more or less successfully, in each and with respect to the nature and handling of their parts. The historian's account of any work will not be complete unless it includes specifications concerning both aspects, and the terms in which these can appropriately be couched will necessarily differ according as, for example, the work is imitative or didactic (a "plot" is not at all the same sort of thing as an allegorical fable) or as its subject is an extended action or a concentrated manifestation of feeling, thought, or moral choice. In all cases, however, the primary problem is that of the specific nature of the whole, and it is adequately solved only when this is stated formally— that is, as a principle of construction ordering the concrete materials of incident, character, thought, imagery, and the like—and in such a way as to permit us to distinguish the particular problems which the writer faced as a consequence of his choice of form. The form or effect of any work depends immediately, as we have seen, upon the form of its principal part, whether this is a plot form of one kind or another or something else having a similar architectonic function. This must be analyzed, as precisely as is possible or useful for the historian's purpose, in terms of its distinctive organization and intended effect on the thoughts and emotions of readers. (For a simple example see below, pp. 283 ff.) The problem of the parts is secondary, but not therefore, for the historian, any less important, inasmuch as in any group of works having the same essential form there may be radical differences in the treatment of its characteristic qualitative elements, depending in part upon the special character of the writer's material *données* or of his extraformal ends, in part upon his special choices of technique. Instances of the first sort of difference are the relatively slight magnitude of the action in *Coriolanus* as compared with Shakespeare's other tragedies and the relatively greater development of its thought over its plot and character; and, again, as between *Cymbeline* and *Philaster*—both tragicomedies of much the same species—the much completer subordination in Shakespeare's play as compared with Fletcher's of the particular scenes to the demands of the overall form. These are relevant observations for the historian of literature if only because they—and the innumerable similar observations that may be made on other works—present causal problems of a peculiarly literary kind. And the same thing is true of the differences he must observe in his writers' uses of traditional or novel devices of technique —both dictional and representational—in relation to such formal ends as depicting character, externalizing thought, or making the activity represented in the work seem probable, important, or emotionally effective in proper degree.

The task of analysis, at least for the works that are to be given special prominence in a history, is thus not simple, and its performance can easily be vitiated by one or another of the faults of method which constitute the characteristic corruptions of this critical mode. One of these is "formalism," or the disposition to reduce problems of artistic form to questions of "structure" merely, in abstraction from the humanly interesting and moving aspects of works upon which their form in the full sense of its peculiar moral and emotional quality essentially depends. Corruption also results from the confusion of artistic principles with techniques, from the substitution of a conception of literary kinds as "norms" for the conception of them as first principles of construction, and finally, and perhaps most disastrously, from the natural tendency to force individual works into formal molds that are either inappropriate to them (as when the *Essay on Criticism* is read as an instance of theoretical rather than practical or moral argument) or too rigid or generalized in definition to fit their peculiar characteristics (as in all discussions of tragic or tragicomic or comic plays and novels which neglect to consider these terms as embracing a considerable variety of distinctive plot forms).

Against such errors, given a historian with some sensitivity to differences of literary effect, the necessary safeguards are of two sorts. The first is experience: whatever his period of specialization, it will be better if he has read widely and critically in works of all kinds written in other periods and languages, especially those which exhibit the sharpest contrasts in the species of literature cultivated and in the character of the preferred techniques. Acquaintance with the ancients is thus indispensable for intelligent work in any modern period, and sympathetic knowledge of contemporary literature, particularly in its more revolutionary and experimental aspects, is essential for any properly discriminating study of the past. It will be better also if the historian has himself written or attempted to write poems or novels—and has meditated on the varieties of problems they present. The second safeguard is an adequate grounding in the theory on which this method of analysis depends. This will include both an understanding of its underlying assumptions about the nature of poetry and criticism and a constantly increasing set of critical tools. The latter are inductively tested differentiae for discriminating, literally and appropriately, the forms of works, distinguishing their parts and the varied functions they serve, and particularizing among their technical devices with respect both to the constitution of these and the specific uses to which they are put.

If it is asked where such an apparatus may be obtained, the answer must be, I think, that it exists as yet only in fragments. The *Poetics*, for all its limitations, is still an essential text, useful for its analysis of one species of tragedy, for its indications of criteria for the general consideration of plot, character, thought, diction, narrative manner, and the like, in imitative works, and, most important, for its exemplification of the methods of analysis and reasoning requisite to a literal inquiry into poetic works viewed concretely as products of different poetic arts. The historian can learn much, also, from the scattered remarks of poets and other creative writers, from Dante to Henry James, on the artistic and technical problems they faced in their works; a comprehensive list of references to these, indexed according to the questions at issue, would be an invaluable tool. But there is clearly much theoretical work still to be done. This could profitably include, for one thing, a systematic reconsideration of the devices of literary language—both the familiar devices codified in the older traditions of rhetoric and the newer devices invented by modern novelists and poets—from the point of view of their possible functions relative to poetic ends. It could very well include also an attempt to reduce to greater analytical precision such fashionable but extremely vague concepts as "symbolism," "pattern," and "myth." What is chiefly needed, however, is the inductive development of distinctions sufficiently numerous and refined to permit us to deal more accurately than we now can with modes of artistic synthesis of which Aristotle took no account. These modes include, for example, various forms of imitative drama and narrative intermediate between tragedy and comedy, the numerous shorter forms commonly referred to loosely as "lyric poems" and "short stories," and the many poetic species which are organized by extrinsic principles rather than by principles intrinsic to their matter, such as Ibsen's *Ghosts,* Orwell's *Animal Farm,* or C. P. Snow's *The Masters.*

To define the artistic particularity of works in the light of such relevant poetic theory as may be available is, then, the first task of the historian in this mode. It is not, however, his only task, since the peculiar effect and significance of individual poems, novels, and dramas is obviously a function not only of their formal constitution (although it is primarily a function of this), but likewise of two other factors which the historian can hardly neglect.

The first of these is the nature of the *données* which the writer has drawn from his experience, reflection, or reading and ordered to one poetic end or another in his work. It is not a matter of indifference, for contemporary readers at least and hence for the historian, whether the locales of plays and narratives are domestic or foreign, near or remote in time, familiar or novel; or whether their characters are depicted in ordinary or extraordinary people, acting and thinking according to a generally received code of morals and manners or according to one considered "advanced" for the time; or whether the events represented are such as may occur normally to any man in a given society or such as happen only rarely or in circumstances of a special sort or such as are impossible except to the imagination; or whether the "thought" of a work is derived from common and popular opinion or from some system of science or philosophy; or whether the stock of imagery from which a lyric poet (or novelist or playwright) draws is large or small, secondhand or original, traditional to a certain kind of poetry or "modern" and new, organized in a coherent set of myths (as in Yeats) or existing only as discrete parts; or whether the writer's language is selective or inclusive, old-fashioned or current, literary or conversational; and so on. These are all distinctions of a material order, such as a merely philological criticism is competent to investigate. They bear directly upon the task of the historian concerned with works as artistic syntheses, however: they signify differences which determine to some degree expectations and probabilities in plots and lyric poems and so inevitably qualify the effects of various works having the same formal principle; and differences of these kinds have often constituted the matter of significant or even revolutionary changes in literary practice. For these reasons the historian of the literary arts must unite statements concerning them with his propositions about the more purely formal aspects of the works he examines; he must take pains, however, to order and interpret all such material or conventional traits in the light of his poetic distinctions.

The second factor is the nature of the writer's mind. Here the historian will be involved with characteristics of literary works, over and above their distinguishing formal and material attributes, which enable him to say, for example, of various works by a single writer, that they are products of a naive or sophisticated mind; of a mind disposed to reduce experience and moral issues to simple oppositions or of one consistently impressed by the complexities of things; of a pioneering or iconoclastic mind or of one inclined to build upon, while transcending, the intellectual or literary past; of a mind dominated by limited interests or of one given to a wide-ranging concern with the problems of his time. It is needless to argue that the degree of pleasure afforded by different works and the seriousness with which mature readers can regard them are strongly influenced by such considerations. They are the sort of considerations that have motivated the many attempts of critics in the qualitative tradition to state the conditions of "greatness" in literature, either generally (as in Longinus) or particularly (as in the essays of Matthew Arnold or, more recently, in books like Eliot's *After Strange Gods* and Leavis' *The Great Tradition*). The historian must accordingly take differences of this kind into account in formulating his characterizations of works; the only difficulty is that they lend themselves more easily to dialectical or metaphorical statement or to some species of biographical, psychological, or doctrinal reduction than to literal definition in terms of the analyzable elements of thought, feeling, and diction through which they are realized in particular dramas, novels, and poems. Of all the theorists who have occupied themselves with the problem, only

Longinus, perhaps, saw clearly what a causal and problematic inquiry into qualities, as general qualities of literature, might be; and what seems to be needed, therefore, if the historian of literary forms is to combine coherently with his other judgments of works judgments concerning the moral and literary personalities reflected in them, is a modern development and extension of the art devised by Longinus for the attainment of the "sublime."

It is clear that both these factors, though in different ways, are related to what may be called the preconstructional and postconstructional aspects of a literary work—that is, with what precedes and what follows the shaping of the writer's materials into *this* individual production. It is, however, with the aspects of the work as thus constructed—its constructional aspects—that the historian who bases his analyses on the concept of artistic synthesis is primarily concerned, and he must consequently seek to frame his elementary propositions about works in such a way as to bring these other aspects into causal connection with the aspects defined by his poetic theory. The solution of this problem depends upon the solution of another problem, even more fundamental. This problem is posed by the fact that although literary works in any critical view are essentially objects of contemplation, the values of which as finished products of art are analytically separable from the processes of their composition and hence not resolvable into history, the literary historian is necessarily committed to regarding such works *sub specie temporis,* in relation to the careers, interests, and environing circumstances of their writers. The problem may be solved in a variety of ways, but the solution most consonant with the premises of this third mode of criticism is one that consists in taking the concrete wholeness of a work as the proximate end of its author's productive activity and reasoning back from what the work is, as an object of critical analysis, to the particular problems and decisions—defined artistically rather than psychologically—which its production entailed, and thence to the particular materials and qualities of mind which set the conditions in which the author's choices of form and of formative devices took place. It is only, indeed, by such a translation of products into processes that the historian in this mode can bridge the gap between the two kinds of statement which, as we saw in the beginning, all literary historians have to make and compose a history which will be a history of forms as well as of writers and deal with the artistic uses made of materials and conventions as well as with the historical causes that brought these into vogue and determined their character and appeal.

2. PRINCIPLES OF ORGANIZATION

The minimum principles of organization of any literary history are obviously succession in time, distribution in space (which we need not consider here), and likeness and difference in character. When these principles alone are operative, unmodified by others, the result will be what for lack of a better word may be called *atomistic history.* Among the innumerable histories, ancient and modern, which belong to this species by virtue at least of their general construction, it will suffice to mention the historical chapters in Quintilian's *Institutes,* Joseph Spence's pioneer account of the English poets, Johnson's *Lives,* Warton's *History of English Poetry,* the *Histoire littéraire de la France,* Hallam's *Introduction to the Literature of Europe,* Stopford Brooke's *Primer of English Literature,* the Petit de Julleville history of French literature, the Cambridge histories, the first part of Legouis and Cazamian's history, and the volumes thus far published in the Oxford history; a complete list would include a majority of the histories, comprehensive or selective, erudite or popular, which have undertaken to survey systematically the literary productions of a nation, an age, or a class of writers.

In all these the primary units of interpretation are either works or, more commonly, authors viewed as the most immediate cause of the characteristics exhibited by their works, but the individual histories differ widely according to the fashion in which the basic principles of succession and of likeness and difference are construed. The minimal extreme in this respect is perhaps best represented by the *Histoire littéraire,* especially in the volumes edited and in part written by Charles-Victor Langlois: here the comparison is conducted in the strictest philological terms, and the primary succession is of individual writers or anonymous works (the latter occasionally grouped in subject-matter classes) ordered solely by their known or conjectured dates without partition into periods. This is too austere an ideal, however, to have satisfied many historians of this type. At the very least, even among those whose conception of criticism has remained predominantly philological, it has appeared necessary to classify the authors dealt with, or all except the most eminent, in terms of some particular criterion, or combination of criteria, of likeness and difference. The most common determinant has been the literary genre to which the major efforts of a given writer were devoted—as in the familiar divisions into writers of verse and writers of prose; dramatists, novelists, poets, essayists, and critics; tragic dramatists and comic dramatists; religious poets and secular poets; poets of the town and poets of the country. These distinctions have usually been combined, however, in either a subordinating or a subordinate relation, with other kinds of distinctions. At times these have been based on the personal, professional, social, political, or ideological affinities of writers—as, for instance, Pope and his friends as distinct from the group surrounding Addison or Johnson and his circle; amateur writers and writers who lived by their pens; clerical and lay writers or middle-class and aristocratic writers; Whig writers and Tory writers; orthodox writers and deists. At other times such distinctions have been based on the traditions of matter or manner writers professed to follow as the disciples of Spenser, Jonson, and Donne; or on the characters of the audiences they wrote for as courtly and popular dramatists; or on their preferred modes of publication as anthologists, pamphleteers, or journalists. The temporal succession of writers is also broken, in most histories of this type, by divisions into periods or ages, the definitions of which are sometimes drawn merely from the calendar (as in Hallam, whose story from 1500 on begins afresh every fifty years), sometimes from changes of rulers or other political transformations, sometimes from phases in the general history of culture (for example, the Middle Ages, the Renaissance, the Enlightenment), and frequently, as in many "survey" histories of the standard sort, from an eclectic mixture of these and other similarly external criteria.

Beyond this only one further step is possible without abandonment of the principle of atomistic succession on which these histories are based. This step is taken whenever historians, not content with an exclusively philological approach, resort to one of the numerous varieties of qualitative criticism in their comparisons of writers and works. The succession still remains one primarily of writers, whether these are considered separately, one after the other, as in Johnson's *Lives* (which typifies the minimal extreme of this mode) or are grouped according to one or more of the classifying devices just mentioned; but the writers are no longer treated merely as authors of such and such works exhibiting such and such material traits of content and form as a result of the circumstances of their origin, but as exponents, in varying combinations and degrees of completeness, of the "values" which the historian demands in poetry or literature generally or those which he thinks distinctive of the age. The history thus becomes a record of successive manifestations of literary characteristics—those of individual writers in the first place, but those also, at least in most histories written since the middle of the eighteenth century, of schools of writers, traditions, movements, tendencies, periods. And as these can be defined and related to one another only in terms of some pattern of dialectical distinctions and oppositions (the historian having no causal theory of literary kinds to supply him with variables and unifying ends of a more literal sort), the parts of the history, from its statements about authors and their works to its statements about schools, traditions, and ages, tend to display those traits of organization which we have already seen to be consequential on this method. If there is to be ordering of qualities at all, its basis, in any particular context, must be a single principle of division under which all the more specific distinctions the historian may hit upon can be subsumed. Hence the frequency, in such histories, of sharp and schematic contrasts between writers, schools, traditions, or periods considered en bloc, as when Ben Jonson's poetry is opposed as a whole to the poetry, similarly unified, of Donne; or as when, in like fashion, the "line of wit" (which now includes both Jonson and Donne) is set over against the "line" which runs from Spenser through Milton and his eighteenth-century imitators to Keats and Tennyson; or as when in numerous histories and in terms of many different criteria of division, the literature of the Restoration and early eighteenth century is defined in antithesis to that of the Renaissance, or the Romantic period differentiated, by a series of compendent contrarieties, from the preceding Neoclassic age.

Such single-principled oppositions of authors and of large or small groupings of authors have become so familiar in literary historiography that we tend to think of them as generalizations of the same order as those made by a military or political historian when he distinguishes between the generalship of Lee and that of Grant or between the Old and the New Whigs in the 1790's or between the social state of England before and after the Industrial Revolution. In fact, however, they are generalizations of a very different kind, resting not upon a matter-of-fact causal analysis of events in terms peculiarly appropriate to the nature of the phenomena—military, political, economic, and so on—which happen to be in question, but upon what Hume called "relations of ideas," that is, general abstract distinctions applicable to many or all kinds of things. In other words, the qualitative particulars to be discriminated, are taken in abstraction from their immediate literary causes or reasons in individual works and interpreted as instances or manifestations of one or another of the metaphysical contrarieties or dialectical commonplaces which constitute the historian's analytical stock in trade. The differences between Wordsworth and Shelley are thus resolved, in F. R. Leavis' history, into two contrasting relations between thought and feeling and two contrasting attitudes toward tradition. In Hallam the distinctions among schools of English poetry in the early seventeenth century are derived from a basic schematism of the mental faculties—imagination, reason, and emotion—which for him ultimately determine all literary effects. In Stopford Brooke's *Primer,* the history of poetic style from 1600 to 1800 is reduced to a series of permutations of those familiar terms of all work, "nature" and "art." In Paul Van Tieghem's book on the Romantic movement in Europe, the major division of Romantic subject matter, which is then used to organize the accounts of Romantic poetry and Romantic fiction, is based on the even more general distinction of internal and external. And in *The Great Chain of Being,* A. O. Lovejoy has brilliantly subsumed the differences between the so-called Romantic period and the Enlightenment, in both subject matter and style, under the simple antithesis—which may serve to organize many other histories besides—of a liking for diversity and a craving for the uniform and simple.

It is only to be expected that different histories of this type, though dealing with the same period or literature, should exhibit a remarkable variety of divergent classifications, emphases, and interpretations. Many of these, of course, are the natural result either of progress in scholarly discovery and proof or of changes in literary taste (so that the judgments on many writers in the histories of a generation ago now seem comically dated); others merely reflect different notions of what the term "literature" properly includes. All these are fruitful sources of polemic among historians or between historians and their reviewers, but they are less relevant to our theme than are the differences which originate in the many possibilities of variation implicit in the method itself. Thus there are few histories in this tradition that do not combine the results of philological and biographical research with their dialectical characterizations and estimates; but individual histories differ greatly according as one or the other of the two elements is made to predominate and according as the two are more or less closely related in the historian's exposition. There are few histories, also, in which statements designed to show what each author had "by distinction" are not supplemented by statements designed to show what all the authors included or all the authors belonging to a particular group had in common; but here again in practice the extremes lie far apart. There are likewise few histories employing dialectical principles which do not allow the historian to mingle propositions about the historical "values" of his authors with propositions about their "values" in terms of some universal scale; but in this respect, too, the diversity is very great. And, lastly, although there are few histories of this type which do not treat in some fashion of both content and form in their descriptions and generalizations, the widest differences prevail with respect to the relative emphasis placed on the two aspects and with respect to the conceptions entertained by the historian of the nature of each and of its relation to the other.

Out of these divergences innumerable controversies have sprung, in which partisans of philology, or "history" pure and simple, have been ranged against critics; biographical and psychological critics against "historical" critics; "absolutist" critics against "relativist" critics; "formalist" critics against those who find the values of literature in its moral or sociological implications; and so on. In the nature of things no easy resolution of any of these disputes is possible, since all of them turn on the dogmatic opposition of half-truths; but that is not to say that there are no criteria for appraising the species of literary history which has given rise to the quarrels. That better and worse histories of this kind can be written is clear enough: they will be better, obviously, in proportion as the historian uses and makes available to others the findings of the best scholarship on the topics he treats and in proportion as he is himself an original and perceptive critic in the qualitative mode; who can be other than grateful for comprehensive and well-arranged repertories of information about literature and for fresh literary judgments on authors of the past? When this is said, however, we must admit that something is wanting in histories of literature conceived and organized as these are. They have all the limitations of the two modes of criticism on which their propositions are based, and in addition, as every one knows who has tried his hand at constructing one of them, if only in class lectures, they are very hard to do well, for two main reasons. In the first place, given only the principles of succession and of likeness and difference, the historian must perforce fall back on extrinsic criteria of relevance for determining what things or even what kinds of things he ought to say. He may aim at the ideal of bio-bibliographical completeness which has inspired the editors of the *Histoire littéraire,* but short of this his only guides in the selection of authors to be included, in the proportioning of space to these, in the elaboration or suppression of biographical, bibliographical, and other circumstantial details, and even in the choice of topics of qualitative characterization are such vague and arbitrary standards as those set by his private interests, theories, and tastes, the current fashions in scholarship and criticism, or the custom of the trade. And for the same reasons, secondly, there can be, in histories of this type, no principle of historical continuity of a more specific kind than the general persistence throughout the ages treated of a more or less widespread impulse to compose works of the various sorts included in the historian's definition of literature or poetry. They are necessarily wanting, therefore, in the dynamic quality which the best histories of political or military affairs have always had. The structure of the narrative, if it can be said to be a narrative structure at all, is distinguished by perpetual fresh starts—with each new period or subperiod, with each new topical division of a period, even with each new author; and the historian is compelled to exert all his dialectical or literary ingenuity in devising transitions from one large or small part to the next which will not betray too obviously the static character of his construction.

These difficulties have been felt by many literary historians as keenly as by most of their readers, and two principal efforts—sharply opposed in their conceptions of method—have been made to go beyond the simple principle of atomistic succession which has been chiefly responsible for the trouble.

One of these, based on an extension to the history as a whole of the devices of dialectical organization which we have seen operating in subordinate parts of the histories just considered has led to what may be called integral or organic literary history. The integration has been effected in a great many ways and in terms of many varying or conflicting theories of the nature of literature and of the connections between literature and other things. Sometimes these connections have been largely suppressed or relegated to a secondary or incidental rule, with the result that unity is achieved by the application to successive writers of a single dialectic of combination and separation having as its elements a compendent set of "literary" qualities or values, the necessity pervading the history being that of the disjunctive major premise of critical theory which holds it together. Examples of this are some of Eliot's early essays (especially those dealing with the progress from the seventeenth century to the nineteenth of the celebrated "dissociation of sensibility"), Leavis' *Revaluation* (which has a similar theme but with more intrusions of the social correlatives of the poetic traditions), and Cleanth Brooks's "Notes for a revised History of English Poetry" (composed, he tells us, in the belief that "the orthodox histories . . . will have to be rewritten . . . with more consistency than they now possess, and with emphasis on a more vital conception of the nature of poetry than that which now underlies them"). To this general class belongs also the conception of literary history expounded and exemplified by René Wellek, although the dialectical mechanism Wellek prefers to use is quite different. He too proposes a history which will be a history of literature "as literature and not another thing," as free from dependence on external factors as histories of music and painting have commonly been; and he insists that such a history can be written without treating literary development either as a meaningless flux, a mere series of differentiated works, or as a reflection of some absolute value "extraneous to the process of literature." His solution depends upon an analogy of literature to language as this is interpreted in the theories of the Genevan School and the Prague Linguistic Circle; it consists in "relating the historical process to a value or norm"—that is, a system of standards and conventions—which stands platonically as the One to the Many given by the historian's observations of particular writers and works (that is, it determines the common predicates to be applied to the latter) while being itself subject to change. By means of such a normative idea, which will differ from one historical context to another, we may constitute integrally, in exclusively "literary" terms, the history of an author, a literary genre, a period or movement, a national literature (even though this is "harder to envisage"), or an international literary development.

More frequently, however, the emphasis in the integrating dialectic has been on the other things with which literature in its general evolution, or in a particular phase of this, has been thought to be connected in a peculiarly intimate way. The simplest class of such histories consists of those in which writers or works are characterized in terms of their varying "expressions" or "reflections" of some single situation or line of development—sometimes described in a relatively literal fashion, sometimes simplified into a historical myth —in the general life of the time. There are many partial exemplifications of this device in histories based generally on the principle of atomistic succession (for instance, in Legouis' chapters on English poetry between 1580 and 1660) and, as every one knows, it has been often used, especially since the beginning of the nineteenth century, to organize whole histories, of a considerable variety of types, in which likenesses and differences among writers and works are defined primarily, though not always exclusively, by "correspondence" or "equation" with characteristics attributed to the unifying state of affairs or process of change. The latter has sometimes been conceived broadly as the shifting temper of a nation, as in Barrett Wendell's *The Temper of the Seventeenth Century in English Literature,* or, more specifically, as this temper modified by the circumstances of a new environment, as in Moses Coit Tyler's history of literature in colonial America. The unity, again, has sometimes been found in the continuity of political development, as in W. J. Courthope's *History of English Poetry* (based, as the preface informs us, on the postulate that the study of English poetry is in effect "the

study of the continuous growth of our national institutions as reflected in our literature"); sometimes in the persistent opposition,
in a given society, of antithetical political ideals, as in Virgil Par-
rington's history; sometimes in the manifestations of contemporary
economic life, as in L. C. Knights's *Drama and Society in the Age
of Jonson;* sometimes in the "moral history" of a people in a period
of cultural crisis, as in Alfred Kazin's *On Native Grounds* (in which
American writing between 1890 and 1940 is interpreted—but without neglect of its artistic traits—in relation to the widely felt need,
created by the "moral transformation of our American life, thought,
and manners under the impact of industrial capitalism and science,"
to learn "what the reality of life was in the modern era"); sometimes in the pattern of contemporary intellectual activity, as Sir
Herbert Grierson's *Cross Currents in English Literature of the
Seventeenth Century* (in which the literature is discussed as "reflecting
the spiritual conflicts" of the age); sometimes in the evolution of
the language, as in F. W. Bateson's *English Poetry and the English
Language*. All these histories—and the many others that could be
added to the list—are in their varying fashions dominated by a concern with "the relation between literary modes and ways of thinking
and feeling, between quality of writing and quality of living"; it
is the peculiar paradox, however, of their dialectical method that in
proportion as they clarify "the ways of thinking and feeling" mir-
rored in their authors, the particularity of "the literary modes"
tends to be obscured or reduced to a common denominator or political, social, intellectual, or linguistic terms. Their characteristic
limitation is therefore the opposite of that inherent in the "literary"
histories of Brooks and Wellek: just as those histories have the effect of unduly separating poetry from life, so these run the risk of
unduly collapsing the history of poetry or literature into the "moral"
history of the society it reflects.

The necessity present in such histories derives typically from the
assumption that literary works must inevitably be mirrors of their
age as well as, more immediately, of their authors' experiences and
minds. This assumption underlies also another important group of
modern literary histories, which differ, however, from those just considered by introducing another level of necessity—and hence of
schematic integration—in the form of a dialectical analysis of the

underlying causal factors. The primary determinant has sometimes been the economic or political structure of society, as in the many attempts to write the history of literature in terms of Marxist theory or some variant thereof; an example, with special features of its own, is Bateson's *English Poetry: A Critical Introduction,* in which the major schools of English poetry are reduced to five (with a sixth not treated in detail), each with its "basic form of poetic statement" which is the "reflection" in its poetry of the peculiar character or "dominant incentive" of the contemporary "social order"; there have been five such orders from Chaucer's time to the present, the distinctive character of each being determined by a permutation of two pairs of contraries—collectivist and individualist, rural and urban. More commonly, however, the ultimate unifying causes have been given a psychological status in the common faculties or impulses of the mind; as, for example, in Taine's *History of English Literature,* in which all historical phenomena, including literature, are deduced from the operations of the understanding and the will as modified in the lapse of time by the three factors of *race, milieu,* and *moment;* or in Louis Cazamian's account of English literature from 1660 to the present, in which the literary evolution is plotted in terms of a necessary alternation of phases dominated by intelligence with phases dominated by imagination and feeling; or in Leslie Stephen's *History of English Thought in the Eighteenth Century,* in which a complicated dialectic of historical progress is built out of similar basic contraries; or, most recently, in Hiram Haydn's *The Counter Renaissance,* in which the distinction of two types of temperament— that which "believes in the essential congruence and relatedness of the ideal and the empirically actual" and that which sees only an irreconcilable discrepancy between the two—is used to schematize the whole intellectual and literary development, in England and on the Continent, between the later Middle Ages and the period of Newton. In the lengths to which they carry the principle of dialectical integration, these histories, it is evident, go far beyond any of the other varieties of this type of construction, and in doing so they encounter the characteristic danger, not only that the individual and specific traits of the literature will be submerged in the abstractions of the unifying scheme, but that the history itself will take on the character not so much of history as of philosophy and so be judged as good or bad in terms of its dialectical adequacy alone.

There can be no doubt, however, that these various modes of organic history do achieve a solution of the twin problems of continuity and relevance posed by literary histories of the traditional atomistic kind: of the first by substituting a logical progression or schematism of ideas for simple chronological succession; of the second by providing a matrix of common terms and distinctions capable of being applied analogically to all writers and all species of works. The attractions of the method for such minds as tend to identify intelligibility in history with a reduction of its multifarious particulars to some principle of unity can readily be understood; the difficulty is that there are and have always been other minds, no less concerned with making sense out of the literary past, for whom any such dialectical reduction is bound to seem at once too easy and too destructive of the observable literal distinctness of works and of the reasons thereof to hold their interest for any length of time.

It is from historians of this latter kind that the second major solution of the problems of continuity and relevance in literary history has proceeded. Its model has been not dialectic but the narrative-causal sequences characteristic of those histories of political or military events which have developed beyond the stage of annals. And its principles, which determine the variety and interrelation of the propositions the historian has to make, are the general factors implicit in any concrete instance of change, of whatever sort, in nature or human affairs. These are: (1) an initial situation from which the change proceeds; (2) a final situation in which the first situation eventuates and which contrasts with the first in kind, quality, or amount; (3) a continuing matter which undergoes change and of which both end terms can be predicated; and (4) a moving cause, or convergence of moving causes, capable of bringing about the particular change defined by the other variables.

The possibility of constructing a literary history according to these principles depends, in the first place, upon the discovery, in any succession of works with which the historian may be concerned, of a continuing subject of change that can be stated in more or less specific and literal terms. (1) This may be interest in a particular subject matter, myth, or body of doctrine which writers continue to exploit (as the world of natural phenomena, the Arthurian legends, the conception of romantic love); (2) it may be a special technique or type of medium to which successive writers devote themselves (as the writing of novels in letter form, the use of symbolic devices of representation, the heroic couplet); (3) it may be an established model, or corpus of similar models, which persists as an effective tradition (as the early poems of Milton, the comedies of Terence, the Cervantean manner in fiction, the prose style of Seneca); (4) it may be a particular genre, the conventions and rules of which continue to be used as a norm in creation (as dream allegory, drawing-room comedy, the verse tale, the detective novel, the Western story); (5) it may be a specific end or artistic problem which, once it has emerged, continues to direct literary practices (as writing poems in the service of religion, composing tragedies that will move the tender affections, devising meters suitable to drama, giving a lifelike quality to dialogue in fiction); or (6) it may be simply the persistence of a general desire, for example, to use language imitatively or to prevent drama, fiction, or poetry from degenerating into fixed routines with little immediate relevance to contemporary life.

The continuum of a narrative history may be drawn from any one of these, and the form of the change it sets forth is then constituted by taking as the initial and terminal points any more or less contrary sets of literary characteristics, exhibited successively by the works under consideration, that involve differences in the practice of writers which can be related causally to whatever is taken as the constant factor in the development. The differences thus may be differences of kind or form relative to the persistence of a given subject matter, technique, model of imitation, convention, problem, or general end, or they may be differences of quality in subject matter or technique relative to the continued cultivation of a given form, or they may be differences in the extent to which successive writers manifested a given complex of traits of whatever character. Similarly, the contrarieties basic to the history may range from contrasts between an initial non-existence of something and its eventual emergence fully formed (with its possible later disappearance) to clear-cut oppositions of characteristics of the same order with or without intermediate gradations between the first and the last. The immediate moving causes, finally, are the productive acts of the writers involved in the change as these are conditioned, immediately or remotely, by the artistic or extra-artistic ends which the writers sought to realize in the process of construction, by the character of their literary, moral, and intellectual habits, and by the accidents of their social status, education, experience, and reading or of the events or circumstances which occasioned the writing of particular works.

It is evident that here again, as in organic literary history, we have moved beyond the simple principles of succession and of likeness and difference, though without ceasing to employ these as guides in the ordering and interpretation of data. The structure of a narrative history, like that of an organic history, is continuous and dynamic rather than atomistic and static, and its constituent elements, like those of an organic history, are related to one another as contraries or opposites. In both types of history, moreover, the problem of relevance is solved through the use of a previously determined system of concepts, and in both types there is an assumption of necessity.

At this point, however, the contrast begins, and philosophically considered, it is a fundamental one. In the first place, the continuity achieved in narrative history is the continuity not of a dialectical integration of historical differences in terms of a single analogy or scheme. Rather it is the continuity of a sequence of distinct events connected causally by whatever individual men or groups of men, through a period of time, happened to do with respect to the element constituting the continuum of the change. Accordingly, the degree of integration attainable in such a history depends upon the possibility of discovering causal connections, in materials, techniques, forms, or ends, among the different sequences with which it deals. The particular contrarieties in a narrative history, therefore, cannot be deduced from any unified scheme of common terms as, for example, in the dialectical histories of Taine and Cazamian. Inasmuch as their function is to signify initial, terminal, and intermediate points in a change, their selection (out of the store of possible significant differences in literary practice possessed by the historian) must always be a posteriori and relative to the specific matter of the change which is being traced. The concepts, furthermore, without which the ordering of a narrative history and the determination of its criteria of relevance would be impossible are concepts of a very different sort from those on which the organic historian relies. What they represent is not a particular pattern of universals reflected in the history but simply a specification of the general causal factors which may be distinguished in any occurrence of change. They are not therefore constitutive concepts, determining the substance of the historian's elementary propositions, but heuristic concepts, determining the number and nature of the questions he must ask with respect to literary events about which he has already, and independently, made elementary propositions. And finally, although the construction of any coherent history entails the assertion of necessary connections among its happenings, the connections asserted in a narrative history are necessary not in any sense that implies determinism of a Marxist or psychological kind but only retrospectively, in the meaning of necessity involved in our saying, of something which has actually come about, that it could not have taken place as it did unless certain other things had happened previously.

That there have been many successful attempts to deal narratively with literary phenomena—taking these as events in particular sequences of change rather than as manifestations of more general principles and causes—hardly needs to be pointed out. Brief examples could be cited from many histories which, considered as wholes, are basically atomistic in structure (for example, Henry Hallam's *Introduction* and Douglas Bush's volume in the Oxford series), from a great number of scholarly articles and monographs, and from the writings of many literary critics (such as J. L. Lowes's *Convention and Revolt in Poetry* and several of Eliot's essays). The method has also been applied, on a larger scale, in the construction of literary biographies, of some of the better accounts of the origins and early development of drama and fiction, and of numerous studies in the history of genres, traditions of subject matter and technique, literary schools and movements, and the reputation and influence of writers. The characteristic virtues of the mode can be seen in such works—to mention only a few at random—as Alfred Jeanroy's *La Poésie lyrique des troubadours*, C. S. Lewis' *The Allegory of Love*, Ernest Bernbaum's *The Drama of Sensibility*, Paul Van Tieghem's *Ossian en France*, George Williamson's *The Senecan Amble*, and, more comprehensive in scope than these, William Minto's *Literature of the Georgian Era* (a much neglected account of the changes in English poetry between Pope and Byron, interpreted in the context of other literary changes, which seems to me one of the least doctrinaire and most sophisticated books on its period I have read). Written with a minimum reliance on dialectical devices of historical construction, these histories, as well as a good many others like them, have the great merit, which is rarely encountered in the more ambitious histories, of telling, interestingly, complex and significant literary stories. Their limitations are chiefly the result of the kind of critical principles their writers have employed in discriminating the changing characteristics of works. For the most part, these historians have tended to rely either on grammatical or qualitative statements about the content and form of works or on inferences concerning the artistic intentions of writers of which the critical premises are at best definitions of techniques or generic differentiations of literary kinds. Their narratives, as a consequence, admirable as many of them are, have tended to stop short both of the fullest possible literary particularity and of the completest possible adequacy of historical explanation.

The next logical step, therefore, seems to be an extension and further refinement of narrative literary history on the basis of the one critical concept which is here left out, or utilized only inexplicitly and with respect only to its most general implications.

We have already said that in any history founded on the principle of artistic synthesis the central though by no means exclusive emphasis would be on the constructional aspects of literary works considered from the point of view of the problems faced by writers in the process of making poems, dramas, or narratives of different kinds. The collective enterprise of historians in this mode would consequently have as its ultimate purpose the writing of a narrative-causal history of the various literary arts in terms of four things: (1) the successive shifts in the artistic or formal ends which writers at different times and in different places have pursued, (2) the successive changes in the materials through which the different ends were realized, (3) the successive discoveries of more effective or at least new devices and techniques for the achievement of the different forms in the different materials, and

(4) the successive actualizations of all these changing possibilities in the production of artistically valuable or historically significant works in the different arts with which the history deals. For reasons we have noted, the relation between the first three of these elements—forms, materials, techniques—is such that they must be viewed, relatively to the preconstructional choices of writers, as independent variables; so it is possible to make any one of them by itself the organizing line of change in a history, as has often been done for materials and techniques in the partial mode of narrative history just discussed. It is the distinguishing assumption, however, of the kind of history we are now considering that complete historical intelligibility demands not only the inclusion of all three elements but the recognition that the first is necessarily prior in importance (though not always prior in the historian's order of inquiry) to the other two, since in the actual construction of literary works of a given kind the latter either depend upon it as a principle or are fully explicable, in all their peculiarities as combined in particular works, only by reference to it. It is appropriate therefore to describe this mode of literary history as the narrative history of forms.

The crucial problem, then, is the discrimination of the various artistic ends pursued by writers from time to time and the organization of these differences into significant lines of change. We need only recall here what has been said earlier about the first part of this task: it is not a question either of classifying works grammatically in terms of their conventional genres or of schematizing them dialectically in terms of a predetermined pattern of rational oppositions to which their differing characteristics are reduced; rather it is a question of distinguishing with adequate precision, in terms of the constructive principles operative in each, the generic and specific natures of the concrete wholes which writers, for one reason or another, chose to produce, and of doing this in such a fashion as clearly to indicate, for any group of works thus differentiated, the peculiar formal requirements which the choice of this principle rather than of some other, in the shaping of the material, imposed upon their writers. And the problem is solved, we may also recall, when the historian is able to say, for any work distinguished thus and so in medium and manner, that its principal part is an organization of such and such specific elements of action, character, thought, or emotion, accomplished in such and such a way, and endowed consequently with the power of inducing in attentive and perceptive readers such and such a sequence of specific effects.

How seldom discriminations of this sort have been attempted in literary history can be easily illustrated. It is impossible to learn, for example, from any of the elaborate accounts we have of the serious English drama of the seventeenth century how many of the plays commonly called "tragedies" had plot forms of the highly particularized type analyzed by Aristotle in *Poetics* 13 and 14 (although we may suspect that apart from Shakespeare the number was small) and how many, on the contrary, owed their peculiar character to their authors' preference for various other formally distinct though allied ends. If then we are to trace with any precision or artistic intelligibility the history of English "tragedy" during this and subsequent periods down to the present, we need to have, as a starting point, far more adequate answers to this question than can be inferred from the existing histories, valuable as many of these are for their accounts of dramatic materials and conventions.

It is much the same with the histories of the English novel. Where can we discover, for example, how Fielding's novels are related, not materially and technically only but formally, to the fiction and drama that preceded him—or even to one another; or what were the formal innovations, if any, of Jane Austen; or to what different artistic forms Henry James adapted his various techniques of narrative and how far these forms were carried by him beyond the stage of differentiation they had already attained; or how the "modern" adventure stories of writers like Graham Greene differ in their formal principles, if they do, from the "classic" adventure fiction of R. L. Stevenson; or whether the historical significance of Ernest Hemingway is exhausted when we have finished discussing his contributions of fresh subject matter and new tricks of technique.

Nor is the case different when we turn to the histories of English poetry. Although much has been written about the changes in materials, attitudes, and dictional devices between Metaphysical poetry and Augustan, between Augustan and Romantic-Victorian, and between Victorian and "modern," can any one be justified in saying, on the basis of these discussions, that this is the whole of the story or that there were not likewise far-reaching shifts, in each of these periods, in poetic forms, the consequences of which for the other aspects of the successive revolutions in poetry the historian ought also to consider? And even if, contrary to all probability, this was not the case—even if, during the whole period from 1600 to the present, no important new forms of lyric or didactic poetry emerged and no important new possibilities of further differentiation were discovered in the old ones— should we not at any rate be told precisely what the various forms were in relation to which, collectively or separately, the various material and technical changes took place?

It could well be that a concerted effort by many historians, equipped with sufficiently delicate tools of analysis, to give us the accurate discriminations among formal ends now so generally wanting would have the effect of renewing decisively our understanding of the course of English or any other literature in its various periods and branches. It would in any case serve to direct our attention more sharply than has yet been done to a major cause of both continuity and variability in literary practice. The history as finally constructed would not be exclusively a history of forms, although it would be this primarily in the sense that the historian's formal distinctions among works would serve to order narratively, as either lines of continuity or end terms of change, his propositions concerning the materials and technical operations in and by which the forms were achieved. Such a history would stop short of the kind of "integration" that presupposes, throughout or at any stage, a single analogy or a fixed and necessary scheme of development, but the historian of forms would be able to find partial substitutes for these devices, more in keeping with the a posteriori assumptions of his method, in certain theoretical considerations about the causal relationships of literary ends. Thus we may say that two distinguishable kinds of poetry are related subsumptively when the kind developed later implies as one of its necessary conditions of existence the previous development of the other kind, different though the two are in the specific nature of their organizing principles. We recognize, for example, that before writers can make unified structures having a sustained emotional power of a certain specific sort they must previously have learned how to achieve emotional interest and suspense of a less formal kind in the parts of works. It goes without saying that in the actual history of literature the movement is not always or everywhere from the more material to the more formal stages of such theoretically established relationships. It may be, for instance, that in a given historical situation, while writers of prose fiction are going from relatively general and diffuse emotional effects to more unified and particularized effects (as in the evolution of the "comic romance" between Scarron and Fielding), writers of tragedy are moving in the opposite direction (as in the history of tragic forms between Shakespeare and the later eighteenth century); or that shorter forms are at one time elaborated into larger (as in the relation of Richardson's first two novels to the earlier "pathetic" tales) and at another time longer forms as compressed into shorter (as in the relation of the full-length Gothic romances to the later short stories of Poe and others); or that, within a given species like tragedy, the development is at one stage characterized by the addition of new plot elements to those already in use to yield more complex emotional structures (as in the relation of Shakespeare to Kyd and Marlowe) and at another stage by the simplification and re-ordering of earlier plot forms in terms of one of their subordinate elements (as in the relation between Robert Dodsley's *Cleone* and *Othello*).

Employed as a heuristic device rather than as a constitutive principle, however, this notion of subsumptive relations among forms may be of the greatest utility to the historian in the analysis and ordering of his data. And it may be supplemented by similar general considerations bearing on the relative importance of different lines of formal change. From a historical point of view, the most significant shifts in literary ends are clearly those to which the historian can refer—as their necessary or probable consequences—the greatest number or variety of other changes in the kinds of materials writers chose to exploit and in the kinds of devices of construction, characterization, thought, imagery, diction, prosody, or representation they invented or revived for the purpose. Generally speaking, it may be assumed—again as not a dogma but a rough guide in interpretation—that a widespread shift on the part of the ablest writers from the cultivation of mimetic to the cultivation of didactic forms (such as occurred after the middle of the seventeenth century) is likely to have more far-reaching results of the kinds mentioned than a shift from serious forms to comic in drama or fiction, and that a shift of the latter sort is likely to be considerably more consequential than one involving only such formal differences, significant though these are, as can be discerned between Shakespeare's earlier and later tragedies or between Congreve's *Double Dealer* and his other comedies or between *Pride and Prejudice* and *Emma* or *Persuasion*.

The problem of changes in literary ends can be treated apart from the problem of changes in literary materials, but only at the cost of rendering the statements about forms unhistorical and abstract; and conversely, although changes in materials can be, and repeatedly have been, made independent objects of study apart from forms, this has always been at the risk either of leaving the changes unexplained or of finding the explanation in causes which have only a remote bearing on the transformations necessarily effected in any body of materials when it is used as the matter of literary works. The historian of forms must therefore talk about changes in materials, but from the point of view not of the history of religion, culture, ideas, society, or language merely but of the history of the literary arts. Taking materials broadly, as comprising everything in the diction of a work or in the things signified by the diction—that is, story (as distinct from plot), environing circumstances, types or signs of character, objects or indexes of emotion, attitudes, conceptions, images, modes of argument, and the like—that can be referred to antecedents other than the writer's formal end and technical skill, whether the antecedents are in real life or in conventions of earlier literature, the historian will concern himself with these primarily as they have been formed for literary use either by particular efforts of previous artists or by the more general influence of past or contemporary ideas in attaching special significances and values to this or that aspect of experience. The most important changes will be those which necessitated or made probable the development of new formal effects or new technical devices on the part of the writers touched by them. Many instances of this could be given: the romances, lyrics, and allegories which in the twelfth century exploited the recently articulated doctrines of courtly love; the Renaissance dramas in which the plot materials of Greek romance suggested new effects; the rise of new formal varieties of comedy, tragedy, fiction, and poetry during the eighteenth century in response to the contemporary exaltation of "good nature"; the proliferation of new species of poetry, drama, and romance after 1750 as a consequence of the Medieval Revival; the emergence in our time of original plot forms in drama and novel in obvious adjustment to the fresh conceptions and values made current by Freud, and of new types of diction and rhythm in poetry and narrative in similar adjustment to modern linguistics and the general relaxation of verbal taboos. The historian of forms will avoid unduly schematizing such changes (as is done, for instance, in Stopford Brooke's account of changes in poetic subject matter between Shakespeare and Wordsworth and more completely still in Bateson's *English Poetry*). At the same time he will look beyond short-run and accidental differences to the broad lines of continuity that connect the successive major importations into artistic literature of new regions of physical, moral, and psychological experience: the successive shifts of interest, attitude, or knowledge which bring it about in a given age that certain themes or aspects of life formerly central in literary creation become incapable of stimulating any except the most old-fashioned writers or that situations and characters once thought appropriate only to comic forms are now exploited for serious effects, or vice versa; and the successive changes in literary opinion and practice with respect to the kinds of language or meter which are or are not proper, at different times, to literature or any of its kinds. In this consideration of such problems, finally, the historian will attempt to make clear the relation of particular material changes to contemporary changes in forms, discriminating between those changes in matter which affected simultaneously a number of important forms, those whose consequences were limited to one or two forms, and those which, emerging first in one form, were later, perhaps much later, extended to others.

The problem of changes in techniques is susceptible of generally similar treatment. The term techniques may be given a somewhat extended meaning, in this context, to signify any distinguishable modes of procedure which are the consequences, in a particular work, of its author's desire to impose on certain selected materials, invented by him or borrowed from earlier writers, a certain specific form or power, whether imitative or didactic; it includes thus a wide range of things, from the material organization of the plot or argument or lyric situation, the establishment of probable or necessary relations between its parts, the depiction of characters, and the elaboration of thought, down to the handling of diction, imagery, symbols, and verse and of all the devices of representation, literal or symbolic, which may be used to keep the minds of readers or spectators properly directed and to enhance, functionally or decoratively, the intended effect of the whole or of any of its parts. These are all things which writers can learn from other writers and then develop further in response to the material or formal exigencies of new works; they can therefore have a history of their own distinct from the histories of the materials and forms in relation to which they are used. Many parts of this history have indeed been written, so that the historian of forms has already available to him a considerable body of relevant data. He will need to review existing knowledge, however, in the light of his understanding of the varied artistic functions which the devices hitherto discussed—usually with exclusive reference to their material characteristics—may serve in works of different kinds. He will also need to supplement these observations with observations of his own. For example, there is nowhere in print, so far as I am aware, an adequate study of the many experiments in narrative manner which preceded Fielding and upon which he built. Again, despite all that has been written about the dramatic conventions of the early seventeenth century, I can think of no one who has inquired analytically into the extraordinary variety of choral devices (of action, character, thought, diction, and representation) which Shakespeare employed, especially in his tragedies, to affect the opinions and sympathies of his audience relative to the action in its successive parts. And similar gaps could be pointed out in other fields—most glaringly, perhaps, in the history of the modern lyric, where research has hardly gone beyond questions of versification and the grammatical or dialectical study of imagery.

In constructing a history of changes in techniques the historian of forms will attend to the particular artistic uses for which new devices of all kinds were invented; he will distinguish between the kind of invention that consists in adapting new devices to old formal uses and the kind that consists in finding new formal uses for old devices; he will dwell on the numerous efforts of writers to renew forms of poetry, drama, or fiction by borrowing devices from other forms, poetic or not (as eighteenth-century novelists, for example, obtained new effects by taking over devices from comedy, satire, and the essay), or by borrowing from the same or similar forms as cultivated in a more novel way in other literatures (as Eliot revivified English poetry by bringing into it techniques already developed in France); he will concern himself with the survivals of old devices in the face of belief by the more advanced or sensitive writers that their utility is exhausted; and he will call attention to the curious results that come about when, as often happens, a device appropriate and powerful in one species of poetry is adapted to uses it is incapable of serving effectively in another (as in the attempts of the Warton brothers to employ Miltonic blank verse in poems much closer in form to *Il Penseroso* than to *Paradise Lost*). He will not commit himself to an assumption of steady progress in the techniques any more than in the principles or forms of art, but he will be directed in his interpretations of successive technical differences by general considerations similar to those available to him for tracing changes in form. We may thus say theoretically, though with the proviso that in any given situation in history the order may be reversed, that there is a tendency in the literary arts to move from generality to particularity in the construction of plots (or their lyric equivalents) and in the definition and depiction of characters, from a concern with the immediate and external aspects of actions to a concentration on their internal aspects or their indirect consequences in the feelings of the agents or their friends, from simple and explicit indications of character, thought, or motive to elaborate and subtle indications, from highly articulated modes of speech to more elliptical and suggestive modes, from a fashion of imagery in which the reference is primarily to objects to one in which the inner state of the characters is more fully involved, from simple metaphors to complex and difficult ones, from verse having relatively few rhythmic dimensions to verse having many, from contentment with "statement" to insistence upon "rendering," from a minimum reliance on inference or indirect representation to a maximum reliance on these—and so on through many analogous probabilities of development by which the historian of forms may be guided, with due respect to the facts before him, in defining his lines of continuity and change.

The final problem of the historian in this mode arises from the obvious fact that the three elements so far considered, treated in abstraction from their synthesis in completed literary works, have the status only of possibilities, that is to say, of materials separated from the forms actually achieved by writers in constructing individual poems, plays, epics, or novels. The concrete realities and hence the distinctive characters of all the various arts reside in their products; it is to the successful making of these that the formal, material, and technical decisions of artists are directed, and it is of these, as made thus and so, that we predicate, in the first instance at least, significance or value. The historian of the literary arts must therefore find ways of dealing with the individual works within his field of interest that will do justice at once to their multiple historical relations and to their qualities as unique artistic wholes the production of which marked the coming into being of values, great or small, such as the world had not previously known.

Of the problem as stated in these terms no complete solution is possible in any of the other modes of literary history we have examined. For those historians who have been content with philological devices of analysis, the question of artistic value remains implicit, or rather is answered prior to the history itself in their decisions about what writers to include and what relative space to give to each; their characterizations of individual works, as we have seen, are restricted to grammatically distinguishable traits of "content" and "form"; and their judgments of historical significance dwell exclusively on such topics as the priority or originality or the typicality of particular works in relation to developments in materials and techniques and the extent of their popularity with readers or of their influence on subsequent production.

For those historians who have been concerned dialectically with general qualities of poetry or literature, these same devices are still available, but they are supplemented by others the general effect of which is to shift the locus of both literary value and historical significance from works to their writers, in terms of some variant of the ancient doctrine which made human discourse, of whatever kind, a reflection or "imitation" of the soul. In histories thus conceived, as we noted earlier, the emphasis may be either primarily "literary" or primarily "historical."

In the former case (well illustrated in Quintilian, Johnson's *Lives*, and the histories or historical essays of Hallam, Eliot, Leavis, and Cleanth Brooks) the values imputed to works are values which they possess by virtue of their authors' approximations to or departures from an ideal definition of literary or poetic excellence, statable in terms either of a dialectical composition of contrary general qualities or of a particular canon of writers who have most completely realized the ideal or, most commonly, of the two together. Much of the literary part of Hallam's history, thus, is an account of the triumphs, partial triumphs, and defeats of "good taste" or the "classical style" in poetry, drama, and literary prose; and the ruling concern of Leavis in his *Revaluation* is to discriminate between those poets and "lines" of poets who most adequately exemplify the proper adjustment of intelligence and emotion in poetry and those who depart from this norm in either of the two possible directions; his canonical writers include Shakespeare, Donne, Jonson, Pope (at times), Wordsworth (in certain respects), and Keats, and his remarks on individual poems turn consistently on their degree of participation, irrespective of their specific forms or ends, in what is thus constituted as the best "tradition."

When the primary emphasis of the historian is not literary in this sense but "historical," the two kinds of valuation tend to become identical (as notably in Taine and Leslie Stephen), and the relative greatness or importance of works is referred to the relative greatness or importance of their writers as men representing, more or less completely, major combinations or disjunctions of the psychological or social factors discriminated in the underlying dialectic. Occasionally, of course, the two extremes are combined, with the historian's judgment moving from the first level to the second, as when Eliot remarks that the "quality" he sees in Marvell is "probably a literary rather than a personal quality; or, more truly, . . . a quality of a civilization, of a traditional habit of life" or when Leavis discusses in similar fashion the "representativeness" of Jonson, Carew, Dryden, and Pope.

It is evident that in any of these histories, for all their radical differences, the judgments of literary value and historical significance are relative to either the preconstructional causes and conditions of works or to their postconstructional effects, seldom, and then only remotely, to the artistic ends of writers and the problems encountered by them in the actual process of making artistic syntheses of such and such kinds. The result is that individual works tend to lose their integrity as unique products of art and to appear in the history only as causes, consequences, instances, or signs of something else.

Now it would be foolish to assert that this is not an important part of the truth about works, which the historian, if he aspires to give an adequate view of the literary past, must somehow bring into relief. And there is nothing in the assumptions underlying the narrative history of forms that makes it impossible for a historian of this school to formulate judgments which take this truth into account. His characterizations of works, as we have seen, can be made to include all the material discriminations possible in the philological method and at the same time general distinctions of quality derived, as in the dialectical method—but with a stricter attention to the literary causes of their manifestations in works—from the author's moral and intellectual personality and his relations to the culture and ideas of his time. He can deal likewise and as fully as historians of any other sort, with questions of material originality or conformity to tradition, with the effects of works on the writing of later works and on the taste and moral or doctrinal attitudes of readers, and with their representative character relatively to the literary practice or ideological currents of their age.

The important point, however, is that he is not restricted, in either his historical or his critical judgments, to a consideration of literary works merely in these somewhat general preconstructional and postconstructional terms. For, historically considered, individual works are not for him simply causes, consequences, or signs of other things. They are unique events in their own right: their significance cannot be adequately stated by treating their novelty as a function either of residual differences only (after the other traits of matter and manner have been assimilated to antecedent sources or traditions) or of any kind of dialectical division or recombination; rather it has to be exhibited, for any given work, in a narrative account of how its author solved the special problems of object, means, and manner set for him by his decision to give to his subject matter a certain specific artistic form and effect—in the course of achieving which he not only inevitably modified to some degree the traditional materials and techniques available to him but also revealed new possibilities in the form itself, perhaps even discovering a form as yet unattempted. In telling such a story the historian will necessarily adjust his statements to what he knows or can find out concerning the prior developments in forms, materials, and techniques employed by the work in question, but he will do this always with a view to the new state of affairs brought about by the work's appearance. He will make clear, thus, whether the consequences of writing it were to endow literature with an art form hitherto unknown, or with a masterpiece, having greater or less formal novelty, in a species already in process of development, or with a fresh variety of materials, or with new or more refined devices of technique of such and such kinds, or with some combination of these distinguishable types of value. The "placing" of any work in a history, and the character and proportions of the treatment accorded it, will depend upon what is thus revealed: of some works it will appear that their significance in these terms is multiple, of others that it is limited to one aspect alone; and although all works are events and no work is merely representative, the historian will often have to decide that the nature and magnitude of the novelty achieved by some works necessitates the fullest discussion of them as events, whereas others which innovated artistically in slighter degree can be introduced into his narrative, if they are introduced at all, merely as instances of what was generally being done. And the same work, of course, can appear as an instance of more than one thing.

The transition from such historical judgments of works to the consideration of their intrinsic and comparative literary values requires no change in the structure of the historian's narrative. For his first concern, we may repeat, is with the peculiar values which any literary work possesses by virtue of its writer's success in imposing on certain materials chosen by him for reasons of his own, a certain humanly interesting form, new or old, in such a manner as to enhance to the fullest extent the specific emotional or didactic force of which the form is capable. The intrinsic judgment of any work is therefore a judgment of its artistic success in the light of its distinctive end and of the writer's invention or selection of better or worse means, from among those relevant to his task, for its maximum realization. Such a judgment and its verification of course presupposes sensitivity to the peculiar effects of different work on the part of both the historian and his readers. It also presupposes analytical insight into what the general and special requirements of the form attempted are and into the comparative effectiveness of different ways of actualizing it in words. The judgment itself, however, is relative always to the specific nature of the task in hand and hence not dependent on any particular standard or canon of literary or poetic excellence determined in advance and thereafter applied dialectically to all kinds of works. In addition, comparative judgments of two sorts are possible. The starting point of the first is again the experienced effects of the work, and the judgment consists in tracing these to their causes in the relative scope, maturity, or penetration of the ideas and moral attitudes presupposed by the construction of the work as a whole when it is compared with other works of the same or an earlier time. The starting point of the second is the peculiar difficulties which confronted the writer of a given work either because of the character of his materials in relation to his intended form or because of the state of development attained by the techniques of his art when he wrote, and the judgment consists in pointing to the traits of his achievement which it possesses in spite of or by reason of these. It can easily be seen that for the indication of any of these three kinds of judgments in a history no interruption of the causal sequence is required—no systematic intrusions, as in many histories, of summarizing paragraphs of praise or blame—but only such a shaping of the narrative statements about works, both those treated singly in detail and those treated collectively, as will allow the various reasons of success or failure, of development or decline, in the author's choices to appear. And the values so revealed will have a historical status inasmuch as they are the values that have emerged successively, and always in a clothing of historically determined conventions and accidents of material, in the actual course of development of the various literary arts. But at the same time, inasmuch as their realization involves the universal elements and principles contained in these arts, they will also appear as values of an absolute sort, in the sense that, once embodied in works, they can never again be resolved completely into the history from which they came.

These, then—forms, materials, techniques, and individual achievements—are the major variables which must be combined somehow in any adequate narrative history of literary forms. The possibilities of combination are many, but what these are and to what extent they permit the writing of unified histories dealing with many species of works, we shall be better able to see after we have inquired into the kinds of causal efficacy which, in this mode of history as contrasted with the other modes, may be assumed to bind literary events and changes together and to connect them with other things.

3. PRINCIPLES OF EXPLANATION

The contrast is sharpest, as one might expect, with the conception of causality found in histories of the organic type. The possibility of constructing a history of this sort depends, in the first place, upon the assumption that the "real" as distinguished from the "apparent" or "superficial" causes of what writers do are to be found in a single factor or complex of factors present throughout the particular history, or in history generally, to which all the more specific or local factors can be related as consequences or manifestations. Explicit statements of the assumption frequently occur, especially in those historians, like Taine and Cazamian (to say nothing of the Marxists), who exemplify its implications most consistently. "Comprendre," writes Cazamian, "c'est unifier"; and he illustrates his maxim in a sketch of English literature between 1660 and 1914 in which each phase of the development is treated as the necessary product of two factors, one internal, the other external: "l'évolution psychologique d'une part, la pression du milieu historique et social de l'autre." The problem of the historian at each successive point, he remarks, is to examine the joint effect of these two forces. Not all integrating historians have been as systematic in their search for unitary explanation, but the taste for it has been constant in this tradition and has infected also the thinking of a good many critics and scholars who would undoubtedly repudiate the notion of causal monism if it were put to them in so many words.

The tendency has taken many forms. It can be seen in the disposition of innumerable historians to prefer one type of causality to all other possible types—to insist, for example, that diction is the most important element in poetry and that consequently differences between particular poets and general changes in poetry are determined primarily by differences or changes in "the attitude to language"; or that the fundamental determinants are alterations in subject matter; or that they are to be looked for in the relations of authors to their contemporary audience; or that the only real explanation is a psychoanalytical one; or that the operation of causes runs always in a single direction (for example, from having something to say to finding a suitable form in which to say it); and so on. The tendency can be seen also in the common belief that the history of literature is always most intelligible when it is correlated with some one other line of development, this being identified variously by different historians—sometimes as the history of religion, sometimes as the history of culture in the anthropological sense, sometimes as the history of philosophic or popular ideas, sometimes as the history of the class struggle or of some other socio-economic classification of phenomena. And these presuppositions have usually gone along with the conviction that each age or period distinguished in literary history possesses a characteristic unity of "spirit" from the statement of which (however radically different this may be in different histories) consequences follow as to what writers did, or even had to do.

Whatever the unifying cause or hierarchy of causes in any particular history of this type, it is obvious—as a second trait of the method —that the relation of such a cause to the concrete effects in literary works it is designed to explain can be only that of a more or less remote antecedent. The quest is typically, indeed, for "underlying" causes, such as the national character, the temper or "sensibility" of the age, the broad movement of society or of collective thought, the dominant spirit of the ruling class, the particular "moment" of a profound psychological evolution, the prevalence of a certain all-inclusive Weltanschauung, the "general conditions of culture and civilization"—for causes, that is, which do not affect writers immediately as artists of a certain kind struggling with the problems of individual literary works but more remotely as men belonging to large groups, classes, or generations of men all but a few of whom are not artists at all. Authors of such histories rarely introduce any mediating causal steps between the integrating principle and the peculiarities of content and form exhibited by the works it purports to explain. The result is that we are never given the sufficient causes of literary works considered as concrete objects or events (if we are given causes at all) but only the conditions *sine qua non* of the presence in some works and the absence from others of certain combinations of general traits. It is as if, seeking to explain the fact that I sometimes make good fires in my fireplace and sometimes poor ones, I should take into account only the shape and size of the chimney and the economic origins of the logs.

The reasoning used to connect causes and effects, moreover—and this is a third trait of the method—seems to proceed normally from general antecedent conditions, as better known, to particular observable characteristics of writers and works, as relatively more obscure, that is, forward from the cause or principle, as in mathematics, rather than backward to it, as in ordinary history or in our attempts to diagnose practical situations in common life. It is thus habitual among these historians to speak of authors and literary styles or movements as being "produced" by their "age" or by the social or cultural "conditions" amid which they flourished. This kind of language has become so common that it takes a second or third reading to see anything curious in a statement like the assertion, in a recent essay, that the "limited sense of continuity" said to be characteristic of the eighteenth-century world view "led Pope and Johnson to prefer certain sorts of literature to others," namely, to neglect narrative and connected argument, although it is conceded that these forms were being cultivated by many writers during the same time.

Such statements are indeed curious if they are taken in the literal sense suggested by their words. For their validity as causal propositions is then made to depend upon the illicit assumption that we can deduce particularized actuality from general possibility, the emergence of completed forms from the prior existence of their elements. It is reasonable to suspect, however, in view of the widespread use by intelligent historians of this mode of inference, that we are wrong in thinking it to be literal causal inference at all. The truth is, as we recognize increasingly the more we examine the histories in which such propositions occur, that most of their writers are not primarily interested in individual literary works for their own sake but in these chiefly as signs of deeper or larger realities and that what we tend to interpret as causal explanations are not really assertions of causal efficacy in any literal sense but rather quasi-Platonic statements of a quite different sort, resting on assumptions in which we may discern, for all the intrusions of literal or "Aristotelian" language, the notions of the divided line and of the participation of the Many in the being of the One.

It is this philosophic bias rather than methodological incompetence, we must suppose, that has led the better historians of the organic school to concentrate on the discovery of single "causes," to seek these by preference in factors remote from the constructed particularity of works, and to argue the connections of "causes" and "effects" in a seemingly a priori way. The result in the more elaborate histories is an interpretative dialectic that moves in two stages, the first of which is a simple application of the principle of the divided line, the second of which involves also the idea of participation. The consequences of the first assumption we have already noted—in the universal tendency of these histories to treat the characteristics of literary works as "reflections" or "symbols" of the (comparatively more "real") traits of their authors and, through these, taken again as "images" or "expressions," of the society or state of civilization or age which "produced" them, through a hierarchy of imitation-object relations the final term of which is the unifying reality of the history. The consequences of the second assumption are seen most clearly, perhaps, in the extreme developments of the organic method which have distinguished the German tradition of *Geistesgeschichte*. Here the interpretative relationships run horizontally, so to speak, from particular masses of phenomena to other particular masses in terms of likeness or analogy, the unifying "causal" reality being the dialectical whole which, whether it is explicitly named or not, is constituted by the pattern of these relations between its parts. The device, pushed to the limits of metaphorical daring through the discovery of what Spengler called "deep uniformities" among the most disparate historical phenomena, is exemplified to the point of parody in Paul Meissner's *Die geistesgeschichtlichen Grundlagen des englischen Literaturbarocks*. Employed somewhat more modestly to bind together concurrent qualities or changes within limited fields of generic difference, it is to be met with nowadays in the writings of nearly all critics and historians whose starting point is a conviction of the interrelatedness of the arts with one another and of any or all of these with the general movement of society or thought in any age; for instance, in the reproach directed against a recent critic of Matisse for not perceiving the significance of "that great change from three to two-dimensionality which modern art has effected in pictorial space—a change that expresses our industrial society's abandonment of Cartesian rationality for empiricism and positivism"; or in the insistence by a more sober historian of the American mind that "no one who studies the career of Ezra Pound can doubt that the search for obscurity was related to hatred of democracy." That a lurking presumption of causal efficacy underlies, or can easily be read into, statements like the last is of course obvious; the point is that the historian who makes such assertions in an organic history is under no obligation to render this explicit or to argue its plausibility for the relationship in question or even to commit himself to saying that of two terms thus related one represents cause and the other effect. It is true that in relationships in which one term is literary and the other social, political, psychological, or ideological, the second is usually assumed to be more fundamental, but this means, at least in the stricter applications of the method, being either closer to the nature of the complex which is being constituted or else better known. It is enough if two or more things can be brought together by analogy in such a way as to make them parts of a common whole, small or large, the qualities of which, as signified by their likeness, they all share (though some or one of them more fully or obviously than the others).

This is a perfectly legitimate method of interpreting the literary past, capable of giving us, in the hands of philosophically minded and trained historians (like Leslie Stephen, for example), illuminating insights not easily arrived at by any other way. The typical corruptions of the method are two: on the one hand, irresponsible analogizing, uncontrolled by any dialectically rigorous criticism of terms and hence often debased to the level of mere verbal equivocation, as constantly in Spengler, Meissner, and other extreme devotees of *Geistesgeschichte;* and on the other hand, overliteralization, uncontrolled by any clear understanding of the ideals and limits of the procedure and hence frequently leading to statements of equations, correspondences, and identities among disparate phenomena which are hard to distinguish from bad or unverifiable propositions of cause and effect; as, for example, in the sentence about Ezra Pound—we can hardly help asking, apropos of this, whether there is indeed any necessary or probable relation between "obscurity" in poetry and "hatred of democracy" such as would justify, in any concrete instance, making the latter in a literal sense the cause of the former.

There are many traces of this kind of ambiguity in recent works, especially British and American, in which historians trained in critical or philological techniques—and hence more respectful of texts than their German contemporaries—have attempted to relate literature, in various particular ways, to the evolution of society and ideas. It can be detected in Douglas Bush's interpretation of early seventeenth-century literature in the light of the conflict between the

Christian-Humanist tradition and the new materialism, where, although writers and literary schools are consistently treated as "parts" and "signs" of "larger" movements, there is at the same time a considerable admixture of the literally causal; in F. R. Leavis' correlations of poets, in his *Revaluation,* with changes in "civilization," where it is often hard to know whether we are being given highly suggestive analogies or merely amateurish social history; and in René Wellek's papers on the unity of Romanticism, where our appreciation of the synthesizing insights is often thwarted by a sense of the literal differences in form or method among particular writings which his system of equations does not wholly conceal. Lastly, and in a rather striking way, the same ambiguity is seen in the series of books by Hardin Craig, Theodore Spencer, E. M. W. Tillyard, and others, on the relations between Shakespeare and the Elizabethan "world picture," where a dialectically constructed scheme of ideas, pieced out from many texts, among which passages in Shakespeare are of key importance, is first predicated of the age as a whole and then used as a principle in the explanation of the plays: we are tempted to cry out against the circularity of this until we realize that despite these authors' frequent assimilation of their method to that of ordinary philological history they are not dealing really in causal sequences of events but only in relationships of participation among phenomena joined by analogy.

Whatever compromises or confusions may be exhibited by particular historians of this school, their basic procedures in effecting links between the elements of their histories remain clearly distinct, as founded on quite different aims and philosophic assumptions, from those of the narrative historian of literary forms. The historian of forms cannot indeed dispense with analogies, but he will use these not as principles of interpretation but as heuristic devices in the discovery of dynamic connections among facts which it will then be his business to try to explain in literal terms. For his task, unlike that of the organic historian, is not to clarify literary particulars by treating them as "parts" of more easily apprehended wholes. Rather it is to preserve the integrity of particular literary achievements while making them intelligible historically in terms (a) of the individual acts that resulted in their production and (b) of the context of continuous changes in literary forms, materials, and techniques to which these acts were related as effects or causes. He is therefore compelled to seek for causes in the ordinary sense of the word: causes, in the first instance, of what particular writers did in solving the problems presented by particular works and, beyond or behind these, causes of the various collective changes with respect to which the works were events. The only ultimate realities he will be concerned with are literary works conceived of as concrete wholes possessing distinctive powers by virtue of the peculiar manner in which their diverse elements were selected, treated, and combined. He must attempt both to trace the separable elements to their origins and to account for their treatment and combination, and this with reference always to observable differences in the principles of construction upon which the final result depended in different works.

He cannot assume, accordingly, that the causes he is looking for will always be of the same kind or operate in the same order of priority or exert the same relative degree of compulsion, or that they can ever be resolved into or deduced from any single "underlying" cause valid for the whole history. He will not of course suppose that there are no causal interrelations among the happenings or developments he assigns as the causes of particular acts or that he can never uncover "general causes" linking many different kinds of works with one another or with contemporary changes in society, politics, and thought. But he will treat these remoter causes as secondary to the proximate or immediate causes which account for the specific literary phenomena he is primarily concerned to explain, and he will not insist on them unless he can indicate at least a plausible series of intermediate causes connecting them with their assumed literary effects.

He will distinguish, however, between the necessary conditions of an event or change, in the sense of those antecedents without the occurrence of which we cannot imagine how it could have taken place (as we may say, for example, that the development of dramatic blank verse by Marlowe was a necessary condition of Shakespeare's achievement in writing dialogue) and the sufficient conditions, in the sense of the convergence of proximate material, final, and efficient causes upon which its actual occurrence as an event or change of such and such a character can be shown to have depended in a positive way;

and he will always seek, as far as his data permit, to move from the former to the latter.

His procedure will differ, finally, from that of the organic historian (or what often seems to be the procedure in organic histories) in being analytical rather than synthetic—in treating causal statements, that is to say, as a posteriori hypotheses made necessary or plausible by the peculiar character and combination of the elements discernible in a given work or group of works. These he will always take as better known and reason back from them to what had to happen or exist, including accidents as well as purposeful actions, before they could have become what they evidently are. He will argue, thus, from completed works to the specific artistic ends and problems they presuppose; from the ends and problems to the reasoning implicit in the particular choices and combinations of means affected by writers in relation to them; from the means as used to the antecedent events and circumstances implied by the writers' preference for these means over others as well or better suited, theoretically, to their ends; and from the ends as chosen to the previous happenings, in the minds of the writers and in the general situation, necessitated hypothetically by their choice.

It follows from these three differences that the causal explanations offered by the historian of forms will have much in common with, and will indeed subsume while supplementing and reordering, the kinds of explanation commonly found in literary histories based on a philological approach to texts. The causes asserted in these histories have normally been of two sorts: (a) those which relate the elements of subject matter and technique combined in particular works to their sources in earlier literature or in the life and thought of the time; and (b) those which relate those elements to requirements or opportunities imposed by the tastes or demands of audiences, critics, publishers, censors, stage managers, and the like (even when these are resisted), by the character of the special occasions which inspired particular works, and by the nature of the writers' constructive tasks as defined conventionally in the accepted rules and customs of the genres being cultivated (whether these are complied with or reacted against). I shall return later to the uses which the narrative historian of forms can make of both these types of causes; it is sufficient here to point out the limitations inherent in this mode of "literary history" or "historical criticism" when it constitutes the only resource of the historian or is made dogmatically exclusive of other principles of explanation. It is true enough, as one enthusiast for the method has insisted, that Shakespeare—or any writer—"must be reckoned a man among men, a man who can be understood only against the background of his own time," but surely the converse of this truth, which has been a commonplace since antiquity, is the further truth that any explanation which considers a work only against the background of the writer's own time, without taking account also of the specific nature of his art, is bound to be incomplete as historical understanding. We can know, for example, by philological means, that Shakespeare took the story of *Othello* from a novella by Cinthio and made certain changes in the sequence of events there set forth; but not why, in writing his play, he went to the trouble, for instance, of altering so drastically the events after the murder. So too, thanks to one of the triumphs of modern philology, we can trace a great proportion of the words in *Kubla Khan* to certain miscellaneous books of travel; but the delicate method by which these facts are established does not enable J. L. Lowes to make clear, except in terms of a myth about the creative imagination, why it was that only these few words, out of the hundreds of thousands which Coleridge must have read in the same sources, became part of the poem. And again, although Shakespeare, as we have been told so often, was doubtless a man of the theater, ambitious for immediate success in competition with his older and younger contemporaries, to argue from this cause alone to what he did in his tragedies is patently to make intelligible only the not very significant respects in which, in these plays, he relied on established conventions of plot, character, diction, and stage technique. It is to leave unexplained not only the peculiar uses he made of the conventions but the highly important fact that the tragedies he wrote were essentially different in kind, no less than in degree of excellence, from those of any of his rivals.

It is a natural tendency of scholars trained in this presumably "objective" method to assume that the questions it makes possible are the only questions concerning the causes of literary effects that can ever be properly answered or indeed require to be asked. An example among many others of this methodological dogmatism is a note by G. L. Kittredge on the curiously unhistorical character of Caesar in Shakespeare's play. "Was the historical Caesar," he asks, "so antipathetic to Shakespeare that he either could not or would not portray him adequately?" To answer the question, he says, is not difficult. "Caesar's lordly style, his pompous habit of speaking of himself in the third person has been adequately explained by reference to the Latin tragedy, *Julius Caesar,* by Muretus, first published in 1553. Muretus invested Caesar with the style and manner of Seneca's braggart Hercules, and this device had established a fashion: the audience expected the Caesarian dialect." That this is part of the story, and hence needs to be considered by any historian who aspires to causal sufficiency in his narrative, probably no one will question, but can we ever safely assert that any such important fact as the characterization of a key figure in a play by a first-rate dramatist is "adequately explained" until we have asked ourselves whether or not the peculiar plot form of the play could have been preserved had the characterization been of another sort—that is, had Shakespeare represented Caesar as other than "lordly" and "pompous"?

The conception of causality underlying the narrative history of forms would make provision for precisely such questions as this as well as for all the other types of causal problems now considered by philologists and literary historians which can be solved in literal terms.

We have seen why in a history of this kind there can be no unified structure or hierarchy of causes and effects. This does not mean, however, that the historian cannot attempt a general analysis of possible sources of novelty or change in literature which would serve him as a guide in his inquiries by suggesting, if not fixed relations of priority or dependence among causes themselves, at least a rough logical order in the questions he may ask concerning them. The basis of the order is given by the primary assumption upon which this mode of history depends, namely, that the values achieved in literature at any given time and the changes occurring with respect to these are what they are by virtue, immediately, of decisions made by individual artists in the process of thinking out and composing individual works and, more remotely, of antecedent conditions, influences, accidents, and so on which helped shape their purposes and habits as both artists and men. Of these two levels of causation—

constructional and preconstructional, proximate and more or less remote—neither can be neglected, but it is clear that though the first presupposes the second as its necessary substrate, it cannot be deduced from or resolved into it. It is also clear that we cannot know what causes of the second kind were operative in a given literary event or sequence of change until we have analyzed the more immediate causes in terms of which these become historically relevant.

The logically first inquiry of the historian is therefore into the constructional causes of the literary happenings he has to deal with. These may be divided into three groups, the first depending primarily on the nature of the specific art form which is being attempted, the second primarily on extraformal motives, incidental to this, in the writer himself, the third on the material circumstances of his productive acts.

Although critics and historians have hitherto made little of the fact, it cannot be doubted that once a competent writer has determined in a general way the material subject and scope of a work, as well as the general traits of its medium and manner, and has come to know, more or less clearly, what specific form, or emotional or didactic effect, he wants the completed work to produce, he must then begin to feel a certain objective compulsion, as to what he can or ought to do in the different parts of his work, that stems from the peculiar nature of the artistic task he has set for himself. There is plenty of testimony to this fact from writers who, like James in his *Notebooks*, have spoken in detail of their constructional problems, and it can be verified by any one who will recall the various necessities, not of his own making, he has had to face in writing anything, even an essay like this. Given a particular matter and a formal end of a particular sort, whether often successfully accomplished in earlier works or now for the first time discovered, it follows necessarily that some devices of plot (or other structure), character, thought, diction, or representation will be impossible for the writer to use, other devices indispensable, and still others advantageous in a lesser or greater degree if the form in view is to be realized with some approximation to its maximum power; and a writer becomes an artist when he knows, instinctively or upon reflection, why these things are so, and is able to embody his knowledge appropriately in what he writes.

For the historian these reasons, connecting the particular decisions of a writer in handling the parts of a given work with the requirements of a whole he is aiming to achieve, constitute what I shall call artistic or poetic causes; their operation resembles that of reasons of state, which, diverse as these are, tend to lead to strikingly similar choices when similar situations present themselves at any time no matter what the idiosyncrasies or ideologies of the statesmen concerned. And just as reasons of state are not always equally determinative, so the efficacy of artistic causes varies greatly from work to work or even in the production of a single writer specializing in a single form. We call those works masterpieces in the writing of which such causes appear to have operated with maximum compulsory force in the author's conception and treatment of all the parts both in themselves and with respect to their functions in sustaining and enhancing the effect of the whole. Such among no large number of others are *Hamlet* and *The Brothers Karamazov*. The historian will distinguish between the few works of this class that have ever been written and the many works in which, although an overall effect is achieved, some of the parts have been neglected, or in which, although all or some of the parts, such as diction, thought, and character, are highly developed, the whole remains comparatively unaffecting or obscure; and between these and those others, still more numerous, in which causes having little to do with art in any serious sense have tended to predominate.

We may divide reasons of art into two classes: those which pertain to conditions of success in writing common to all or to a number of literary forms and those which pertain characteristically to one or another specific form. For each of these the problem of the historian is double—to specify clearly the locus of the trait he is attempting to explain (as a trait of object, manner, or means) and to conjecture the principle or, as usually in the better works, combination of principles which makes intelligible, when this is not obvious or when the reason is not patently extra-artistic, what the writer has done.

The better known principles, and hence those most commonly invoked in the literary histories which do not eschew artistic explanations altogether, are naturally those operative in all or many distinct species of works. Explanations are relatively easy when we are dealing with skills generally desirable in all or in most works: methods of achieving clarity in diction or its avoidance, or of stating something economically or diffusely or leaving it to inference; of writing lively or stately dialogue, of rendering unspoken thought, of making characters or circumstances vivid, of giving probability to a sequence of acts, of effecting suspense or surprise; or generally of evoking or enhancing a particular emotion; or of deciding between a dramatic and a narrative manner, or a special variety of dramatic manner; or of choosing verse of one sort or another rather than prose.

Some of the causal discussions in the *Poetics* relate to effects of these general kinds, as in the connections indicated between Sophocles' introduction of a third actor and his desire for greater magnitude in his plots or between Homer's avoidance of speech in his own person and the conditions of imitation in narrative poems; a modern instance is T. S. Eliot's deduction of the differences between the actions and characters in Seneca's plays and those in Greek drama from the necessary limitations of plays written to be declaimed.

In artistically successful works, however, the operation of these general causes is bound to be controlled, to a greater or lesser extent, by causes arising from the specific requirements of the form relative to the matter being shaped by it. In such works, therefore, the historian's primary concern will be with these causes.

What, for example, would be the first interest of the historian of forms in dealing with a play like *Cymbeline?* Starting with the concrete plot as experienced and with a definition of the peculiar pleasure the play in fact yields, he would attempt to reconstruct the artistic reasoning which in effect, if not consciously at all points, guided Shakespeare's decisions as to what combination of what kinds of incidents linked by what kinds of probability this form demanded; how these ought to be developed, ordered, emphasized, or toned down in the dramatic representation; who the protagonist ought to be and what other character roles were necessary or desirable; what moral traits or mixtures of traits the dramatis personae ought to have and by what kinds of devices their respective qualities and thoughts could be best rendered and in what degrees of particularity; what varieties of suspense in the various parts should be aimed at and what avoided; how (since the form was to be that of a reconciliation tragicomedy) long-run confidence in the eventual reunion of the heroine and her husband could be sustained without lessening unduly the interest of the short-run expectation of evil and for this purpose what kinds of choral devices would be most effective; and what, finally, for any of the scenes or speeches, ought to be the structure and tone of the diction. Before Shakespeare could write *Cymbeline* as we have it, he had to solve all these as well as many subsidiary problems, and his achievement becomes intelligible as a literary event in proportion to the historian's success in linking the solutions Shakespeare hit upon with the final and intermediate formal ends they served in the play. And this link is discovered by means of general premises applicable to all works in which the ends and problems are the same. The middle terms in such causal arguments will be the "rules," specific to the different forms of literary art, which, as Pope said, are discovered not devised. They are thus distinct, as principles, from conventions and traditions, although they may be obscured, for poets as well as for critics, by the particular historical conventions poets have necessarily used in applying them, and although they tend to be forgotten easily, except as embodied in the traditions of the various poetic kinds effective on poets at a given time.

The history of the poetic arts considered as arts is the history of the gradual discovery by poets of such principles for one new literary form after another—for "punitive tragedy" after tragedy as Aristotle defined it, for the imitative lyric after the panegyrical ode, for the lyric of character or of "metaphysical" thought after the simple lyric of feeling, for sympathetic narrative comedy of the *Tom Jones* type after the dramatic satirical comedy of the ancients and Jonson, and so on. It is the history also of the refinement of such principles and their extension to new materials, of the invention of new techniques for their more effective operation in new subject matters or on the sensibilities of poets and readers weary of the older techniques, of their partial or complete neglect (as notoriously in English tragedy after the seventeenth century), of their rediscovery for particular forms (as for the various dramatic forms in the Renaissance and notably for the tragedy of pity and fear by Shakespeare), and so on in a complicated and often accidentally determined sequence which can end only when the desire to create new works of art disappears from mankind.

The first interpretative task of the historian of forms will thus be the recovery, for the works constituting the major events of his narrative, of the various reasons of art which presided in their making; in this he will rely on such theoretical studies of literary forms as are available to him, supplemented by his own insights into the psychological preconditions of particular literary effects. And he will also be able to generalize in these terms about the artistic causes operative collectively in large or small groups of works having in common the same formal end. It was noted by Aristotle, for example, that Greek writers of tragedy had tended to retain the historical names and many of the historical circumstances of the stories underlying their plots, and he found the reason for this in the fact that the tragic effect requires a high degree of probability in the incidents through which it is to be produced and in the further fact that we tend to take for granted the complete probability of anything we believe has actually occurred. This line of reasoning clearly makes sense out of their procedure, if we assume that the writers who established the tradition of historical subjects knew what they were about. And the artistic reason is logically prior, if it is really operative, no matter what extra-artistic reasons may be supposed to have contributed to the use of historical names, and no matter what alternative devices might have been used instead.

It is the same with many other equally general literary phenomena which are usually either left unexplained in histories or explained merely as instances of prevailing conventions or of the ineptitude of writers. A case in point is the tendency exhibited by most of the Gothic novelists of the eighteenth and early nineteenth centuries to endow their principal agents, whether heroes, heroines, or villains, with relatively little character and to represent them acting from simple, uncomplicated motives easily intelligible in the light of the situations they face. This doubtless detracts from the interest such works can have for serious minds, but the historian, before passing judgment, will ask whether the neglect of specificity and roundedness of character in the Gothic stories may not have been dictated, in some sense, by the artistic end their authors had in view, namely, a concentration on the mysteriously terrifying quality of the events portrayed. To portray character in more vivid detail would either introduce moral issues conducive to something like tragic pity and fear or divert the reader's attention from the unusual and sinister happenings to the persons involved in them. What the form demanded, in short, was enough character to impel readers to take sides with some of the agents against others, as a result of natural sympathy, and nothing more; and that being precisely what the writers of these works tended to give, their practice becomes to the same extent understandable as a fact in literary history.

There is finally—if another example is needed—the famous problem of obscurity in contemporary poetry. The historian of forms will have little patience with large analogical explanations of this in moral or sociological terms until he has satisfied himself that the "obscurity" of at least the better poems is not made sufficiently intelligible by treating it as the consequence, partly indeed of their authors' desire to go beyond the relatively easy and explicit techniques of their immediate predecessors, but primarily of their interest in representing poetically complex and evanescent states of emotion and trains of associative or subconscious thought.

The intelligibility in all these cases depends on the possibility of reconstructing the artistic reasons of poets, novelists, and dramatists relatively to concrete poetic tasks, that is to say, of deducing what any such writer did with the *données* of a given work from the peculiar nature and requirements of its professed overall form insofar as this can be identified by the historian. That this can be done with illuminating results for many species of works even in the present state of our theoretical knowledge, I think there can be little question; the doing of it is indeed the distinguishing contribution of the narrative history of forms to the inquiry concerning the causes of literary events.

The clearer the historian is about the artistic causes of works, moreover, the better equipped he will be to assess properly the remaining factors in poetic production, those which stem from other causes besides the pure and impersonal desire to realize adequately a known poetic form or to experiment with new formal possibilities. It has been one of the limitations of contemporary criticism that its emphasis has been placed almost exclusively on these other ends—as in the current tendency to collapse the formal intentions of Shakespeare and Jane Austen, for example, into the "profound" moral convictions which were undoubtedly also effective in shaping the peculiar artistic character of their several works. The historian of forms will keep the two types of causation analytically distinct, but, on the other hand, he will give due weight—never quite the same perhaps for any two works even of the same author— to those traits of the works he discusses for which an explanation in terms of the form is either insufficient or irrelevant.

The distinction between poetic and other causes is most difficult in those works which most fully realize the potentialities of their respective kinds. We cannot doubt, on the one hand, even in the absence of external testimony, that works like *King Lear, Tom Jones,* and *Emma* would not be what they are except for their authors' preoccupation with significant moral issues. But so complete is the subsumption, in these and other masterpieces, of the moral by the poetic that in the historian's causal analysis the status of the former element, important as it is, necessarily becomes one of means rather than end. Masterpieces are exceptions, however, and the historian must also deal with a great many works the construction of which has obviously been influenced by competing aims, formal and extra-formal, with consequences ranging from incidental intrusions of matter difficult to explain on formal grounds to a more or less complete wrecking of the form. Between these extremes lie many works in which, as in Fletcher's tragicomedies, a concern with enhancing the separate effectiveness of parts leads to a general relaxation of the whole; many others in which, as in Dickens' *Hard Times* and perhaps Orwell's *1984,* the author's practical zeal, though quite compatible with the production of a fine didactic or imitative structure, is satisfied with immediately strong effects on a narrow audience through the use of frequently inferior means; and still others in which, as in *Don Quixote* and *Joseph Andrews,* although it is possible to discriminate two distinct ends, the extraformal end is not only kept subordinate to the other but, for the most part, made to serve simultaneously its peculiar needs. Works of the third kind present special problems of causal interpretation, the solution of which requires of the historian both a precise awareness of what the competing ends and their constructional consequences are and an analysis of their effects which will relate these clearly to the various elements of the work. To do justice to them, the critic must distrust facile explanations at the expense of the author, deriving from the oversimple assumption that any particular trait or device in a work must be accounted for by a single cause. The ends which compete with the specific dictates of the poetic form need not be extraliterary, however. The realization of a certain form in a certain matter may still be the controlling aim, but the choice of means for its realization may be determined in part at least (as in the composition of the *Lyrical Ballads*) by a desire to test or exemplify a new theory of poetic subject matter and language, or again (as in *Samson Agonistes*, Pope's *Imitations of Horace*, and Fielding's *Amelia*), by admiration for a particular model or tradition of writing and a desire to utilize its devices in giving form to new or different materials.

There are, lastly, many works belonging in neither of these two classes about which it would be futile for the historian to attempt to deduce much of what was done in the parts from the nature of the form—for the simple reason that the form was not the controlling end pursued by their writers. Their primary interest, that is to say, was not in achieving finished and moving works of imitative or didactic art but in exploiting, apropos of some more or less emotionally indifferent subject, the resources of a particular type of medium or technique either newly discovered by them or recently come into vogue. Their writers fall into two easily distinguishable groups: those in whom the technical or dictional interest is genuinely experimental (for example Ezra Pound, some of whose early poems, though historically of great importance, have the limited significance as poetic art of what A. R. Orage liked to call "studio work") and those in whom the same interest is predominantly ritualistic (as many of the technically minded minor poets who have written since Pound, Eliot, or Auden).

The historian of forms will take account of all such competing, supplementary, or partial ends in his interpretations of literary events; and he will not overlook, in the second place, the various material compulsions and accidents to which writers are subject, in differing degrees, while engaged in constructing works. A writer has always, for one thing, a contemporary audience in view, the specific character of which is bound to influence to some extent, often without full awareness on his part, the invention and handling of his matter—his choices among possible kinds of incidents and circumstances, his preferences for particular types of character and of signs for rendering these, his use of certain maxims and topics of argument or commentary rather than others, his selection of imagery, diction, and verse, and his decisions, frequently, as to what has to be made explicit and as to what can or should be left unsaid. Every work, no matter how perfect its art, inevitably reflects its audience in these and other similar ways through the moral, social, psychological, and literary conventions it employs. Less distinguished works do this more completely and obviously than the better ones; indeed, the least distinguished works of any age tend to be mere formulary productions in which nearly everything is determined by their writers' preoccupation with what the general public expected, or would resent, in writings of a certain kind. This historian must attempt to place himself in the points of view of his authors and try to understand their extraformal problems of this order, and their modes of solving these, in the light not necessarily of what con-temporary playgoers and readers really were—which is always a some-what vain inquiry—but of the images of them which his authors had formed and were guided by, insofar as these can be inferred from indications in their works, supplemented by such external evidence as is available. He will ask also, in the same connection, how far in the construction of particular works their writers appear to have deferred—often with formal or technical consequences one would not otherwise expect—to current critical prejudices or doctrines, and make an effort, when this is clearly the case, to locate the effects as exactly as possible in the constituent parts of the works. He will ask likewise what special traits of object, means, or manner in any work can be made fully intelligible only by a reconstruction of the particular occasion which inspired its writing: an excellent example of such inquiry is E. N. Hooker's study of Dryden's *Annus Mirabilis.*

He will consider, again—and for some works the question is of great importance—the relation to a poet's formal ends of the in-trinsic or conventionalized character of the matter with which the author worked. The question includes but goes beyond the ques-tion of "sources" in the common philological sense. It arises when-ever we know the "sources" of a work, literary and non-literary, basic and incidental, and then ask what the consequences were, for the author's handling of the formal problems peculiar to the work, of his choice or invention of such and such a story or argument, such and such characters, such and such a mode of language or verse, such and such conventions of plot construction or representation, and so on. It seems clear, in general, that when an author has once committed himself to material decisions of this kind, even if they were determined originally by his conception of the desired form, he is thereafter limited, to a greater or lesser extent, in what he can do. The great difficulty is of course that any unqualified statements we may be tempted to make about the limitations inherent in this or that specific kind of matter are likely to be contradicted, sooner or later, by the achievement of some artist. Who would have thought in advance, for example, that Dostoevski could have made a great tragedy out of so inferior a plot formula, theoretically considered, as that of *The Brothers Karamazov?* A writer can say of two subjects that one seems to him more promising or interesting than the other, but that means merely that he happens to see more possibilities of doing something with it; and he is therefore an uncritical historian who ventures to argue from the fact that a work is, or appears to him to be, artistically unsuccessful to the conclusion that this was due to the author's choice of subject or his decision to write within the conventions of a certain verse form or literary genre. An extreme instance is J. M. Robertson's argument that Shakespeare was necessarily condemned to failure in his effort to achieve unity of character in *Hamlet* because of the intractable nature of the "plot" he took over from the old play; as if, in the first place, he did fail and as if, in the second place, the difficulties Robertson points out could not have been overcome, within a certain range of invention, even by a dramatist of much less genius!

The problem, nevertheless, is a real one and, to a historian who approaches it in a less a priori spirit, one susceptible, frequently, of illuminating solutions. It is obviously easier for writers to see artistic possibilities of a certain kind in certain subject matters at one moment in history rather than at another; for example, the difficulties involved in getting serious emotional effects out of materials once appropriated to comedy are certainly less arduous at present than they were at the beginning of the century. It is a great advantage to an original artist also, as Eliot has remarked, if the "form" in which he proposes to write has already been extensively cultivated by his contemporaries and immediate predecessors, since in that case much of his work of material or technical invention has already been done. (It is of course true that some artists have thought this a disadvantage and that there is, besides, for any given art, a point beyond which the development of its conventions tends to yield diminishing returns, although we can perhaps never know beforehand when this point has been reached.)

The historian will not neglect such considerations in his attempts to reconstruct the circumstances in which particular works were composed, but he will also be able, occasionally at least, to show in more concrete ways how what writers did or failed to do was influenced by the matter they used. It is not hard, for instance, to trace the partial failure of Stevenson's *The Master of Ballantrae* (a failure which every one, including the author, has noted) to his inability to fuse together the two emotionally somewhat discrepant stories out of which its fable was built. And it requires no very sophisticated analysis, again, to see that, as between *Othello* and *Macbeth* and *Julius Caesar* and *Coriolanus*, the given plot materials of the earlier plays in each pair were such as lent themselves much more readily to the effect of tragic pity and fear which Shakespeare apparently desired to produce, in some degree, in all four plays—for example, they demanded much less in the way of choral and representational assistance for the sake of keeping the opinions and emotions of the audience in the right artistic line than did the given plot materials of the other two.

It is possible, finally, to say of any literary work that it would undoubtedly have been different from what it is had its author been in a different psychological state at the time of its inception and writing —had his mind been working more rapidly or sluggishly, had he been more absorbed in his task or more indifferent to it, more intent on doing something new or more content with repeating the kinds of things he had already done, or had luck been more with him or more against him in the moment when he conceived its design. The trouble is that, although such factors obviously help to determine the variations in artistic quality in successive works of the same kind by the same writer, there is little or nothing the historian can say about them over and above what is implied in his critical analyses of the works.

He can talk more easily, as many historians and biographers are fond of doing, about such accidents of production as where a certain work was composed or under what circumstances the idea for it occurred to the writer, and whether it was written rapidly or slowly, with much revision or little, without or with advice from wife, cook, publisher's reader, theater director, or friend, in longhand or on a typewriter, in sickness or in health, and so on. These things are undoubtedly also causes, and some of them have been made into recipes for literary success addressed to intending writers. The difficulty is to know how to deduce from such variables any of the literary effects exhibited by particular completed works and hence how to give them any other status in a literary history than that merely of interesting or trivial incidental facts. And although it seems that there ought to be a somewhat greater significance in the circumstance that some works (Pope's *Epistle to Dr. Arbuthnot* is an example) were put together finally out of fragments originally composed with quite different ends in view, it is usually impossible, here again, to find acceptable premises in terms of which the causal connections can be made.

Perhaps I have said enough, however, about the kinds of extrapoetic causes that may immediately affect, in ways more or less susceptible of historical investigation, the outcomes of particular acts of literary construction. Taken by themselves apart from the influence necessarily exerted by the intended form, they are obviously capable of explaining only the presence and material character of certain of the elements of subject matter and technique which an author has invented or borrowed in conceiving and writing a given work. They are essential to a full understanding of what was done, but such understanding is possible only when the historian concentrates in the first instance on the artistic causes of a work and then estimates in relation to these the other causes stemming either from the author's extraformal aims or from the conditions set for him by his conception of his audience of readers or critics, the occasion of his writing, the peculiar nature of his materials, and his personal situation at the time. The convergence of verifiable statements involving the interrelation of factors of all three types will bring us as close as we can get to the sufficient immediate causation of a literary work, and the same criterion of causal adequacy will guide the historian in his explanatory generalizations, at this level, concerning the various works of a given author, a given school, or a given period.

A similar relation holds—given the premises of the narrative history of forms—between this whole group of three proximate constructional causes and the more remote, preconstructional causes of literary events as holds between the artistic causes of a particular work and the other two immediate causes just discussed. Of preconstructional causes the least remote, it goes without saying, is the author himself; it is only as mediated through him that the general or collective causes of literary change can produce their effects in works, and it is only in him, as a continuing substrate of abilities, habits, memories, feelings, interests, and aims, that the immediate particular causes of these effects can operate. He is an individual man, and hence can never be sufficiently explained as a product of the society or culture in which he acts—except in that mode of history which substitutes relationships of participation for causes and effects. He is also, insofar as he interests the literary historian, a maker of works of art, and hence never, considered merely as a man, a sufficient cause—except again on some theory of organic participation—of the particular works he creates. These are distinct from him as he is distinct from his age or the literary and intellectual traditions to which he attaches himself: there is nothing in what we know, or can learn, about the life, personality, education, reading, moral convictions, or literary theories of Fielding, for example, by which we can make intelligible causally, without other principles, either the peculiar artistic synthesis achieved in *Tom Jones* or the formal differences between that novel and *Amelia*.

It is necessary to insist on this obvious point since its implications have seldom been acted on by historians even of the most literal kind. But having done this we may proceed to the converse, and not less obvious, truth, that the productive acts of any writer, however original and unpredictable in advance even by the writer himself, nevertheless presuppose as their necessary conditions characteristics of the man, as an individual molded by and molding the circumstances of his career, which the historian may investigate independently of his inquiries into the immediate causes of the writer's works. He may uncover thus, depending upon the availability of documents, an indefinite number of biographical facts; his problem is to know which of these have causal relevance in the literary history he is constructing. It is clearly not the same problem for him as for the writer of a literary biography as such a work is usually conceived, nor can he solve it, in the manner of many literary historians in other modes, by falling back on the easy formula *sa vie et ses oeuvres*. He is writing a narrative history of forms designed to make intelligible the successive achievements of writers in relation to concurrent changes in formal ends and in the artistic devices and conventions of material used in actualizing them in works; and his principle of continuity is therefore something distinct from and over and above the particular careers of the authors whose individual accomplishments and whose functions as agents or signs of change he has to account for. Accordingly, his criteria for the selection and arrangement of biographical facts must be extrabiographical; that is to say, his guide in each instance must be his prior knowledge of what an author's achievements were in themselves, as concrete wholes distinguished by such and such material and technical accidents, and of what their relation was, as events productive of more or less extensive or significant innovations in form, matter, or technique, both to one another and to earlier and contemporary works by other authors in the same kinds. Knowing these things, he can then reason back from them to the biographical conditions and happenings which made them possible insofar as these can be connected by reasonable premises with particular characteristics of the writer's productions. In short, he will proceed from the works to the man, as what at this stage of his inquiry is less well known, and his method will consequently be the reverse of that favored by many modern biographical critics, who begin by conjecturing the nature of an author's private interests, moral problems, or childhood fixations, from his letters or other records, and then resolve his literary works, often on Freudian assumptions, into necessary consequences or signs of these.

The biographical causes thus arrived at will inevitably be multiple in kind, ranging from the author's native powers and temperament, through the diverse formative influences exerted upon him by the social, cultural, and religious circumstances of his family, by his youthful experiences, education, and reading, and by his methods of earning a living, to his development of personal convictions about morals, politics, or art, his decisions as between different literary kinds and traditions, his chance encounters with persons and books, and the effects on him of public events of one kind or another during the course of his career. From the point of view of the historian's problems these causes will fall into two classes: those which account for the likenesses between an author's works, however progressively different these may be, and the literary or ideological traditions in which he was working; and those which account for his divergences, in both kind and quality of achievement, from past or contemporary practice. The historian's method is such that it is much easier for him to do justice to causes of the first type than to those of the second, whether the effects to be explained are the writer's choices of forms or shifts from one form to another, his selection and elaboration of subjects, his uses of certain techniques rather than others, or his preferences in language and verse. In all these respects, if comparison is possible at all, it is simple enough to point out lines of filiation with earlier or contemporary literature and thought, some of which at least can be established as probable cases of direct borrowing, reminiscence, imitation, emulation, or influence, and, on the basis of an accumulation of such cases for the various works of an author, to generalize to his character as a representative figure in a movement or age.

It would be absurd to minimize the value for literary history of this kind of information, which the techniques of philological scholarship are peculiarly well fitted to uncover. But it would be equally absurd to suppose that it can give us, taken by itself, more than a part of the story—a very small part, indeed, for any writer of more than ordinary originality and power. Such a writer, as we have said, is by definition, and antecedently to the writing of any particular work, a man who cannot help altering more or less, at the same time that he assimilates, the ideas and materials of his age and the traditions of art he has elected to follow. The historian of forms, while not neglecting the question of sources, will thus seek to handle it in such a way as to make clear the extent to which a given writer is himself a cause as well as an effect of the influences playing upon him. He will observe, for example, that though Fielding's moral doctrine, as set forth explicitly in his essays and used in various ways in his novels, has an obvious affinity with the doctrines of numerous divines since the days of his favorite Barrow, it yet takes on a form of its own when viewed in the light not merely of its elements and catchwords but of the particular patterns of arguments which define it in Fielding's statements. The historian will be as much concerned with noting such transformations as with tracing the matters transformed to their origins in the writer's education, experience, or reading. He will attempt to exhibit the special features which differentiate a particular writer's response to a common influence from the responses of his contemporaries; he will emphasize the peculiar conjunctions of materials from heterogeneous sources which tend, even when the borrowings (as in Montaigne) are extensive, to set a writer of some originality of mind apart from others; above all, he will take pains to discriminate causally among instances of indebtedness or influence by showing how much, precisely, they explain in an author's works, that is, whether the debt to an earlier writer or tradition is for subject matter, or for suggestions in handling the medium, or for devices of technique, or for the structural formula of a plot or of certain incidents or characters, or for the idea, directly or indirectly imparted, of formal effects to be aimed at, or for some special combination of these possibilities. It is only when such distinctions have been made, for example, that we can say exactly what peculiar meaning "the manner of Cervantes" had for Fielding or what was characteristically Thomson's in his use of Newtonian ideas.

The ideal, in short, is to relate a writer's preconstructional assimilation of the various external influences that molded his habits of thought, feeling, and writing, or supplied him with particular materials and intentions, as closely as the data permit to the quality of inventiveness he displayed, successively in his different works, in solving the peculiar complexes of problems, never quite the same on any two occasions, which confronted him immediately in the composition of each. It is thus that the historian would proceed if his problem, for instance, was to make intelligible Pope's innovations in the couplet: having analyzed Pope's performance on the basis of an adequate literal prosody, he would attempt to interpret it in the light of converging inquiries into (1) the nature and extent of his adherence to and departures from previous practice, (2) his choices of earlier poems as models or as starting points for further developments, (3) his doctrines concerning versification as such independent of its uses, and the immediate and remote origins of these, (4) the nature of the problems of verse technique set for him generally by his decision to write didactic and satirical poems designed to affect a certain kind of audience by virtue both of their particular modes of argument and of the special qualities of moral character displayed by their speakers, and (5) the peculiar and differing poetic problems of this order presented by his successive poems.

Beyond such convergences of biographical and artistic causes it is perhaps impossible for the historian to go with any security in his attempts to explain the achievements of an author or his role in contributing to literary change. It is obvious that the writing of a notably original and powerful work or the discovery of a significantly new form presupposes genius as well as art and experience, but there is no way in which the historian can talk about a writer's genius apart from a critical analysis of his productions and it is seldom possible to reconstruct the process of invention by which a new form or technique was conceived. It is doubtless true that a writer who has something new to say will tend to seek a new form of expression, but this does not imply that another writer may not start with the intuition of a new form and then cast about for new matter to embody it in. There have been instances of both procedures, and the historian will not ordinarily be in a position to say, for a given instance, which was which. The extent, moreover, to which a writer departs from his predecessors or deviates from his own early manner will depend in large part on how impatient he is with doing merely what has already been done well or often—a spirit common to all artists, scientists, and scholars who, even if not geniuses, have succeeded in revealing fresh possibilities in their subjects. But here again there is nothing the historian can say that is not contained in his descriptions of the novel things achieved; the most he can do is to make clear whether the novelty was the result, in a given case, of a revolutionary rejection of the past or of a more or less thoroughgoing adaptation of traditional materials to new ends and uses. There will consequently always remain a margin of chance or mystery after the historian has done his best, and this will be true not only of the divergences of certain authors in the direction of greater artistic excellence or technical sophistication in a particular species of writing but of the lapses of others from the standards previously attained in works of writers well known to them or in earlier works of their own. The English tragic playwrights of the eighteenth century certainly included few men (if any) of notable dramatic talent, but this is scarcely a sufficient explanation of the fact that, although they knew Shakespeare well and wrote for audiences nourished on his tragedies, they yet neglected notoriously all the formal and technical lessons he might have taught them. And who will say that there is compelling necessity in any of the numerous attempts to account for the supposed artistic failure of *All's Well That Ends Well?*

4. THE SAME SUBJECT CONTINUED

The causal problems we have so far considered are relatively easy in comparison with those which arise when the historian of forms undertakes to make historically intelligible not merely the construction of individual works or the successive productive acts of individual writers but those larger changes in literary characteristics which manifest themselves in many works by many writers through a more or less extended period of time. Where is he to look for the causes of such great collective events as the rise and flourishing of Elizabethan drama, the development and decline of the "metaphysical" tradition in poetry, the general shift from mimetic to didactic, satirical, and occasional forms after the Restoration, the emergence of the novel of common life and then the Gothic romance in the eighteenth century, the Romantic movement, the new English and American poetry of the twentieth century? Or such less conspicuous yet in their way important things as the disappearance in the later seventeenth century of the older conventions of court poetry, or the increasing interest of dramatists at this time in serious plots turning on alternatives of choice for the hero or heroine neither of which could bring happiness, or the slowness of the early novelists to adapt to their uses the techniques of dialogue available to them in drama, or the greater success of eighteenth-century writers with comic than with serious forms, or the shift in didactic poetry, between the eighteenth and nineteenth centuries, from a primary concern with moral philosophy to a primary concern with philosophies of nature, or the modern taste, in serious fiction, for plots of disillusionment or frustration, with bewildered or fearful protagonists?

There are endless causal problems of these sorts, for many of which variant solutions have been suggested or insisted upon by historians of other schools: all of these the historian of forms will consider and some of them he will be able to use. Success in finding "explanations" for general literary developments or changes has been greater, of course, in proportion as historians have looked not for causes in the literal sense but for correspondences or correlations based upon analogies of characteristics—as, for instance, between difficult techniques of contemporary poetry and the methods of modern science or the disappearance of formerly common beliefs from modern life. The analytical commitments of the historian of forms prevent him, fortunately or unfortunately, from utilizing such easily manipulated explanatory devices. He can consider as causes of the highly particularized literary effects he is trying to make intelligible only those events or changes which he can connect with the literary effects by showing their direct or indirect operation, as humanly likely conditions or stimuli, on the intellectual, moral, and literary habits and aims and, through these, on the productive acts of the writers in questions; so that, for example, if the Industrial Revolution is proposed as a major cause of Romantic poetry, he will want to be shown in precisely what ways the language, rhythms, imagery, thought, character, situations, and effects of the great body of Romantic poems would necessarily or probably have been different had the Industrial Revolution not occurred. And he can discover causes in this sense, as we have frequently said before, only by reasoning back to them from the literary facts or changes which are to be explained; by looking, that is, for those antecedent things or conjunctions of things without which they could not in all likelihood have come about or come about thus and not otherwise, with this rapidity or to this extent, at this time, in this place.

The first prerequisite to any search for collective causes in the history of forms is therefore such an analysis of the literary ingredients of the development under consideration as was outlined in the second section of this essay. The historian, in other words, must be clear to begin with as to exactly what it is he is trying to explain: whether its full definition (as in the case of the major literary events mentioned above) entails more or less complex discriminations of formal ends, materials, and techniques and of the varied interrelationships of these in many works, or mainly distinctions appropriate to materials or techniques; and whether the facts to be accounted for with respect to any or all of these variables are chiefly facts of persistence or chiefly facts of change, and, if the latter, whether the change was gradual or sudden, piecemeal or wholesale, a change of kind (as the emergence of a new poetic species) or only a change in quality or in extent of activity relative to a species or a number of species already in the tradition.

There is in the history of forms no other principle of relevance than this for the judgment of what causes, among those the historian may think of looking for, he ought to consider seriously and what he ought to reject. The judgment will ever be a delicate one, since the causal explanations offered by a history, whatever its subject matter, can never be framed in terms of general laws but must always remain hypotheses, chosen in preference to other possible hypotheses about why something happened, merely because of their arguably greater power of rendering the particulars in the history intelligible.

The best, therefore, that the historian of forms can do is to see to it that any general causal suppositions he may advance conform as closely as the data permit to the several criteria which the experience of historians and of practical men has indicated for inquiries of this kind.

The first of these is clearly sufficiency of explanation, and for the literary historian this implies two things: negatively, that he will proceed on the principle that wherever, as in any instance of collective change, multiple literary variables—formal, material, technical— are involved, the causes will likewise be multiple; and, positively, that in his interpretations he will seek to conjoin propositions about all the factors necessarily present in the kind of change he is dealing with. He will thus recognize that we understand any human event or development most fully when, given a sequence of happenings of a certain order, we know (a) the specific purposes which animated the agents and determined their problems, (b) their individual characters, backgrounds, habits, and ideas, and (c) the nature of the antecedent situation, as they saw it, out of which came the actions by which they altered it in such and such respects.

The second criterion is equally obvious: it is simply that the causes proposed must be appropriate to the effects they are intended to clarify, that is, they must possess the capacity, mediately or immediately, to bring about results of the particular kinds in question. We may suspect, thus, at least until some one shows the chain of intervening steps more convincingly than has been done, that the special consti- tution of the audiences in the private theaters of London *ca.* 1608 is an inappropriately assigned cause of the "romantic" tendencies dis- played in the dramas written for these theaters by Shakespeare and Fletcher. The standard literary histories are full of causal conjectures concerning which the same doubts may be felt; the best remedy against them is a prior inquiry, such as the historian of forms will al- ways undertake, into the immediate artistic causes of the works they are supposed to explain.

The final criterion is commensurateness: causes are incommen- surate when they are either too particular or too general, in their nature and probable efficacy, relative to the extent or complexity of the phenomena they are used to account for. Of the first sort are the current clichés about the effect of the Royal Society on the general development of prose style after 1660, the influence of Hobbes's psy- chology of the imagination on the rise of Augustan poetry and taste, the contribution of Shaftesbury to the formation of "sentimental- ism," and, more notoriously still, the tyranny of Rousseau over the European Romantic movement; it is perhaps not unfair to add that the sin of incommensurateness in this first sense has been cultivated with peculiar assiduity by the devotees of "comparative literature" in the usual narrow meaning of that term. Of incommensurateness in the second sense many illustrations will doubtless suggest themselves, such as a recent attempt to explain the contrast between Pope's "love of conciseness" and the preference of most nineteenth-century poets for a more distended manner of writing by positing as the main cause the greater leisure prevalent in the eighteenth century as compared with the later period; as if this same cause did not operate also on such contemporaries of Pope as Thomson and Young, who were far from loving, or at least manifesting, "conciseness."

These are general criteria, and their proper application to ques- tions of causality in the history of forms requires that the historian keep in mind also a number of other distinctions. The facts to be ex- plained at this stage of his inquiry, as we have said, are those pre- sented by the spectacle of many writers of varied origins, characters, and outlooks exploiting, simultaneously or successively, a certain range of materials and techniques to the end of making literary works of certain more or less clearly differentiable kinds; and causal problems distinct from those involved in the analysis of individual works and authors necessarily arise for the historian whenever he is confronted by collective similarities and differences either in the literary species cultivated by his writers or in their choices of materials or in their preferences in techniques. The great temptation in such cases is to assume that since the facts are general—that is, statable in terms of generalizations from numerous particular acts—the causes must also be general, in the sense of involving collective stimuli operative on the writers as a group. The prevalence of this assumption accounts, at least in part, for the inclusion in most literary histories of descriptive chapters or sections on the "background" of the literature of a period or of one of its branches, setting forth much miscellaneous and not always strikingly relevant information concerning political habits and activities, social conditions, the state of education and learning, the tastes of the general public, the major movements of ideas, the development of science, the circumstances governing publication, and so on. This is much less misleading, however, than the equally common propensity of historians to suppose that the occurrence of a large and complex literary development, such as the revolution in English poetry after the middle of the seventeenth century, must remain a mystery unless some similarly large and complex development in another sphere of contemporary life, such as, in this case, "Rationalism" or "Materialism" or "the Newtonian world view," is asserted to be its essential cause.

The historian of forms will be skeptical of such hypotheses (if they are indeed hypotheses and not, as surely in many histories, *geistesgeschichtliche* analogies based on mythical constructions of the history of ideas) on the ground that they beg the question of causes by discouraging adequate inquiry into the more immediate factors, both formal and extraformal, which necessarily operate in literary production. He will ask—to go with the same illustration—whether a sufficient or nearly sufficient understanding of what happened in English poetry after 1650 may not be arrived at by a process of adding together the various proximate causes he has discovered, so that a telling of the detailed story of why poet after poet from before the Restoration into the eighteenth century chose the particular forms, materials, and techniques he did would by itself go far toward making the collective changes intelligible. However this may be, he will at least recognize the possibility, familiar to all who have studied in local detail the mechanism of general elections, that an outcome statable in common terms does not inevitably presuppose, as its decisive cause, common antecedents in the opinions, interests, and actions of individuals.

He will give due weight, therefore, to causes of this additive or coincidental type, but without minimizing the importance, where this can be established, of collective causes of various kinds. In dealing with these he will be careful to differentiate, in the first place, between causes in the positive sense of influences or stimuli tending in a certain direction and causes in the more negative sense of antecedent and environing conditions. The latter may be either literary or non-literary, and of these the first are ordinarily much the easier to handle. We can thus say that the popular English drama of the late sixteenth century would not have been what it was except for the peculiar character of the earlier dramatic developments, although the most complete analysis of these is not in itself sufficient to explain the forms the new drama took; or that the directions followed by English poetry after about 1914 would certainly have been different had it not been for the distinctive poetic tendencies of the Edwardians; and we can make many similar propositions connecting particular literary changes with the state of literature in general or of some species of literature or of some tradition of materials or techniques or of the language in general or the literary language or the language of poetry or the language of tragedy, at the time when the change began. It is of course indispensable to do this; the difficulty is to distinguish between what the antecedents were in themselves—that is, as analyzed objectively in their own terms—and what they appeared to be to the writers involved in the change, since it is obviously only in an account of the latter aspect that their causal relevance to what happened becomes clear.

The same principle holds for the treatment of non-literary conditions, although here it is much harder to trace the connections. We can assert as a general rule—or at least many historians have done so —that certain political, moral, economic, social, or intellectual circumstances are more stimulating or more discouraging to literary activity or to literary activity of a certain kind than others; with greater probability we can say the same thing about modes of literary patronage, situations in the theater or book trade, and changes in the composition and tastes of readers; but we know from our experience and observation that objective facts of this order are likely to be interpreted differently by different writers and consequently to be followed by actions often quite unpredictable in terms of the rules: the most ample provisions for encouraging learning do not always give us learned men, nor does the badness of an educational program mean that all the students who suffer under it will get a bad education. The point, of course, cannot be pushed too far: it is difficult, for instance, to conceive of a flourishing drama in a society which has banished the stage. The historian, however, is not apt to go astray in such cases; his besetting temptation is to find not too little but too much causal significance in the known antecedent or concomitant circumstances of literary change, and he can be easily deceived into oversimple explanations, especially of revolutionary or reformist movements in literature, by what the actors in such movements say about the immediate past and the obstacles it interposed between them and desirable new achievement.

A case in point is the new American literature of the 1920's as represented by such men as H. L. Mencken, Van Wyck Brooks, F. Scott Fitzgerald, Ernest Hemingway, Sinclair Lewis, and Ezra Pound. The movement is often treated, somewhat naively, as if it came about in spite of the restrictive moral and cultural conventions, the deadening standards of the colleges and magazines, the tyranny of the sanctified older reputations which, as its exponents insisted countless times, had thwarted originality in the United States since the Civil War. These men were certainly justified in attacking American culture as they saw it, and their revolt led to much excellent new writing. The historian, however, before making too much of their courage in breaking with the old bad traditions, will be inclined to ask whether this very badness was not actually, for them, rather a rich opportunity than an unfortunate impediment; for what, after all, would Mencken have been without his Bible Belt and his Van Dykes and Mabies, or Lewis without his Main Street, or Pound without the Y.M.C.A.?

The inquiry concerning conditions thus leads into the inquiry concerning causes in the stricter sense; and here again the historian will distinguish between relatively general and relatively particular causes and, among the latter, between those more and those less immediately determinative of the constructive choices of writers and hence of the formal differences of literary works. Out of the many particular causes of the first sort to which historians have rightly attached importance we can mention only a few. Any list would include, obviously, the kind of happenings which, when they take place on a large scale, we call renaissances: the gradual or sudden shifts of interest that bring back into prominence, as exemplars of form or technique or as sources of literary materials, works or writers of whole literatures of the past— the new studies of Virgil in the twelfth century, the successive waves of enthusiasm for Greek models from the fifteenth century to the nine- teenth, the Celtic and Scandinavian revivals of the eighteenth cen- tury, or the "return to Donne" of our own day. There have been few literary historians of any school who have not attempted to do justice to such phenomena, although we could often wish for greater par- ticularity in the analysis both of the peculiar values in the revived authors which different writers or generations selected for admiration and of the special artistic uses to which these were put in new works. Justice has also been done more or less adequately to a second type of cause which is in a way the counterpart of this: the power of success- ful new works or authors to inspire imitation, adaptation, or parody among contemporary writers at home and abroad—we need consider only how much has been written about the "schools" of such writers as Chaucer, Spenser, Donne, Jonson, Milton, Wordsworth, and Scott, or how freely contemporary Continental novelists have acknowledged the stimulus of Hemingway and Faulkner.

Somewhat less attention, perhaps, has been given to a third type of cause, closely related to this, which William Minto was tempted to erect into a kind of law: the peculiar power of attracting literary tal- ent which seems to be inherent in new and developing "forms" in the generation after their discovery. "The stimulating novelty of the form," writes Minto, "must stand first in the list of 'causes' of the greatness of Elizabethan drama. The significance of this simple fact, as generally with obvious facts, has been overlooked by aetiological speculators." Both the Greek and the English drama, he notes, at- tained their height within a generation of their birth, and subsequent efforts to revive their magnificence have proved unsuccessful. "To put it somewhat mathematically, in the first generation of their existence they drew towards them irresistibly a larger proportion of free intellect than they were ever able to attract in subsequent generations. This is the law of all subjects of disinterested intellectual effort, whether artistic or scientific. The most ambitious intellects rush after the newest subjects with which they have affinity: if the subjects are great, and succeed in fascinating congenial minds, then the results are great." Properly qualified, as Minto qualifies it in his final sentence, this is clearly a valuable insight, verifiable in the experience of most of us; it has the advantage, furthermore, of suggesting a realistic causal hypothesis for the interpretation of large collective facts which have often been treated, somewhat mystically, as instances of the imagination or sensibility of an age finding its most effective and characteristic expression.

The converse of this species of cause has been much more frequently invoked, though usually without sufficient attention to its positive implications: the strong urge to change which is normally felt by ambitious or original minds when they become convinced, for good or bad reasons, that the possibilities of a particular form, technique, or body of materials have become exhausted as a result of either much or outstandingly successful cultivation; as when Dryden remarked of the Elizabethan dramatists that there is "scarce an Humour, a Character, or any kind of Plot, which they have not us'd" and added that this is "a good Argument to us either not to write at all, or to attempt some other way." It is not hard for the historian to discover evidence in nearly every literary generation of the existence of such feelings; the difficult thing is to find sufficient reasons for the particular choices of "some other way" which the writers made.

There are at least three directions in which the historian may look. He may ask whether the suggestion might not have come from abroad, as in Eliot's attempt to renew English poetry by borrowing technical devices already developed to a high degree of sophistication in the French Symbolist tradition. Or he may inquire whether the renewal—of poetry, for instance—might not have been effected by importing subjects, techniques, or forms from another literary species, such as the essay or the novel; it is thus that Minto accounts for much that was new and apparently revolutionary in the poetry of Cowper,

Wordsworth, Scott, and Byron; and in a similar way, perhaps the historian can find a partial explanation of the directions taken by the so-called "lyric revival" after 1740 by examining how far the characters, situations, thoughts, and emotions of the many short lyrics of this period exploited materials previously worked up in the episodes of large-scale didactic poems like Thomson's *Seasons*. Or he may consider, finally, in the manner suggested in the second section of this essay what were the theoretical possibilities of further innovation in a particular literary species at a particular time, given the stage of development which it had then reached, so that, for example, the various lines of specialization followed by writers of serious drama after Shakespeare or the so-called "breakup" of the novel in the generation after Richardson and Fielding become at least partly intelligible as natural, though not inevitable, next steps beyond what those masters had done.

All these are "literary" causes in the sense that they all involve factors the origin and efficacy of which lie within the relatively closed world of men specializing, as writers of poems, plays, novels, essays, and the like, in the production of literary works. The influence of literary criticism on literary practice clearly falls in the same class, especially in those periods when the doctrine and judgments of critics have had only a remote or indirect relation to the development of philosophy; the great exceptions have been the dialectical and "scientific" criticism, respectively, of Plato and Aristotle, the "philosophical" criticism of Hume, Burke, Kames, Dugald Stewart, and many others in the eighteenth century, the "transcendental" systems of Coleridge and the Germans, and the more recent efforts in speculative criticism of Croce and Dewey.

That the practice of writers in the different literary arts tends to be affected, more or less decisively, by contemporary or earlier formulations of the ends and appropriate devices and materials of these arts or of the principles of art in general and by the pronouncements of critics on the merits and faults of particular works is one of those general probabilities which no one ever thinks of denying but which few have been able to use convincingly in the causal interpretation of literary events. It has been a commonplace at least since David Hume that humanistic and social studies differ radically from the natural sciences in that their data are never immune from the formative or distorting influence of the theories set up to explain them. It is a much older commonplace that the forms of all the arts must first exist in the minds of artists before they can be embodied in works and hence must inevitably be subject to the pressure of whatever historically determined opinions the artists may hold as to how works of such and such kinds ought to be made. And anyone who has ever tried to write anything for publication knows how hard it is for an author, no matter how independent in spirit, to avoid altogether considering what critics and reviewers are likely to say of his performance. It seems to follow, therefore, that the relations between changes in literary production in any age and changes in critical theory and taste constitute one of the more pressing topics of causal inquiry for the literary historian.

And so indeed it must; the only trouble is the extraordinary difficulty which the problem presents, except now and then in the case of an individual work or writer, to the historian who wants to talk literally about causes and effects rather than analogically about correspondences and equations. For the peculiarity of the relationship between criticism and production is that the causes never run entirely in one direction. When a historian has discovered clear affinities between a particular body of literary works and the particular critical rules and criteria generally favored in the same age, he cannot always be certain how far the works are what they are because of the criticism and how far the criticism is what it is because of the works. Surely to some extent at least the writing of poetry in Britain and America since the 1920's has been directed as well as encouraged by the "new criticism" which emerged during the same period—there is probably more than malicious gossip, for instance, in the charge that a certain young poet has set himself deliberately to achieve Empsonian "ambiguity" in his verse. But it is hardly less certain that the "new criticism" itself, much of which has been written with the "new poetry" in view and with the promotion of a taste for such poetry as one of its objects, would not be exactly what it is had not the pioneers of the poetic renascence written as they did. This is one great difficulty. Another, scarcely less important, arises from the complementary fact that, although criticism may affect production and production criticism, the two activities remain distinct (even when the artists are also critics) by virtue of the operation in each of special causes or reasons foreign to the other. The critic, thus, may attempt to set forth principles for tragedy or the novel, and in doing so he will naturally be influenced by the tragedies or novels he has read or perhaps written, but he will also be influenced by the traditions of critical discussion itself and by the general premises of critical argument he has happened to choose. The artist, similarly, although his tragedies or novels may be affected by the criticism he has read or perhaps written, will tend to do as an artist, insofar as he is a good one, what his peculiar task and the traditions of his art indicate that he should do. There can be no easy or simple inferences, therefore, from the one field to the other, and the historian must always reckon with the possibility that in any period or in any writer, for this or another reason, the development of doctrine and the development of practice may follow quite divergent roads. The relations between the tragedies written in the eighteenth century, for example (some of them by men with considerable critical learning), and the statements of contemporary critics and theorists on what tragedy ought to be are by no means conspicuously close except on a few points; and anyone who argues from E. M. Forster's *Aspects of the Novel* to the principles of form which guided him in the composition of his own novels will have his eyes closed to a good part of the truth.

The historian of forms will show his awareness of these complexities in whatever he may say about the influence of critical ideas on the course of literary production. He will approach any possible influence of this kind from the point of view not of what he knows concerning the history of doctrines but of his prior analyses of the artistic problems which his writers faced because of their choices of formal ends. He will then ask how far such ends had been envisaged by critics or by the writers themselves as critics or makers of programs before they were embodied in works; as was the case, for example, with the "sublime ode," the pathetic novel of common life, and the tale of terror in the eighteenth century. He will raise similar questions, also, about changes in technique and conventions of material. How much critical discussion of French Symbolist devices, for instance, had taken place in England prior to the use of these or analogous techniques in English poems? Or what is the chronological relation of the turning away by poets of the eighteenth century from the standardized genres or of the "naturalistic" expansion of subject matter in the late nineteenth-century novel or of the later concentration of novelists on "proletarian" or psychoanalytical themes to the development of theoretical sanctions for these departures? He will distinguish between those cases for which clear connections of cause and effect can be shown and those for which the telling of the prior critical story merely adds in a general way to the intelligibility of what the creative writers did. He will attempt likewise to distinguish, although this may not always be possible, among cases in which (a) the choice of a certain kind of "subject" was dictated by a desire to translate precepts of technique into practice, (b) cases in which, the "subject" having been chosen for reasons quite independent of doctrine, the character of its handling was affected, contrary to the peculiar needs of the form, by current critical teaching, and (c) cases in which, again given the "subject," the harmony of formal requirement and critical prescription was complete, so that the same thing would probably have been done even if no critic had written. The history of the unities of time and place in drama from the sixteenth century to the present day will supply illustrations of all three of these possibilities. He will also consider, in tracing the influence of a particular writer or work on subsequent production, the extent to which this influence was encouraged, impeded, or directed to certain aspects of the achievement rather than to others by the mediating effects of the critical discussions which the work or writer inspired; it should be possible to explain in these terms, at least partly, such things as the nature and course of Henry James's impact on later fiction or the differences between the eighteenth- and early nineteenth-century uses of Spenser. And there are, lastly, the interesting negative cases in which the development of literary production during a certain period has gone beyond or counter to or at any rate has proceeded more or less independently of the development of theory: such was the coincidence in the Renaissance of a rich imaginative literature dominated by imitative ends with critical schools which, however they differed in other traits, agreed in making the controlling purpose of poetry didactic.

The historian of forms will construct his narrative in such a way as to give due prominence to these situations along with the various more positive situations distinguished above; and since the causes of such varying relationships between criticism and practice are likely to be found, as I have said, quite as much in the evolution of criticism as in that of production, he will be led to a somewhat different treatment of the history of criticism from that ordinarily given in literary histories of the traditional types. It will be a treatment which, while making clear the material content of the doctrines and judgments set forth in critical writings and their relation to past or contemporary literary works, will take into account also the distinctive problems the critics were trying to solve and the peculiar assumptions and methods which conditioned the formulation and solution of these. The critical treatises and essays, in short, will be analyzed formally in their own terms no less than the poems and dramas they may have influenced, and their doctrines interpreted in the light of the specific and often widely variant ends and dialectical requirements so revealed. Only after this has been done can the historian feel safe in attributing any particular common positions to the critics of a given period (no matter how similar verbally their statements may be) or say with precision what significance for literary production is to be attached to any of the large critical "movements" (such as neo-classicism) which historians have loved to create.

We come finally to those causal factors the importance of which for the historian arises from the fact that the world of literary creation is after all only relatively a closed one: the audiences writers seek to interest usually lie altogether or in great part outside its bounds, and the writers themselves participate in varying ways and degrees in the esthetic, intellectual, and practical activities of their society and age, not necessarily as artists but as men.

There is less need to dwell on these factors than on some others. They have constituted, as we have tried to indicate, the special province of those literary historians who have sought to integrate literature dialectically with other things and for whom the most revealing explanations of what writers did lie not in their immediate activities and tasks as artists but in the "underlying" or "ultimate" causes of their behavior as men. The result has been to import into literary history a vast amount of discussion of the relations between literature and the other fine arts, literature and the evolution of ideas, and literature and society. The discussion has not always—has seldom indeed—been strikingly competent when judged by the best standards of the various specialized disciplines which have been drawn upon for materials, and the conceptions of extra-literary history thus disseminated have been typically doctrinaire and oversimple.

The problem, however, has been clearly posed, and we may there-fore confine ourselves to noting a few of the respects in which the treatment of causes of this kind by the narrative historian of forms will differ from their treatment by historians of other schools. The historian of forms, of course, is concerned primarily with literal distinctions among works and the causes of these in terms of the character of the works as artistic syntheses. The consequences of this difference in approach can be seen most easily perhaps in his handling of the connections between literature and the other arts.

It has become a widespread fashion to talk about literary works by means of technical concepts borrowed from music, painting, architecture, and gardening, with the result that many poems and novels have been said to have a "symphonic structure" or to con-tain instances of "spatial form." It has been remarked, for example, that a poem of Pope, with "its collocation of a certain number of balanced or contrasted units . . . resembles architecture—houses built by Kent or palaces built by Wren"; and another scholar has under-taken to show the remarkable correspondences between the verse movement of Augustan poetry and the symmetries of the contempo-rary formal garden and then the equally remarkable similarity of the blank verse of Thomson and others to the more sinuous lines of the later English garden, the "antagonism" of the two styles sig-nifying, naturally, a deep transformation in the spirit of the age. For the historian of forms such analogies can be starting points only; insofar as they are not merely lazy substitutes for a poetic analysis of the devices in question, they may suggest problems to him which he might not otherwise have seen; in dealing with these, however, he will proceed on the assumption that the causes of any apparently similar effects in two arts which differ radically in their media and their principles of construction must necessarily be distinct, and he will not be content until he has traced these in terms appropriate literally to each of the arts. The result may very well be, as in most or all of the examples just given, the simple conclusion that the analogy tells us more about the critic's or historian's method than it does about any actual connections of cause and effect between the two arts. This will, of course, not always be true. Apart from the many ways in which writers have exploited their knowledge of the other arts in inventing subjects, descriptions, metaphors, and the like, and apart from the frequent close relations between poets and musicians and between dramatists and designers of scenes, we know that the theories of literature prevalent in certain periods have tended to assimilate it more or less closely, in its general ends, to other arts. Sometimes, as in the eighteenth century, this has been to the plastic arts, sometimes, as in the nineteenth century, to music; the consequences can occasionally be seen in the preferences of writers for certain genres or in their attempts to devise new techniques. We know also that some writers, especially in modern times, have deliberately tried to get effects of arrangement in individual works which they hoped would remind readers pleasurably of musical forms; and we know what uses have been made by certain contemporary novelists and playwrights of technical expedients borrowed from the cinema. All these relations are susceptible, the data permitting, of literal causal treatment; they will never, perhaps, explain very much in the history of literary forms, but they will at least make the historian's narrative somewhat more intelligible here and there than it would have been had he neglected to take them into account. And there may be some advantage, in histories embracing the whole range of literary activity during a given period, in the kind of subsidiary reference to the state of the other arts—without either systematic analogizing or strict causal commitment —which George Sherburn, for instance, has employed in his account of the Restoration and eighteenth century; the illumination of the literary facts is indirect but surely not for that reason to be contemned.

The special uses which the historian of forms will make of what it is customary nowadays, thanks very largely to the influence of A. O. Lovejoy, to call the history of ideas cannot be so easily defined. The difficulties are due, in the first place, partly to the great variety of things covered by that term. The history of ideas has been made to include the formal treatment of principles and doctrines in the systems of philosophers and scientists; the independent development, in application to problems in many fields, of concepts or analytical devices which, having been used in the construction of systems, have then passed into general currency as commonplaces of argument (for example, Plato's list of virtues, Aristotle's four causes, Newton's "universal attraction," Freud's libido); the shifting history of crucial or influential philosophic terms ("Nature," for instance); the persistent disputes over the relative importance of the different sciences and of their systematic relations to one another (as the numerous quarrels over the comparative values of natural and moral philosophy and the current attempts of Weizsäcker and others to rebuild physics on a historical model); the complex evolution, individually and in interrelation, of the arts of stating or arguing intellectual positions or persuading readers of their truth (for example, the Ramean "reform" of logic in the sixteenth century and the architectonic status given to rhetoric in the eighteenth); and, finally, the various institutions and other mechanisms by which ideas have been disseminated or transmitted from one culture or one generation to another.

The history of ideas, being itself a philosophic discipline, has naturally been affected by these many sources of variation in its subject matter, and the task of the literary historian who wishes to utilize its contributions is therefore complicated, in the second place, by the necessity of interpreting these in the light of the philosophic principles which have determined their formulation in the history. For the attribution of ideas to philosophers and others by the historian of ideas is never a simple matter of first discovering and then stating "facts" (as many of the literary historians who have drawn their notions of Elizabethan cosmology from Lovejoy or of eighteenth-century deism from Leslie Stephen have naively supposed). The character and significance of a given philosophic system or doctrine or of the ideological currents of a given age as represented in a history is inevitably conditioned quite as much by the historian's peculiar philosophic and methodological assumptions as by what is said in his texts. The predicament of the historian of ideas is indeed closely parallel to that of the historian of imaginative literature, so that it is possible to distinguish in the history of ideas three fundamental ways of approaching problems which correspond broadly to the three modes of literary history defined above: first, a grammatical way, characterized by the use of philological devices of exegesis and comparison for the sake of restating the explicit content of doctrines, grouping them chronologically and with respect to their topical bases, and explaining on historical grounds their dissemination and influence (for example, Thomas Stanley's *History of Philosophy* and F. T. H. Fletcher's *Montesquieu and English Politics*); second, a dialectical way, characterized by the use of general philosophic concepts and distinctions, not necessarily those of the historical texts, for the sake of ordering a sequence of doctrines or of exhibiting the basic affinities and oppositions in the ideas of an age (for example, in their very different fashions, Stephen's *English Thought in the Eighteenth Century*, Irving Babbitt's *Rousseau and Romanticism*, and Lovejoy's *The Great Chain of Being*); and third, a way, lacking as yet any very good name, the essence of which is a consideration of philosophic or scientific writings, separately and in sequence, in terms of their distinctive assumptions, problems, and ends and of the specifically different modes of argument by which their conclusions were reached and ordered (for example, the historical essays of Richard McKeon). Of these three modes of constituting the history of ideas, only the first and—increasingly in recent years—the second have had an appreciable influence on the treatment of ideas by literary historians. The historian of forms, however, will profit most from the methods appropriate to the third approach, since these alone are capable of giving him a view of intellectual history which neither obscures the literal meanings of doctrines nor separates these from their limiting and differentiating contexts of problems and ends; a view, moreover, which preserves the broad traditions of human thought and the historical interrelations of its divers fields without imposing a unity on any of its chronological phases such as we know from experience with contemporary ideas could never, in a literal sense, have existed.

The problem is further complicated, no matter how the content or method of the history of ideas is understood, by the fact that the relations between it and the history of imaginative literature may be investigated in two clearly distinct ways. The historian may start from an idea or a complex of ideas as better known and argue to the character and extent of the influence these had on literary works, or he may start from the literary works considered in their concrete wholeness and argue to the intellectual events or changes which influenced their forms and upon which at the same time they imposed new forms. The first mode of procedure has been the commoner by far. It is the dominant method—to give only a few random examples representing a variety of approaches to the analysis of ideas—of such recent studies as Marjorie Nicolson's *Newton Demands the Muse: Newton's "Opticks" and the Eighteenth Century Poets;* Theodore Spencer's *Shakespeare and the Nature of Man* and the related works of Hardin Craig and E. M. W. Tillyard; J. W. Beach's *The Concept of Nature in Nineteenth Century Poetry;* McKeon's essay on poetry, philosophy, and rhetoric in the twelfth century in *Critics and Criticism;* to say nothing of numerous incidental passages in larger histories dealing with the reactions of poets, novelists, and dramatists to the "thought" of their time. It is, indeed, a natural method for the intellectual historian whose subject matter embraces poetic as well as theoretical works, even though he may not subscribe to Lovejoy's contention that "the interest of the history of literature is largely as a record of the movement of ideas." For the literary historian, however, who is certainly not likely to agree with this thesis, its use as a basic method of interpreting artistic writings is subject to two serious limitations, one on the side of the inquiry into causes, the other on the side of the inquiry into effects. The latter is obvious enough: it is the danger that, since the continuum of his story is an intellectual rather than an artistic development, he will tend systematically to emphasize only those aspects of the "poetic" writings which can be seen as effects of the assumed cause, thus blurring or destroying altogether differences of artistic kind and hence of the internal causes affecting the poet's use of ideas, and reducing works of all species, even works of great poetic complexity, to a common denominator of simple dialectic or expression of belief, seldom much above the level of an essay by Seneca or Addison; the reader will think at once of many recent efforts to trace intellectual themes in Shakespeare. The other danger is slightly more subtle; it is the risk, which becomes especially great when the dialectical method is employed to constitute a "world view" for a period or to define a "tradition" of ideas, that the historian will attend to only those ideas in his literary texts and hence to only those intellectual causes among their antecedents which he can assimilate to his chosen subject. The reader will recall how many fresh things were seen in both James Thomson's poetry and his background once the influence of Newton was joined to that of Shaftesbury as a topic of investigation; and we may add that surprises still await the student of eighteenth-century literature who will take as his clue the easily demonstrated fact that the philosophical writings of Cicero were more intimately familiar to educated men in that age than most of the later writings which have commonly been treated as the foundation works of the Enlightenment.

The moral for the historian of forms is clear. He will continue to employ the approach through selected causes as a method of investigation, although he will define these literally rather than dialectically; and the retrospective causal sections of his narrative will often be strung on threads derived from the history of ideas, with literary works treated partially, as signs or evidence of intellectual change. These will be subordinate devices, however; the major continuum of his narrative will be literary rather than ideological, and his characteristic starting point in the causal consideration of ideas will accordingly be poems, novels, essays, and plays and the problems involved in the assumption or use by their writers of the same or different ideas for different or the same artistic ends. He must clearly be able to recognize and compare ideas, whether explicit or merely presupposed, when he comes upon them in works of these kinds, and this necessitates some competence in the techniques of intellectual as well as poetic analysis; but once the facts thus obtainable are clear for a given work, writer, or sequence of writings, the task of discovering and stating their causes will entail an inquiry in two stages, the first concerned with origins, the second with uses. The former will carry him back from literature to the history of ideas, only now with highly particularized questions in view which can never be satisfactorily answered in terms of clichés like "the Christian-humanist tradition," "the scientific spirit," "materialism," "rationalism," "antirationalism," "empiricism," "sentimentalism," and so on, and with an open mind as to where he may find the effective intellectual antecedents, if such there were, of the literary traits and changes he is concerned to explain. There are excellent models for researches of this type in some of the essays of Lovejoy and Etienne Gilson and in critical editions of texts such as F. B. Kaye's *Fable of the Bees*, P.-M. Masson's *Profession de foi du Vicaire Savoyard*, and André Morize's *Candide*. For the arguments and attitudes to which writers have given explicit statement in literary works the difficulties of the inquiry are no greater, and no less, than in any investigation of sources and traditions.

The really troublesome problems are those presented by the usually unexpressed assumptions about the beliefs and moral sentiments of the audience which underlie such things as an author's choice and development of a certain plot form or his supposition that certain acts or traits of character or modes of thinking will arouse sympathetic (or antipathetic) reactions. What conceptions of human nature, for example, were implied in the growing preference of eighteenth-century dramatists and novelists for plots, involving ordinary people, the peculiar pleasure of which was determined by the unexpected emergence, in the dénouement, of humane and generous feelings? It has usually been taken for granted that the appeal of such stories must depend on the prevalence of doctrines that insist optimistically on the essential "goodness" of average human nature, and various scholars, by a process of exegesis which has led to much distortion of the ideas of Shaftesbury, Steele, Rousseau, and others, have developed a causal interpretation of "sentimental" drama and fiction in these terms. But what if we argue, on the other hand—as can be done, I think, with much psychological plausibility—that our delight in manifestations of the social virtues, in literature or in life, is in direct proportion to our belief that such occurrences are rare? In that case, obviously, we should look for our causes not in the supposed moral "optimism" of the eighteenth century but in the somewhat more easily demonstrable pessimism of that period, or rather in its characteristic combination of pessimism about the motives from which men generally act with an ethical ideal that identified virtue more or less completely with "good-nature" and "tender generous feeling."

The second stage of the inquiry is the necessary complement of this, although I can think of only a few writings by literary historians in which its distinctive problems have been faced. These problems are set by the evident fact that ideas in literary works are what they are not only because of the circumstances, more or less external to literature, which have brought certain basic views about God, the universe, man, and philosophy, or certain special distinctions, doctrines, terms, methods, or modes of philosophic speech into prominence during a given time, but also, and no less decisively, because of the particular and highly differentiated functions which such materials may be made to serve in various kinds of works and in the various "parts" of any kind.

It seems simple enough, at first sight, to account for the ideas explicitly argued in a given philosophical poem or moral epistle by pointing to the author's adherence to such and such a school or tradition of thought; and this is about all that most literary historians have attempted in discussing works like the *De rerum natura*, the *Essay on Man*, or Thomson's *Seasons*. That the traditional ideas as stated in these works are never quite the same in interrelation, emphasis, and ordering as in the earlier works from which they were drawn is of course notorious. Apart from this, however, it makes a great difference, with respect to the status and causation of ideas in didactic writings of this sort, what the particular end of the poem is. It makes a difference whether the end is the setting forth of an argument as a statement of truth or whether the argument (as in Pope's poem) is a rhetorical means to the inculcation of an attitude toward the things in life to which the poem refers. We judge the value of the ideas by different standards in the two cases and hence we must judge differently concerning the reasons for their use— giving more weight in the first to the convictions of the author and more in the second to his notions of what readers were likely to believe.

So too with the various modes of allegory; although they all have a basis in doctrine, the causal relations between the doctrine and the poem are clearly not the same in the traditional allegories, like *Pilgrim's Progress,* which take for granted that the doctrine is known and generally accepted and in those more characteristically modern allegories, like some of Kafka's mythographic fables, in which a new and presumably difficult doctrine is being adumbrated through the symbolic devices of the work.

And there is a wide difference, which has seldom been sufficiently considered by historians, between the uses of intellectual materials in didactic writings of whatever kind and their uses in the construction of imitative dramas, narratives, and lyrics. Here the historian's problems fall into two groups: those involved in tracing the possible influence of earlier or contemporary ideological discussions, by the writers themselves as well as by others, on the invention of plot forms, episodes, characters, or character relationships (which is clearly not the same thing as inventing any of these for the sake of promoting the discussion); and those involved in accounting for what happened to the historically conditioned ideas when they entered into the "thought" of imitative works either as grounds of deliberation and reflection by the characters or as topics of choral or narrative commentary designed to enhance the effectiveness of the form vis-à-vis the audience. It is hard to see how there can be an adequate historical treatment of the effect of intellectual movements upon literature that does not recognize such differences as these and that does not attempt, in any clear case of influence, to assess the relative importance in the final result of the causes deriving at various removes from the history of ideas and causes deriving more immediately from the special natures of the artistic tasks which the writers faced in constructing their works.

Difficult as these problems are, they are yet relatively easy when compared with the problems facing the literary historian in his attempts to deal in a literal causal fashion with that vast congeries of possible causes of literary effects which is usually labeled, vaguely enough, "society." His common sense must tell him that the question is an important one—else how explain the prestige it has attained, in the minds of historians of all schools, since the eighteenth century? Common sense also tells him that if he is to investigate it with any intelligence or accuracy he must be trained not only in poetic, rhetorical, and intellectual analysis but in the various special disciplines which make up the "social sciences": he cannot get very far if he remains merely an amateur economist, an amateur sociologist, or an amateur political historian. Not many of the literary students who have had most to say about the relations of literature and society have been masters in any of these fields; what has kept the fact from becoming too glaringly apparent has been their reliance on a method of interpretation which makes analytical expertness in the non-literary subject matters they have annexed less essential than an ability to see and develop analogies from hints easily available to them in the writings of specialists. They have been encouraged in their efforts, moreover, by the apparently self-evident truth of the dogma that "literature is an expression of so-ciety." This dogma, as understood by most of its adherents, serves to guarantee the relevance of any collective circumstances in the background of literary production presenting correspondences with the works of the writers concerned. It is even better perhaps, as permitting greater dialectical neatness in the historian's exposition, if the background circumstances come to him already worked up speculatively into some species of myth (as in the works of Max Weber and R. H. Tawney on the relations between capitalism and the Protestant spirit or in the writings about the frontier in America by some of the disciples of Frederick Turner).

For reasons which I have often stated, the historian of forms is prevented, by the principles of his method, from falling back on these alluring expedients. He can have no wish to treat literature in abstraction from "life"; he can even conceive of it "as a part of the process of life itself," although he will not suppose that a poet or novelist ceases to "live" when he turns his mind away from politics or economics to concentrate on the problems of his art, or that to set literary works "firmly in a social context" means dis-cussing them only or primarily in "social" terms. He will accordingly look for social causes, but he will know that a properly realistic (rather than metaphorical) comparison of literary with social phe-nomena requires that he have an independent knowledge of both and therefore a preliminary training which will at least qualify him to criticize on relevant scholarly grounds the conclusions and hy-potheses of the experts in political and social history whom he con-sults. Moreover, his procedure being essentially an analytical one, he will be concerned only with those conditions or changes in the practical affairs of a society to which he is led by the necessity of accounting for traits in literary works and in the habits and ideas of writers which appear not to be adequately explicable in the light of more immediate causes. He will not assume that everything in literature—perhaps not even any of the more important things from his point of view—must have a "social" explanation if only he can find it, or that such an explanation, when found, can ever account fully for the particular effects that interest him. He will treat social causes, like all others, differentially, recognizing that whatever causes of this type he is able to establish will differ widely in significance, at different times or in different places, relative to other causes and to the aspects of literary works they help him to explain. He will keep in mind, above all, the peculiar difficulties that attend reasoning from cause to effect in this field. He will know, concerning any young writer at the outset of his career, how nearly impossible it is to infer correctly, from even the completest information about his political sympathies and his social and economic background, what the character and direction of his output will be as defined by any of the literary variables which are important for the historian of forms. So the best he can do, having examined the completed output in these terms, is to look to the writer's social background for any obvious sources of materials or stimuli in the light of which his works, in any of their aspects, can retrospectively be made more intelligible as events. And this process repeated for many writers will bring him as close as he can come, given the complexity of the subject and the futility of trying to explain particular happenings in terms of general statistical probabilities (such as the conclusions of sociologists respecting the behavior patterns of classes and other large groupings of men), to being able to set the collective facts of literature "firmly in a social context."

The relevance of such findings to his distinctive concerns as a historian of forms will vary greatly in degree of remoteness. In many cases the political or social events he is led back to will turn out to be only conditions sine qua non of literary change, important for the opportunities they opened up or closed off but for nothing much more positive than that. Such, for example, were the Norman Conquest, the Revolution of 1688, the achievement of freedom of the press, the spread of popular education in the nineteenth century, the emancipation of women, and the decline and fall, since 1900, of the older quarterly reviews. I have probably already said enough about how "causes" of this sort must be handled.

A second large class of events consists of those which can be shown to have had somewhat more positive but still very general effects on the state of mind both of writers and of broad sections of the public, so that new hopes or enthusiasms were generated or old illusions dispelled. Such, for example, were the religious struggles and changes of the sixteenth century, the French Revolution, World War I, and the rise of Soviet Russia. No one can doubt that events like these have had an influence upon the spirit of literature at the times of their occurrence or at least upon the comparative fortunes of different writers with contemporary readers; the difficulty comes when the historian tries to discuss the influence in particular detail. As Minto shrewdly remarks of the supposed effects upon the rise of Elizabethan drama of the feelings generated by the triumph of Protestantism and the defeat of Spain, "one must have no small confidence in the power of general conditions over specific effects who would venture to say that our dramatists would never have come into existence, or would have sought some other line of activity, had Mary remained upon the throne instead of Elizabeth, and had England continued at peace with Spain"; it is hard to see "what the stir of the Reformation had to do with the dramatic tendencies of Marlowe, or how the defeat of the Armada was concerned in the migration of Shakespeare from Stratford to the London stage." The connection seems to be much clearer, at least on a superficial view, between the writings of the so-called "lost generation" of the 1920's and the moral impact of World War I; but leaving aside the fact that these writings were highly diversified in form, technique, and matter, can we be sure that they were not themselves as much a cause as an effect of the disillusionment commonly attributed to the war, or that *The Waste Land,* for instance, would not have been pretty much what it is had the war never occurred?

With a third type of events the historian is on safer ground; these are the happenings or changes to which it is possible to trace significant increments in the subject matter of literature or important shifts in the perspective from which old materials are viewed. Such, for example, in addition to some of the events already mentioned, were the geographical discoveries at the end of the Middle Ages, the opening up of America, the beginnings of intercourse with China, the conquest of India, the Industrial Revolution and its consequences, and, in this country, the Civil War, the Westward Movement, and the Great Depression. The literary effects of happenings of this kind, in bringing into prominence new stories, new scenes, new motives, new types of character, new objects of emotion, new words, are relatively easy to investigate, and they have not been neglected by scholars. Nevertheless, only a few of these (among them notably Gilbert Chinard in his three books on the myth of

America in French literature) have made a point of going beyond descriptions of the facts to the discussion in literary terms of the uses to which the fresh materials were put.

With a fourth class of events the difficulties for the historian of forms are much greater, but so also are the rewards. These events are the usually slow and gradual changes in social relationships and attitudes the effects of which can be discerned by comparing successive writers with respect to the propositions about such things which they appear to take for granted or think it necessary to insist upon. These include the social types or actions they choose for sympathetic or unsympathetic, serious or non-serious treatment and in general those traits of subject matter or emphasis which we would expect to be radically different in the works of authors living in and writing for (say) the semifeudal court society of the fourteenth century on the one hand and the largely democratic and semi-collectivist present-day world of the Labour Party and the New Deal on the other. The study of such characteristics is rewarding because it brings the historian fairly close to his writers' materials not in their raw state but as already partly formed for literary treatment. The formal effects a writer will produce with them cannot, indeed, be predicted from knowing merely these things, but the peculiar quality of the effects when produced will depend in considerable measure on the preconstructional, and often quite unconscious, choices which are thus revealed. That the job of discovering and stating them is not easy will be clear to any one familiar either with the many Marxist attempts to define the position of dead or living authors in relation to the class struggle or with the equally simple-minded efforts of enthusiasts for democracy to find the elements of their creed in (say) Shakespeare and Milton. Here the defect lies primarily in the insensitivity and excessively schematic character of the literary analysis, but the results are frequently vitiated also by the too great readiness of historians who specialize in the social relations of literature to look for the cause of a writer's expression of social attitudes (as Ben Jonson's satiric attacks on usurers, monopolists, speculators, and "undertakers") solely in his personal background and conditioning without allowing for the influence of his poetic ends or the literary tradition he is following or his judgments as to the social prejudices of his audience. The consequence is that first-rate studies of such problems are comparatively rare; I can think of few that seem to me more discriminating and generally sensible than George Orwell's essay on Dickens.

By far the closest relations between literature and society, however, are those which involve the active intervention by writers, as writers, in practical affairs. These are the relations which, on the whole, historians of literature have shown themselves best fitted to deal with; witness, to take only two especially successful examples, the works of Daniel Mornet on the literary preparation for the French Revolution and of Louis Cazamian on the English social novel of the mid-nineteenth century. There have been many such studies, though few as competent or interesting within their limits as these, for most periods of literature—and this means nearly all literary periods—in which the ends that have determined, more or less profoundly, the construction of many literary works are fully explicable only when viewed in a context of the practical and propagandist aims of contemporary politicians, political or ecclesiastical parties, or movements for social revolution or reform. The connections have sometimes been only slight or tangential; at other times— as in the cases of the eighteenth-century French "philosophes" and of that characteristically modern phenomenon, the rise in all countries of a powerful class of Socialist "intellectuals"—they have been extremely close. The literary significance of the productions thus inspired has also varied greatly, from novels and plays which are scarcely more than ephemeral pamphlets with fables, to finished and lastingly moving works of didactic art. The great temptation has been to treat these all alike in terms of the social doctrines or "beliefs" they express without attention to the formal principles which, at least in the better ones, such as Shaw's best plays, have subsumed the practical aims and deflected them from any easily recognizable party line. The historian of forms will attempt a more discriminating analysis, and he will likewise avoid the error of supposing that all novels and plays which have "social significance" in the sense that they are built on contemporary conflicts of the sort that interest sociologists or social historians were therefore necessarily constructed with the depiction of these conflicts as their controlling artistic ends.

There remains one important question about causes in literary history to which I can offer here only a somewhat tentative answer. I have tried to make clear in the foregoing discussion that the method of causal investigation appropriate to the history of literary forms is an analytical method presupposing for all literary events a multiplicity of distinguishable causes. The central problem of the historian in this mode is set by his conception of literary works as syntheses of preexistent materials into artistic wholes, the peculiar forms or "powers" of which are determined, within an indefinite range of possible variation among different works, by the specifically different principles of construction their writers have happened to use. His first efforts, therefore, are directed to defining the various forms, in this sense, which have been achieved more or less successfully in the writings he has to deal with. From this as a starting point he proceeds to inquire, first into the extent to which the constitution and handling of the analytically separable elements of object, means, and manner are explicable in the light of the intended forms and the extent to which other reasons must be looked for to account for what was done, and then into the many differentiable antecedent conditions and influences, proximate and remote, without the supposition of which neither the forms aimed at nor the materials of language and human experience in which they are embodied nor the techniques used to construct them would be fully intelligible. This is indeed the only way he can reason if he is to preserve, as completely as possible, the concrete particularity, as artistic objects, of the works that form the events of his history; to reason in the opposite direction would have the effect, as we have seen, of destroying the formal distinctness of the works and of resolving their elements into mere functions of the biographical or social antecedents, whatever these might be, that constitute the historian's preferred causal hypothesis.

It has sometimes been objected to this mode of procedure that it tends to obscure or distort the nature of the facts the historian is studying by directing attention separately to causal factors which in their actual operation are inseparable. And I cannot deny that this is so. It is in one sense false to insist, as critics of the *Scrutiny* school love to do, that such things as plot, character, or thought are merely "abstractions" from the linguistic continuum of a work. For the author they are more than this—they are principles of construction which operate in the process of composition, at times in harmony with one another and at other times in conflict, to determine what he does. Yet, in a different sense, the position of F. R. Leavis and his friends is a perfectly sound one: the immediate response of sensitive readers to a completed work is a response to the synthesis of meaningful words, one after the other, which the writer has effected. And the point becomes clearer still when we turn from the causes in the work which condition its effect on readers to the causes in the author which condition his acts of composition. However these may be differentiated, in relation either to their literary effects or to their personal and collective origins, the manner in which they actually exert their efficacy is again synthetic. The life of an author concentrating on artistic problems in an infinitely complex social and intellectual world, wherein the past is always becoming the present and the present merging into the future, is obviously an indivisible continuity of stimuli and responses. And with respect to these the analytical procedures of the historian of forms, whatever greater understanding they may bring, must always leave one with the sense that much more remains to be said. It is upon these truths that the organic methods of criticism and literary history have been based. But unfortunately, the nature of human language and thinking is such that we cannot have it both ways: either we must sacrifice the organic interconnectedness of things—without denying its reality—for the sake of gaining a sharper understanding of the specific differences among the products of the various literary arts or we must sacrifice these differences—except as they are felt by us apart from what the historian says—for the sake of appreciating the interconnectedness.

There is nothing the historian of forms can do about this objection, therefore, beyond countering it with an equally strong insistence on the limitations of the alternative way of procedure. For his part, he must be content to push his analytical inquiries as far as they can go, and the only question that need perplex him is how far that is. The question arises most acutely when he moves from a consideration of particular lines of development in literature, however complex any of these may be, to a broad view of literary activities that embraces most of the major and many of the minor writings, in all kinds, of several generations or centuries. His first and paramount interest, as a historian of forms, will be to order these in terms of the diversities of ends, materials, and techniques they exhibit and to try to account for them, differentially, in the manner I have suggested. At the same time, however, he cannot help being struck, the farther he goes in his work of comparison, by the extraordinary family resemblances which group together the writings of one generation, no matter how widely different in kind, and separate them as a body more or less sharply from the writings, equally diverse in species, of the generations immediately before and after; a sign of this is his ability to refer anonymous and undated works, with considerable accuracy, to their proper chronological place, without analysis, simply on the strength of the general impressions they make on him. And he will also, as his reading is extended backward and forward in time, come to detect similar strong family resemblances, which likewise cut across distinctions of artistic form, uniting many works of many successive periods and setting them apart as a body from other temporally parallel series of works, in the same language or different languages, the characters of which, though quite distinct, show an equally marked tendency to persist through many generations of writers. From the perception of such resemblances the two complementary ideas of ages and traditions have been derived; and it requires but little reflection to see that they are not, as has sometimes been supposed, merely convenient classificatory fictions but represent real factors in the causation of literary as well as other human activities which no historian of these things is justified in neglecting even though they may not lend themselves readily to analytical investigation.

That there is a peculiar causal force in traditions will scarcely be doubted by any one who has been a member for a decade or more of two universities, or for that matter two well-established institutions of any kind, and has reflected on the different fates which generally befall the same proposals for change, in no matter what aspect of their life, in the one as compared with the other. Each has its own "spirit," hard enough even for those most sensitive to its differentiating effects to formulate and nearly impossible to explain to outsiders, constantly undergoing subtle alteration as new things are done or as new men replace the old yet always exerting, for good or ill, a certain compulsive force on individual and collective choices so that these tend to fall into a general pattern which does not greatly vary, despite ex-

ternal events, from that determined for the institution by its found-
ers. It is the same, as Minto and many others have pointed out, with
the churches of the various Protestant denominations. "You might
find it hard, if you fixed on details, to say where the difference lies;
the same sermon that is preached in one might have been preached
in the other; the same hymns might have been sung; yet we feel under
the influence of a different spirit. And further, these various churches
have probably less in common with each other, though they mix in
the same age, than they have with the churches of past ages, each of
them perpetuating a traditional spirit of its own, and perhaps making it a point of honour to keep that unchanged." It is the same, too,
with philosophy and science; in the long history of these from pre-
Socratic Greece to the present, through all the revolutionary shifts in
problems, materials, and doctrines, it is possible to trace the persistence, sometimes in clear separation from one another if not in systematic opposition, sometimes in more or less eclectic mixture, of
several fundamentally distinct traditions of method, based ultimately
perhaps on different temperamental predispositions and different
conceptions of the powers of language; the result being that in nearly
every period, including our own, we can differentiate among those
thinkers who descend from Democritus and the early atomists, those
whose master, whether they know it or not, is Plato or Augustine,
and those who approach their problems in the spirit of Aristotle. Illustrations could be given from many fields; for our purposes here it
will suffice to refer to the three schools of literary history I have distinguished in this essay.

That the same phenomena, finally, present themselves in literature,
and probably for similar ultimate reasons, will be granted by every
one, although it is harder than in philosophy and science to separate
the few great and inclusive traditions from the many secondary ones,
deriving from the persistent influence of individual writers (Pindar,
Anacreon, Horace, Virgil, Cervantes, and so on), with which literary
historians for the most part deal. There are certainly national traditions, however difficult it may be to say wherein any one of them
consists; thus, although the novel has become a cosmopolitan genre,
we know that we will find some kinds of effects in French novels
taken en masse which we do not expect to meet with in English novels and some things in Russian novels that seem exceptional when

they occur in novels by either Englishmen or Frenchmen; and so too, perhaps even more strikingly, with poetry and the drama. The existence of these continuities is indeed the great justification of national histories of literature; but there are also, clearly, international literary traditions, the persistence of which can be traced, with occasional interruptions and through multitudinous particular changes in materials, techniques, and forms, from the historical beginnings of artistic writing. The sources of these doubtless lie in basic temperamental differences, such as those which, in nearly all ages and countries, incline some writers to choose the serious and others the comic and satiric forms; some to cultivate "realistic" representations of men as they are or as they are thought to be and others idealized imitations or some mode of "romance"; some to base their art, in a quasi-Aristotelian spirit, on the depiction of human experience in literal terms and others, whether with didactic ends in view or not, on a quasi-Platonic use of analogues and myths. These are persistent causes at once of generic differentiation and generic continuity in literature. Not all of the contrasting effects they make possible are equally prominent in all ages or nations, but once any of these divergent tendencies has asserted itself in the early stages of a given civilization and found distinctive modes of expression, it becomes difficult thereafter, so long as the civilization lasts, for even the most original or revolutionary writers with the same predispositions to make a completely fresh start. The existence of these continuities, impossible though it may be to reduce any of them to satisfactory formulas, is the great justification of "comparative" or "general" histories of literature.

All this could probably have gone without saying; it is much harder to disengage the causal realities which warrant historians in differentiating "periods" or "ages" of literature and in attributing to each of these a distinctive "spirit" or "temper." For one thing, clearly, no solution of continuity can be implied: the processes of change in literature as in all human affairs are obviously unbroken from day to day, year to year, decade to decade, century to century. Nor can we ever be justified in describing "ages" or "periods" in such a way that the radical distinctness of the traditions effective in any of them is concealed. During the past thirty years, for example, I have known well a dozen or more men of some intellectual or literary force, in almost as many different fields, all of whom have seemed to me, as compared with many other equally able older men I have known, to exhibit an essentially "modern" or "twentieth-century" approach to things. Yet their individual backgrounds and interests have been of the most diverse kinds, and could they be brought together in the same room and be set talking with one another about almost any question in which first principles were involved, the result would inevitably be a range of disagreement among them, on philosophy, politics, morality, and art, that would reenact most of the major controversies discoverable in the whole past history of thought. And there is no reason to suppose that this has not always been so—whether for the thirteenth century or the Romantic period—no matter how completely the fact has been concealed—by the synthesizing ambitions of historians.

When we talk about the "spirit" of any age, accordingly, we must be careful to bear these two considerations in mind, but, on the other hand, they need not induce us to give up the problem altogether. For it remains true of my friends as a group that I cannot imagine any other period except our own in which they could have flourished or have developed the particular conceptions and attitudes, fundamentally discordant as these are, which they have held. It is in this sense that they are men of "the new age," even though, from another point of view, only a few of them have been avant-garde revolutionaries and some would certainly be described as conservative traditionalists. When I consider why it is that they have stimulated me more strongly in many ways than most past writers of greater achievement whom I have read, I can only attribute the fact to their common possession of this trait of "modernity." The point has been well put, in negative terms, in the remark of a recent critic that if, for example, "a lost poem of Marvell or a lost motet of Palestrina, each perfect in its kind, were brought forth and presented to a twentieth-century audience as a contemporary work of art, its reception would be dubious. It could at best be applauded as an academic curiosity, a feat of mimicry, or at worst ridiculed as an anachronistic absurdity: it could not be received in the same spirit of serious attention which is accorded a work in some sense felt to be of the moment in which it appears."

Here then is a genuine causal problem, arising for all periods in which literature has flourished and taken on new forms, the solution of which clearly entails giving attention to large collective factors in literary production and appreciation that are not easy to discuss by means of the analytical procedures we have been considering. For what seems to be involved in all such cases of general change is, on the one hand, a more or less rapid increment, in a given generation, of new experiences and interests of all kinds and of new and broadly inclusive ideas for interpreting these and assessing their values relatively to remembered experiences from the past and, on the other hand, the emergence of at least a few writers, intent upon doing fresh things of one sort or another in the various literary arts, who have the ability to invent original forms or to develop old ones in response to the new stimuli. The causes of what we call "modernity" in any age lie in the infinitely complex interaction of these factors as modified by the persistence of many distinct and well-established traditions; and its manifestations, consequently, will always be compatible with the widest diversity in literary species, techniques, and materials.

On Writing the History of Criticism in England 1650-1800

SINCE THE APPEARANCE, in 1911, of Saintsbury's *History of English Criticism,* many scholars have done much to correct and amplify the story which he set forth, with so much verve and prejudice, in his chapters on "Dryden and His Contemporaries," "From Addison to Johnson," and "The English Precursors of Romanticism." The bibliography of the subject has been notably enlarged; the contributions of many interesting minor critics, not noticed by Saintsbury, have been examined; the ideas of most of the major figures have been reinterpreted, annotated, and traced to some at least of their sources; the interrelations of British and Continental criticism have been studied with increasing particularity; and the techniques of intellectual history have been used, more and more intensively, to disclose important doctrinal developments the existence of which was largely overlooked a generation ago. Fruitful, however, as all this research has been, it has remained buried, for the most part, in learned editions, monographs, and articles; and even without this handicap, its fragmentary character—as the work of many scholars pursuing many different interests—was bound to restrict the fresh understanding of the subject which it made possible to a handful of specialists in a few academic centers. What has been wanted for a long time, therefore,

Published in the *University of Toronto Quarterly,* Vol. 22 (1953); reprinted with permission of the University of Toronto Press.

is a new and much better Saintsbury, in whose pages those many readers nowadays who are concerned with the evolution of critical thought and method might find a well-informed and intelligible synoptic account of those accomplishments of the first great age of modern English criticism that can still be thought to have more than a merely academic interest.

To provide such an account was clearly the ambition of the late J. W. H. Atkins in the volume on the seventeenth and eighteenth centuries which brings to an untimely close his projected history of literary criticism in antiquity and then in England from the early Middle Ages to the present time.[1] And he has not entirely failed. If his book has none of Saintsbury's sharpness and gusto, it has the advantage of being considerably longer and more detailed than Saintsbury's three chapters, of including a larger number of individual figures and dealing with many of them more amply, and of dwelling somewhat less on the personal idiosyncrasies of critics and somewhat more on the contents of their writings. On the other hand, although Atkins calls attention in his preface to a certain number of novelties in emphasis and judgment, he has neglected to profit in any conspicuous way from the scholarly literature on his subject that was available to him but not to Saintsbury; his identifiable uses of it hardly go beyond a half-dozen or so well-known books or collections of texts; and for all the good they have done him most of the many excellent papers on seventeenth- and eighteenth-century criticism in the learned journals of the past three decades might as well not have been written. This is very disappointing; but even had he made a more diligent use of what he could have learned from other modern scholars about the details of his theme, his book would still be open to the objection that it is based, like Saintsbury's—and also, one must admit, like many of the learned studies he has not used—upon an inadequate and mainly external conception of what a history of criticism in this or indeed any other period ought to be.

Let me give the dull receipt how histories such as Saintsbury's or Atkins' may be made. It is an extension of the simple formula for writing the doctrinal part of the history of philosophy that was em-

1 J. W. H. Atkins, *English Literary Criticism: 17th and 18th Centuries* (London: Methuen & Co. Ltd. [Toronto: British Book Service], 1951).

ployed in antiquity by Diogenes Laertius and in the seventeenth century by Thomas Stanley, among others. You begin by assuming that
the literary criticism of any age is a body of pronouncements about
something, called literature or poetry, which is thought to have a
fixed and determinable nature (however elusive or hard to state) in
much the same sense as any concrete event in human affairs; and you
assume, similarly, that criticism itself is a single discipline, which can
be judged to be better or worse, more or less adequate in its methods,
according to its fitness for making clear the real or full truth about its
supposed common objects and for appreciating their proper values.
You take for granted, in short, that when critics talk of such general
things as imitation, rules, the poetic process, genius, taste, imagination, judgment, tragedy, epic, satire, diction, versification, and so on,
or of such particular things as Homer, Virgil, the medieval romances,
Chaucer, Shakespeare, Spenser, Milton, the metaphysical poets, or
Pope, they are talking—truly or falsely, soundly or fancifully, compre-
hensively or partially, profoundly or superficially, sensitively or in-
sensitively, as defenders of the old or as enthusiasts for the new—of
things that remain what they are irrespective of how critics talk about
them. You therefore concentrate, in your reading of texts, on their
doctrinal content, extracting from them mainly their explicit statements about topics that seem important to you either because you
think them important critical topics in themselves or because they appear to be the favorite topics of critics in the period you are studying.
You thus acquire, as your reading proceeds, a great number of sum-
maries and notes, each with its appropriate subject-matter heading
(Dryden on "ideal" imitation or Shakespeare, Addison on "mixed wit,"
Johnson on the unities or on the defects of the metaphysical poets),
which you then must group together in some fashion if you are to have
a history rather than merely a collection of *fiches*. This you may do in
different ways: by summarizing in succession a critic's different works
or by arranging his doctrines under broad subjects (as Atkins divides
Dryden's mature critical opinions into opinions about the nature and
art of poetry, opinions about the forms of poetry, and "critical standards and judgments"); by grouping your critics either by traditions
or by periods, and within the latter either according to the agree-
ments and oppositions apparent in their critical attitudes or accord-

ing to their relative prominence or distinction as individuals; and so on.

All this, however, will not give you a history, but only the ingredients of one. You can construct a history, at least of the kind written by Saintsbury and Atkins, only when you have hit upon a comprehensive formula for your period as a whole that will allow you to make unified and coherent sense out of the otherwise chaotic mass of doctrines you have extracted from the texts. You must have this in some form, indeed, before you can set to work at all, or you will not know how to select from the many things each of your critics may be saying those relatively few things which can be included in your book. You cannot induce the formula from the facts but must bring it to them; hence the necessity of being equipped with a general view of criticism and of its proper development (again as a single discipline) such as will enable you to make fundamental distinctions of character and value among different critical doctrines; you then merely use the commonplace oppositions inherent in this view as the end terms of your story. You decide, for example, with Atkins, that progress in criticism consists in moving in any direction that is the contrary of any of the narrow and erroneous doctrines about poetry and criticism which you have identified with the "creed" of French neoclassicism in its most "rigid" form, as represented by Boileau, Rapin, and Bossu. You take this "orthodoxy," this oppressive and sterile régime founded on a priori and authoritarian "rules," as your starting point and standard of comparison; and you proceed, with the aid of such simple and general contrarieties as dogmatic-liberal, narrow-broad, outward-inward, dependent-independent, to write the history of English criticism between 1650 and 1800 as a series of efforts, some more enlightened or daring than others, first to challenge and clear away the "errors" of the neoclassical "system," and then gradually to broaden and liberalize the outlook and methods of criticism in preparation for the "great achievements" of the nineteenth century.

The facility of this common way of constructing the history of criticism is, I think, its greatest recommendation; its characteristic and inevitable weaknesses are well illustrated in Atkins' book. It is impossible, in the first place, to avoid distortion or at least oversimplification of what your critics are saying so long as you have committed yourself to a concern only with their doctrines and to an interpretation of these in the context of a preestablished scheme of dialectical oppositions. For you must treat what any critic says about any subject as a sign of his place in your scheme; and if you are to show, as Atkins is bent on doing, that most of the English critics who wrote after Boileau, Bossu, and Rapin were attempting to emancipate themselves from the restricted views and "cold intellectualism" of that school, you must obviously define the "orthodoxy" they were challenging in terms that will not include any of the doctrines or opinions you fix upon as indications of the more "liberal" attitudes that were emerging during the period. The plausibility of the story which Atkins tells would thus be seriously impaired if he were not able to insist that Dryden was trying "to extend the prevailing notion" of imitation when he remarked that poets are not confined to representing things "as they were or are" but might also depict things "as they were said or thought to be" or "as they ought to be" (pp. 111–12); or that there was something both new and out of harmony with neoclassical doctrine in Dryden's discussion of the Roman satirists in terms of "historical factors and the conditions of the age" (p. 142); or that Pope's allusion in the *Essay on Criticism* to the "nameless graces which no methods teach" is a sign of his not being "a representative, pure and simple, of the neoclassical school" (pp. 167–68); or that the opening argument of Johnson's *Preface to Shakespeare,* with its reference of literary judgment to "length of duration and continuance of esteem," is an indication that he had come under the new emancipating influence of Longinus (pp. 237–38); or that Johnson was helping to "dispose" of neoclassicism when he condemned "mere formal 'imitation' of earlier masterpieces" and asserted that "No man as yet ever became great by imitation" (p. 358); or that another fundamental principle of neoclassicism was being denied by Maurice Morgann and others in the later eighteenth century when they contended that there is "something mysterious" in poetry, something more than a "mere formal art" (p. 360); or that it was a conception of poetry "newly won" in the eighteenth century which made its values consist, not in its appeal "to the intellect alone," but in its power to move the feelings, "its impassioned utterances and aesthetic effects" (pp. 185, 362–63). The truth of all these statements is guaranteed, for Atkins, by his account of the neoclassical "orthodoxy" in his opening chapter; but

unfortunately there is not one among the pronouncements he here
singles out as "liberal" or revolutionary that would have been dis-
puted by any critic of importance in antiquity or the Renaissance,
and not one that cannot be found in Rapin himself.[2] But such is the
force of a dialectical thesis, combined with an exclusive preoccupation with doctrines, that absurdities of this sort can be perpetrated
even by a conscientious historian like Atkins, who was surely well
enough read in earlier criticism to know better.

And along with this goes a second weakness, which is likewise, I
think, a necessary consequence of the method. For if you confine your
statements about particular critics and their writings merely to the
explicit content of what is said, you are bound to reduce their arguments to a series of discrete assertions or denials, about generalized
and commonplace topics, the great majority of which can have no
serious interest in themselves for readers in a later age, when these
topics no longer represent questions we think important. It is doubtless well to know what Johnson, for instance, had to say about the
desirability that critics should read the works they comment on, or
about the value of the test of time, or about the evils of imitation, or
about the limited authority of the unities of time and place, or about
the genius of English versification, or about the use of general terms
in poetry, or about romances and novels, or about the distinctive
merits and defects of the various poets dealt with in the *Lives*—to
mention a few of the heads under which Atkins groups Johnson's critical "pronouncements"; but as atomized in his treatment, such opinions can have for us only the value of examination knowledge in critical antiquities; and we wonder how anyone can be thought a great
critic who has to his credit, on the reading of the historian, only such
a mass of miscellaneous platitudes or queer and outdated ideas. It is
the same with all the other critics, whether contemned or admired,
whose "comments," "opinions," or "pronouncements" Atkins pre-

2 See the following passages in *The Whole Critical Works of Monsieur Rapin* (London, 1706): on "ideal" imitation, II, 186; on the relation of literary works to the circumstances of their age, I, 42–54, 156, 157, II, 169, 170, 177, 210; on the "nameless
graces," I, 25–26, II, 173; on length of esteem as a sign of merit, I, 116–18; on the
superiority of original invention to "imitation," I, 198–201; on the element of "mystery"
in poetry, II, 173; on the place of the emotions in literature and poetry, II, 25–26,
75–78, 206–9, 212–14. For the third and sixth of these topics see the excellent article by
Samuel H. Monk, " ' A Grace beyond the Reach of Art,' " *Journal of the History of Ideas*,
5 (1944): 131–50.

sents to us in this scissors-and-paste way. The result can only be dull writing (the writing in Saintsbury would be equally dull except for the often impertinent intrusions of his own much livelier dicta), and, what is worse, writing that is fundamentally unintelligible as history. We can hardly believe that many of these critics were not men of sense, with serious intellectual aims, who knew what they were doing; but of this we get—and can get, I believe, from the method being used —only the slightest inkling. There are no real answers, in Atkins' history, to the surely relevant question of why it was that his various critics took the particular positions they did. He does, indeed, speak frequently of the changing conditions under which the criticism of his period was successively produced—of the French influences in the middle and later seventeenth century, of the rise of periodicals and clubs and the new philosophical temper which characterized the age of Addison and Pope, of the "Longinian revival" and the antiquarian movement in the next generation; but these clearly explain nothing in the peculiar character of the doctrines contemporary with them. And beyond this we get, in the way of causal interpretation, only a set of what I must call occult entities, similar to those which Glanvill, Molière, and others satirized in the seventeenth century: as when we are told that the doctrines of rule and order in French neoclassicism had their roots in "a sense of the urgent need for disciplined order in all spheres of life" (p. 4), or that the emancipation of English criticism from this tyranny "was ultimately determined by the independent native genius" (p. v), or that the reason why the neoclassical "system" was finally rejected in England was that it ran counter to "the innate predisposition of English minds to empiricism" (pp. 146, 356), and so on, as if we explained anything merely by translating a general quality predicated of a text into an equivalent abstraction predicated of the writer or his age.

I have called this an inadequate and external conception of the history of criticism. It is external because it views what critics say from the outside, so to speak, as statements to be classified and judged in terms of the historian's superior knowedge of what is true or relevant in criticism, rather than from the inside, as statements to be understood in terms of the reasons that governed their authors in making them; and it is inadequate because it presents only the material content of doctrines in abstraction from the purposes and presuppositions that determined their precise meaning and validity in the writings from which they are taken. When I assert or deny something in criticism, either in setting forth a general position or in discussing writers or works, what I say is conditioned undoubtedly by my taste and sensibility and by my knowledge of the pertinent facts; but I could not say anything at all unless I also had in mind a particular problem, or complex of problems, which I wanted to resolve, a set of assumptions or basic distinctions by means of which I could both formulate the problems, as problems of this rather than some other kind, and argue to conclusions about them, and finally, some notion of the mode of argument best suited to my aims on this occasion. These are the three determinants of the internal character of any critical discourse; and it is impossible to talk understandingly and fairly about any critical "pronouncement" apart from this threefold context of the question to which, for the critic himself rather than merely for the historian, it was an answer, the assumptions about literature and criticism which underlay the asking of the question and the determination of the answer, and the devices of reasoning by which the answer was established.

The first step, therefore, toward a more complete and intelligible history of English criticism in the seventeenth and eighteenth centuries would be a systematic reexamination of the relevant documents in the light of these internal and logical causes of what their writers said.[3]

Consider, for instance, Pope's *Preface to the Iliad:* whatever we might ultimately conclude about the value of this work and its place in the critical development of the century, our first task would be to

---

3 For examples of the type of analysis I have in mind, see Bernard Weinberg, "The Poetic Theories of Minturno," *Studies in Honor of Frederick W. Shipley* (St. Louis, 1942), pp. 101–29; "Scaliger versus Aristotle on Poetics," *Modern Philology*, 39 (1942): 337–60; *Critical Prefaces of the French Renaissance* (Evanston, Ill., 1950), Introduction; his essays on Robortello and Castelvetro in *Critics and Criticism: Ancient and Modern,* edited by R. S. Crane (Chicago, 1952), pp. 319–71; and his *History of Literary Criticism in the Italian Renaissance* (2 vols., Chicago, 1961); Elder Olson, Introduction to the "University Classics" edition of Longinus and of Reynolds' *Discourses* (Chicago, 1945); W. R. Keast, "Johnson's Criticism of the Metaphysical Poets," *ELH*, 17 (1950): 59–70, and "The Theoretical Foundations of Johnson's Criticism," *Critics and Criticism*, pp. 389–407; Robert Marsh, *Four Dialectical Theories of Poetry: An Aspect of English Neoclassical Criticism* (Chicago, 1965).

read it in its own terms, as a possibly coherent argument, without preconceptions about the nature of "neoclassicism" or "romanticism" or any other such abstraction, or about what is and what is not fruitful or progressive in criticism in general. Our problem would simply be: What was Pope trying to do here and on what assumptions about poetry and critical method do his statements come closest to making sense? We should see at once, I think, that the questions he is asking are not at all questions about the formal excellence of the *Iliad* considered as an epic poem, although his remarks are grouped under the general heads of fable, characters, sentiments, expression, and versification, which earlier critics had used in discussing epic art; nor is he interested primarily in the *Iliad* as a product of Greek culture, although he does refer the explanation of some of its characteristics to "the nature of the times" in which Homer lived. His central problem is dictated by the fact that he is translating the *Iliad* into modern English, and that in doing this he wishes to be as faithful as possible to the essential spirit of his great original; he must therefore decide what the essential spirit is. It is not enough, accordingly, to consider the *Iliad* merely in terms of the art of its construction or of its reflection of early Greek manners and beliefs. If the *Iliad* is still to be read by cultivated Englishmen, it must be as a poem simply; and hence the question to be answered first of all is: What are the particular qualities, among those possible in poetry of any species or of any age, that make the *Iliad* a great poem? These are what the translation must strive to preserve, and it is consequently to the definition of these that Pope mainly devotes himself in his *Preface*.

His guiding assumption must obviously be one applicable to poetry of no matter what kind or period; he cannot therefore fall back on the "rules" of epic, and it would be equally irrelevant to look for principles in the tastes of readers, whether in ancient Greece or modern England. He needs principles of the greatest generality possible; and these he finds in the assumption that excellence in poetry, universally speaking, is a function of two powers in the poet—invention and judgment: the first, a pure gift of nature or genius, manifesting itself in the energy, fire, rapture, and animated spirit of the poet's imagination; the second, natural also in its source but capable of being improved by art, manifesting itself in his skilled control of what he invents. He further assumes that in the best poets the two powers unite, though usually with one or the other predominant, but that of the two, the first is indispensable and the source of all preeminence, whereas the second, though always desirable, is insufficient in itself to give us the greatest poetry. It is with this principle that Pope starts, laying it down as a proposition that will be generally agreed to without proof; and his argument consists in showing, by devices of analysis and comparison, that while Homer is not lacking in judgment and art, his supreme and distinguishing excellence—traceable in all the parts of the *Iliad,* from the plot down to the details of language and verse—is the unsurpassed strength, variety, and liveliness of his imagination.

The *Preface* becomes intelligible, as a critical utterance, only, I suggest, when we have related its doctrinal statements and particular judgments in some such way as this to Pope's specific problem in writing it and to the general assumptions which give sense and cogency to its argument and dictate its procedure; and we shall inevitably distort its significance in the history of criticism if we are content simply to extract "pronouncements" or "opinions" from it without interpreting these in the light of the special logical situation in which they came to be stated and the necessities which this involved for the author.

The consistent application of such a mode of analysis to the critical writings of our period would give them a status in our history very different from their status in histories like Atkins': they would appear not as signs or embodiments of the general characteristics defined for the period by the contraries of the historian's dialectical scheme but as historical events, made meaningful individually in terms of the concrete problems their writers actually set themselves and of the principles and methods they thought appropriate to their solution. A history, however, is more than a succession of discrete events; if it is to be fully intelligible, as a history, the events must be exhibited in a context of collective causes sufficient to account both for the common elements that persist through the criticism of the period and for the variant combinations of these that appear in different writers or at different times. And we would look for such causes, initially at least, in a systematic comparison of our critics, read in the way I have suggested, from the point of view, first, of the kinds of general assumptions or principles they tended to use and, second, of the kinds of questions they preferred to ask.

The first comparison would give us the material continuity of our narrative. It would be a continuity—not, as in Atkins, of a common body of doctrines which in the course of time was accepted, modified, and rejected—but of a more or less common framework of characteristic fundamental terms and distinctions which critics throughout the period, for all their disagreements on points of doctrine or appreciation, found it natural to utilize in the statement of their questions and the justification of their answers.[4] The elements of this framework, we should discover, were of two major kinds, both of which can be seen in Pope's *Preface.* In the first place, there were the many descriptive or analytical terms designating the recognized kinds or styles of literature and the constituent parts of literary works: epic, tragedy, comedy, pastoral, satire, ode, and the like; the elevated, middle, and low styles; matter and manner, thought and expression, fable, manners, sentiments, language, verse, and so on. In the second place, there were the still more general terms, or pairs of contrary terms, applicable to the productive conditions, subjects, audiences, ends, and qualities of literature in all its branches, which served to define the premises from which these critics argued in the construction of theories or the discussion of the beauties and faults of authors and works: nature and art, native ability and rules, invention and judgment, imagination and reason, genius and taste, originality and the imitation of models, the imitation of nature and fanciful invention, general or ideal nature and particular nature, the probable and the true, the probable and the marvelous, instruction and pleasure, the heart and the head, men of taste and the common reader, beauty and grace, simplicity and refinement, the just and the lively, truth and novelty, uniformity and variety, the regular and the irregular, the sublime and the pathetic, the sublime and the beautiful, and many others equally familiar to students of the period.

Even in such bare lists as these we begin to get something of the critical flavor of the age as a whole, something better entitled, per-

---

[4] Cf. above, Vol. I, pp. 175–77.

haps, to be called "neoclassical" (if we are to keep that useful word) than the incredible doctrines to which Atkins applies the term. For the commonplaces I have mentioned are not the same, with a few exceptions, as those which have been put to similar uses in criticism since the Romantics, nor are they identical, as a body, with the controlling terms of either Plato or Aristotle. They form, taken collectively, a particular tradition of critical "language"—a tradition that had its origins in the poetic and rhetoric of Alexandrian Greece and of the Rome of Cicero, Horace, and Quintilian; that was reconstituted and enlarged in the Renaissance, mainly through the addition of elements from Aristotle and Plato; and that persisted, with further additions from Longinus and others, to the end of the eighteenth century. It would be a mistake to think of it as a unified system or doctrine; its character was rather that of a large but historically distinguishable aggregate of commonplace distinctions, of a highly flexible and ambiguous kind, out of which many variant critical systems and doctrines could be constructed. In some of these the terms relating to the natural causes and aspects of literature were subordinated to the terms signifying its character as art (as in Rapin, Dryden, and Reynolds) and in others the relation was reversed (as in Pope's *Preface,* Johnson, and Young). In some of them, again, the terms that served as first principles were those relating to the ends of literature or its effects on audiences (as in Rapin, Dryden, Addison, Johnson, and many more)—and these were the systems most characteristic of the period—whereas in others the controlling terms were sometimes distinctions of subject matter (as in Burke's *Sublime and Beautiful* and Hurd's *Letters on Chivalry and Romance*), sometimes distinctions of language (as in Robert Lowth), and sometimes distinctions pertaining to the powers and activities of writers (as in Pope's *Preface,* Joseph Warton, and Young).

Such variations would enter into our history as part of our attempt to make intelligible what individual critics were trying to do; but it is essential to see them as variations within a general framework of critical commonplaces that was accepted without serious question by most critics of the period, however diverse and apparently opposed the conclusions they asserted by means of them. For it is inevitable, otherwise, that we should exaggerate the oppositions by making them more fundamental than they actually were or at any rate fail to interpret them in a properly discriminating way—and this either in our statements about the originality of the period as a whole in comparison with what went before (we must know at least as much of the past history of our critics' principles as any of them knew) or in our judgments of the later critics in the period in comparison with the earlier. We need not question, for instance, that Richard Hurd was bent on saying things in his *Letters on Chivalry and Romance* that would hardly have been said by René Rapin, but it is surely requisite to an accurate historical interpretation of the *Letters* that we should observe—as Atkins, in his enthusiasm for all signs of revolt against his myth of "neoclassicism," does not— how completely Hurd's argument for the poetic value of Gothic manners is framed and carried out in terms of the same basic distinctions, concerning the possible relations of the marvelous and the probable in poetry, as had served Rapin in his *Réflexions.* The two men differed widely, but they talked a common critical language; and that is a kind of phenomenon which the historian of criticism in this period can never safely omit from his account if he is to make genuine historical sense of his facts.

The significant variations apparent in the criticism of this age are a function in part of the different permutations effected by critics among common dialectical principles (these I have just touched upon) and in part of the different major types of questions which critics were concerned to ask; and the result of our second comparison would be to bring into prominence variations of this latter kind, which would serve as collective causes, as well as formal lines of differentiation, in our narrative, inasmuch as the nature of the questions any critic asks is bound to have a determinative effect on his selection of principles and methods, just as his selection of principles and methods is bound to delimit the questions he can ask. If we examine the writings of critics in the later seventeenth and eighteenth centuries from this point of view, we can easily discriminate in them, I think, three major types of questions and hence three dominant modes of critical discussion.[5]

One is the mode to which, because of the great prominence it gave to what were often satirized as the "mechanical rules," the name of

[5] For a different but equally valid classification, based on distinctions of method, see Robert Marsh, *Four Dialectical Theories of Poetry*, chap. 1.

"neoclassicism" in its stricter meaning has been most commonly applied. It is the kind of criticism we get in Dryden's *Essay of Dramatic Poesy* (along with other kinds) and his *Preface to Troilus and Cressida*, in Thomas Rymer's two books on tragedy, in John Dennis' "remarks" on Blackmore's *Prince Arthur*, Addison's *Cato*, and Steele's *Conscious Lovers*, in Charles Gildon's *Complete Art of Poetry*, in Hurd's *Dissertation concerning the Provinces of the Several Species of the Drama* and in his *Letters on Chivalry and Romance*, in Fielding's *Preface to Joseph Andrews*, in Goldsmith's essay on laughing and weeping comedy, in parts of Hugh Blair's *Lectures on Rhetoric and Belles Lettres*, and in a great many less well-known arts of poetry, books and essays on the major and minor literary genres, and reviews of plays, novels, and narrative poems. It is technical criticism in the sense that the questions it seeks to answer are primarily questions of art and construction; and it is "specific" criticism in the sense that it tends to view these questions in terms of the differing ends and ideals of beauty peculiar to the various species of poetic writing. As practiced in our period it drew its terms and criteria sometimes directly from Aristotle and Horace (except in Fielding, however, on the basis of interpretations of the *Poetics* and the *Ars poetica* that largely blurred their radical differences in principle and method) but more commonly from sources in the Italian, Dutch, and French critics of the Renaissance and seventeenth century in which the doctrines of Aristotle and Horace had been fused, in varying ways, with elements from Cicero, Quintilian, Donatus, the Neoplatonists, and the later medieval arts of poetry. We should not be so prejudiced by this bastard origin that we fail to make clear the good reasons why, for all its evident limitations—as compared, for example, with a better understood Aristotle—this version of "specific" criticism continued for as long as it did to be taken seriously by writers of such obvious sensitivity to literature as Jonson, Corneille, Boileau, Racine, and Dryden. We should try to view it, that is, through the eyes of its exponents and practitioners rather than merely of its detractors in the eighteenth century and later, as one set of devices for isolating and dealing with real and important problems of literary production and judgment in ways that seemed useful at the time. And we should not either exaggerate its "orthodoxy" in the earlier part of our period or conclude hastily that the eclipse which overtook it in the eighteenth century was due solely to the emergence of a more modern and "liberal" spirit. For both of the other two rival modes of critical discussion could also claim the prestige of antiquity and hence of being "neoclassical" in any but the narrowest sense of that word.

Of these rival modes the more conspicuous by far throughout the period is the kind of criticism that appears—to mention only a few examples—in Dryden's character of Shakespeare in his *Essay*, his comparisons of the Roman satirists, and his remarks on Homer, Virgil, Ovid, Chaucer, and Boccaccio in his *Preface to the Fables*, in Dennis' *Grounds of Criticism in Poetry*, in Addison's essays on wit and most of those on *Paradise Lost*, in Pope's *Preface to the Iliad*, and, after 1740, in Johnson (for the most part), Joseph Warton, Lowth, Young, Burke, Kames, much of Reynolds and Blair, and most of the new critics at the end of the century. It is criticism of a sort that has always been practiced, in one fashion or another, whenever the questions critics ask have related primarily not to the formal or technical construction of literary works in their different kinds but to the general qualities or values which distinguish one writer from another or great writers from ordinary writers, irrespective of the genres in which they write. As a consequence, it has usually been indifferent to distinctions of literary species or has subordinated them to broader considerations; it has normally reduced the elements of works to matter and manner, or thought, emotion, and expression; and it has sought its first principles, not in definitions of forms, but either in the natural and acquired powers or habits of writers (as in Pope's *Preface*) or in some ideal of good taste (as in Addison) or some analysis of the natural responses of audiences or readers to literary discourse (as in Johnson). No one has attempted its history as a distinct critical approach; but the historian of criticism in our period would fail in his task if he neglected to point out how long and respectable an ancestry this method had had—from admired ancients like Dionysius of Halicarnassus, Cicero, Demetrius, Longinus, and Quintilian, through the early seventeenth-century Continental writers on wit,[6] to such influential French critics as Boileau, Rapin, and above all Bouhours. "Qualitative" criticism (as it may be called) was thus no novelty in the time

---

[6] See Joseph Anthony Mazzeo, "A Seventeenth-Century Theory of Metaphysical Poetry," *Romanic Review*, 42 (1951): 245–55.

of Dryden; but there can be little doubt that a more extensive and detailed cultivation of it was encouraged, after about 1675, first by the rising prestige of Bouhours and especially of Longinus, and then, increasingly in the eighteenth century, by the growing tendency, in writers like Addison (in his papers on the pleasures of the imagination), Hutcheson, Hume, Harris, Burke, Gerard, Kames, Reid, Stewart, Alison, and many others, to look for new bases of critical principles in philosophic analyses of human nature or the mind. For one of the inevitable consequences of this widespread philosophizing of criticism (to which Atkins does scant justice) was to bring into the foreground those general causes of literary effects—in the psychology of genius and taste, in the universal attributes of language, in the affective properties of objects and actions—that are common to all forms of literature and can be traced in the parts of works without reference to their peculiar structural principles. The upshot of these developments was a general turning away of most critics, by the end of the century, from questions of literary species and their forms and techniques to questions of qualitative discrimination and appraisal, with the result that poetry itself came to be thought of more and more, in dissociation from the forms of poetic art, as a certain superior quality, not confined to poems, of language or thought.[7]

The third mode of critical discussion is that exemplified in works like the writings of Thomas Blackwell and Robert Wood on Homer, Thomas Warton's *Observations on the Faerie Queene* and his *History of English Poetry*, Hurd's *Letters* (in one aspect), the last part of Johnson's *Preface to Shakespeare*, and a good many passages in his *Lives of the Poets*—again to mention only a few characteristic samples. It is a kind of criticism in which the primary questions concern neither universal principles of form in the different literary species nor general qualities of mind and expression but rather the relations of literary works to the particular conditions of their production, these being taken either as causes in a history or as facts in the light of which the peculiarities of past writers can be justified or excused; it embraces but is not identical with what we call "historical" criticism, and hence is perhaps better referred to as "circumstantial" criticism. That it was an increasingly popular critical mode in the

---

7 See Norman Maclean, in *Critics and Criticism*, pp. 408–60, and especially pp. 459–60.

eighteenth century is well known; what we should need to make clear in our history is precisely the point about it which Atkins ignores—that the tradition on which it was founded was as old as the traditions of the other two modes, so that the frequent references in critics from Dryden onward to the conformity between older writers and the moral or political temper of their age or to the demands of English as opposed to French or Greek audiences can in no way be construed as signs of an intent to break with the criticism of the past. For it is hard to see how any educated critic in our period could have found anything savoring of radical innovation in a critical principle that had been enunciated with perfect clarity by Quintilian,[8] that had been applied to the interpretation of the Scriptures by Erasmus and many others, and that was invoked on occasion by critics no more "liberal" than D'Aubignac and Rapin.[9] It would then remain for us, with this truer perspective, to do what has not yet been done—to discriminate the different kinds of use to which the criticism of "circumstances" was put in this period and to look for the causes of its undoubtedly increasing vogue.

For the latter we should have to go beyond the bounds of criticism itself considered as the art of formulating and applying literary principles; and the same thing would be true for many other questions of particular causation in our history. Our final major task, therefore, would be to trace the various accidental causes of what individual critics did and of what happened to the practice of criticism in general, in the many other developments of the period that supplied critics with subjects, materials, problems, occasions, opportunities, and directions. Our history would still be a history of criticism in its stricter meaning of reasoned discourse about the literary arts and their products, and it would not confuse this, as both Saintsbury and Atkins tend to do, with the history of shifting literary tastes and scholarly interests; but it would obviously remain only a partial and somewhat abstract history if we failed to make its events and changes as intelligible as the facts permit by showing how they were conditioned, for example, by such events in the history of taste as the "Augustan" reaction against metaphysical wit and the growing cults

[8] *Institutio oratoria* xii. 10. 1–2.

[9] For Rapin see above, note 2; for D'Aubignac, *The Whole Art of the Stage* (London, 1684), Book II, pp. 69–73; Book III, pp. 44–45.

of Homer, Shakespeare, Spenser, and Milton; or, in the history of scholarship, by the medieval and Greek revivals; or, in the history of literary production, by the rise of the heroic play, the domestic novel, and the Gothic romance; or, in the history of philosophy, by the increasing preoccupation with "ideas" and their association and by the emergence of the Scottish school. All this would be an essential part of our problem; the distinction of our history would be that, in approaching the discussion of external causes like these, we should understand more clearly than those historians who attend merely to the doctrinal content of critical works what it is in the statements of critics that such causes cannot explain.

Here, then, in general outline, is the program of a history which I think would have a good many advantages as compared with either of the two comprehensive histories of seventeenth- and eighteenth-century criticism now available to us. It would be a history without prior commitments as to what criticism is or ought to be, its assumption being merely that criticism is any kind of argued writing about the literary arts that has seemed appropriate, at one time or another, to their natures. It would therefore be free to exhibit critics speaking for themselves with respect to problems they themselves had formulated in the process of solving them, rather than problems set for them, after the event, by the historian; and its criteria of praise and blame would be based on no demand for conformity to a particular ideal of excellence in criticism but solely on an estimate of how much different critics were able to accomplish with the principles, devices, and materials at their disposal. Dryden and Johnson would still be the heroes of the story, but not because they helped to emancipate criticism from the tyranny of neoclassical rules. It would be a history, for the same reason, without a thesis. It would attempt to construct a coherent and intelligible narrative of what happened, but the coherence and intelligibility would result not from an imposition upon the facts of a unified scheme of dialectical opposites but from the discovery, through a comparison of what different critics were trying to do, of such evident lines of development and causal interconnection as the comparison might reveal. The governing pattern of the history, in short, would be the last rather than the first thing we would know; and hence we should be able to utilize to the full the factual contributions of other scholars without any of the embarrassment that must necessarily be often felt by historians of the a priori school. And the history, finally, although it would not neglect doctrines, would be a history of these in a context of the specific questions and general principles and methods which entered into and gave form and philosophic meaning to their statement. It could therefore be expected to throw light not simply on the dead opinions and pronouncements of dead critics but on the permanent and still living problems of analysis and reasoning which critics in all times and traditions have faced, and concerning which we ourselves might easily profit, in a good many ways, by knowing in detail how they were defined and solved by our predecessors in the seventeenth and eighteenth centuries.

Questions and Answers in the Teaching
of Literary Texts

I N THIS ESSAY I want to deal particularly with the teaching of literature at a fairly elementary level to students of whom a few will, but most will not, become specialists in our subject. (I must say at once, however, that I cannot think of any general principles applicable to this earlier stage of literary study that are not relevant also to later undergraduate stages and even to graduate work on its less technical side.) And I shall restrict the treatment of the subject still further. The problem of subject matter—of what authors or works, and how many of each, we should include in our general courses— is one we all have to face annually, or at least whenever we get tired of our current syllabi. But it is hardly a subject for fruitful public debate, and even if it were, the necessary criteria for talking intelligently about it depend (as I hope to make clear) upon our first having made up our minds about something else. Nor can I see any profit in recanvassing the problem of our objectives. It may be needful at times to indoctrinate students with the faith that they are not wasting their time in studying literature. But the best indoctrination, after all, is a good course; and as for ourselves, however much we may like to dispute, in the abstract, about the ends of English study, I suspect that we are all pretty well agreed on what, in a concrete sense, we should like

A paper read at Carleton College, at a regional conference of college teachers of English, 1953; not previously published.

to see result from our endeavors, in the way of newly acquired skill and knowledge in our students. We want these students, whatever their intentions in life, not only to have fixed in their memories a certain number of excellent literary works and a certain body of essential facts about their historical relations, but also to carry away from their experience with us a more eager inclination to read literature for its own sake than they brought to it. All this of course; and beyond this, as something again which few will question, we want them to become sufficiently educated in the elements of a critical approach to literature so that, in their later studies and in life, they will know how to interpret and judge for themselves, appropriately and independently, whatever new works they may read.

To specify such a training of critical habits as one of our agreed aims, however, is at once to raise the crucial question of what it is that a good elementary critical education consists in and how it may most effectually be given to our students. The important practical problem for us, in short, is the problem of method; and I mean this not in the pedagogical sense of the relations between lectures and discussions, oral recitation and writing, close reading and extensive reading, organization by periods and organization by literary types, and so on, but rather in the intellectual sense of the kinds of questions about literary works we ask students and train them to ask themselves, and of the techniques we cultivate in them for getting and justifying answers. It is with this restricted aspect of our general subject, at any rate, that I wish to deal.

I shall group my remarks under two principal heads: first, the varieties of questions that seem most pertinent and necessary to the development of a rounded understanding and appreciation of literary works; second, the conditions of formulation and testing under which warranted answers to such questions are to be sought.

The view of critical questions I want to suggest is based on the simple premise that no statement we make about literature in general or a given literary work can have any determinate meaning or relevance, or permit of any intelligent appraisal of its validity, so long as it is considered merely as an isolated statement. This ought to be obvious to everyone; but unfortunately the history of criticism has

been so written, for the most part, as to blind us to both its truth and
its implications. The majority of histories of criticism have been constructed on the assumption that we can give an adequate account of
what critics in the past have done by summarizing, and comparing
directly with one another, the explicit doctrinal conclusions they have
set forth concerning art, literature, poetry, or particular parts and species of these, and by treating similarly their judgments on individual
writers and works. The immediate effect of such a procedure is to resolve the development of criticism into a succession of arbitrary and
hopelessly conflicting dogmas, only a few of which need be taken
seriously, plus an accumulation of equally arbitrary and conflicting
pronouncements in "practical criticism" that seem well deserving of
the satire bestowed upon them in Henri Peyre's witty lectures on
Writers and Their Critics. And the ultimate effect is to encourage in
us one or the other of two attitudes toward the existing body of critical statements, both of them severely limiting in their practical consequences. On the one hand, we may very well conclude, from the
history of criticism as thus told, that any serious concern with the
principles of literature, or systematic application of principles to
works, is a futile business; or, on the other hand, we may restrain our
skepticism to the limited extent of pinning our faith to one particular
system out of the many systems of criticism available to us in the past,
or now being constructed, and treat the others either as modern corruptions of ancient truths or as ancient errors sufficiently refuted by
the discoveries of later times.

To respond in either of these ways, however—as a skeptic or as a
dogmatic adherent to one system or "approach"—is enormously to restrict our resources as critics and teachers of literature. Fortunately,
neither response is justified by the nature of critical statements when
that nature is fully understood. The trouble with the historians I
have been speaking of is that they have disregarded the simple premise I stated a moment ago. They have consistently taken the declara-
tions of critics, on both general and particular subjects, as if they were
capable of being interpreted, and their truth or falsity pronounced
upon, as self-contained assertions, without prior consideration of their
logical status and functions in the critical discourse in which they
appear. But all statements in criticism have logical contexts, apart
from which nothing significant can be said about them; and the im-

mediate context of any statement is the precise question (often not explicitly formulated at all) to which it is an intended answer. Wherefore it follows that two critical doctrines cannot be sensibly compared, no matter how similar their verbal forms, or be judged in relation to one another, until we are sure that both are conceived as answers to exactly the same question. Thus we have no right to say that Croce either refuted or made obsolete the doctrine of poetic genres unless we are prepared to show—which cannot, I think, be done—that his conclusions represent a solution of the very same theoretical problem, or problems, that faced the earlier critics who upheld that doctrine; and conversely, of course, as well.

But we can, and indeed must, go further than this. For no critical question, in turn, is an isolable thing. Just as statements are relative to the questions to which they are answers, so questions are relative, so far as their meanings and the conditions of their proper answering are concerned, to the still larger context of primary terms, distinctions, and premises which make up the conceptual "framework" (as we say nowadays) of the critic's writing, and determine both what questions he will think it possible or important to ask and what kinds of answers he will seek for them. Wherefore it follows, very often, that what appear to be hopeless doctrinal conflicts in criticism are not really doctrinal conflicts at all, but simply expressions of preference among different, but equally defensible, frameworks, within any two of which the seemingly common referents of the critics' statements may be only nominally the same. This is the case, for instance, with Plato as compared with Aristotle (there is no sense in which Aristotle can be said to have refuted Plato on poetry), with the German idealist critics of the early nineteenth century as compared with these ancients, and with the contemporary school of "semantic" critics as compared with their Victorian predecessors.

If all this is true, it has important practical consequences for our initial problem of determining the kinds of questions we will want to ask, and encourage students to ask for themselves, in our literary teaching. It would doubtless be desirable, from one point of view, if we could forget about literary theory altogether and give our attention wholly to the concrete particulars of the poems, novels, and dramas before us. But we cannot do that, since everything we say, every question we ask, about literary works is inevitably dependent upon some assumption as to what such things are and as to how knowledge and appreciation of them is to be obtained. Whether we like it or not, we are inescapably bound to theory; but once we have recognized this, we can, I think, do two things, both of them clearly implied in the view of critical statements and questions I have been trying to suggest. We can accustom ourselves, in the first place, to looking upon the theoretical statements of critics, from Aristotle to the authors of *Understanding Poetry,* not as doctrines to be taught, but rather as more or less useful tools of our trade— as sources of concepts and distinctions from which we and our students may derive significant questions to ask about works in the hope of generating observations on them that might not otherwise be made. We can form the habit, in a word, of treating critical theories heuristically. And having done this, we can emancipate ourselves from the stultifying notion, which is still widespread, that there must be some "proper" or "right" approach to literature, poetry, or Shakespeare, which we are justified in opposing to other approaches and insisting on as the one true way to critical salvation, whether this is contained in the textbook we are using or not.

The truth is that all the critical systems that have been devised, or that can be devised, are finite bodies of ideas, restricted, by the very nature of critical discourse, to one particular selection of aspects out of the many different ones which literary works present. Each has its peculiar power of stimulating observation and making possible understanding; but each, at the same time, has its characteristic limitations, beyond which its utility ceases. The special concern of Aristotle in the *Poetics,* for example, is with those aspects of certain kinds of poems—the kinds which, as he says, "happen to be imitations"—that emerge when we ask what are the principles of artistic reasoning presupposed by their obviously different structures and effects; it is with these aspects, but only with these, that the conceptual apparatus he provides will permit us to deal.[1] The special concern of Coleridge, again, is with those aspects of poems and poetry, considered generally not specifically, and in terms not so much of artistic principles as of natural causes, that appear when we ask about the effects produced on the mind by poems as distinct from other

[1] See Elder Olson, "The Poetic Method of Aristotle: Its Powers and Limitations," *English Institute Essays, 1951* (New York, 1952), pp. 70–94.

modes of composition and especially about the degree of participation achieved by poets in the universal synthetic workings of the imagination; it is to these aspects that he consistently directs our attention and it is with respect to these, but these only, that he is a useful and inspiring guide. The special concern, finally, of Brooks and Warren in *Understanding Poetry* is with those aspects of poetry, considered as one homogeneous kind of thing, that are isolated when we make poetry a mode of discourse sharply opposed in its materials and methods to science, and ask questions mainly about the characteristics of "poetic" form and meaning which this comparison discloses; what is valuable and suggestive in their approach is strictly relative to this basic decision as to the aspect of poetry they will talk about.[2]

We have here three critical systems that neither overlap nor contradict one another at any significant points; and there are many others, both past and contemporary, of which the same can be said. I think this is a great reason for self-congratulation—that we have available for our needs in teaching, if only we will take advantage of the fact, so many different and well-tested instruments for helping our students see more in works of literature than they have been accustomed to seeing. It should be our obligation as teachers, therefore, first to try to grasp what is positive and still valuable, within the limits of their respective frameworks, in at least the major critical systems of the past and present. We ought then to bring this understanding to bear on the problem of devising a general scheme of critical questions that will include, and set in significant relation to each other, the different fundamental aspects of literary works which our predecessors and contemporaries have defined, and which our students ought to be led to consider.

I want to propose such a scheme here, but without implying that I think no other equally useful schemes could be devised for the same purpose. It consists of five groups of critical questions, corresponding to five distinguishable aspects of literary works—their verbal elements and the actions, thoughts, and feeling revealed by

[2] For this general view of critical questions and statements, see further *Critics and Criticism: Ancient and Modern*, edited by R. S. Crane (Chicago, 1952), especially pp. 2–12, 63–64, 148–49, 174–75, 317–18, 463–66, 522–23, 530–45, 546–52, 594; and Crane, *The Languages of Criticism and the Structure of Poetry* (Toronto, 1953).

these; their overall forms; the qualities of thought and sensibility in their authors which they reflect; the circumstances of their composition; and the moral, social, or intellectual effects they are capable of exerting. I shall speak of them in ascending order of complexity.

1. We may ask questions, in the first place, that depend for their content and for the data of their answers, merely on a consideration of literary works, irrespective of their specific kinds, in their common aspect as verbal compositions. This is the distinctive sphere of *explication de textes,* in its various lexicographical, syntactical, prosodical, logical, and stylistic applications. We may call the results, for short, the criticism of elements and devices.

The objects of such criticism are literary works considered from the point of view of their basic literary constituents—their words, lines, sentences, paragraphs, speeches, and so on; and the categories which determine its questions are, first, meaning or content and, second, diction or style. Meaning (as I use the term here) is the immediate power exerted by the language of a composition as selected and arranged by the writer; it embraces everything from the individual significations of the words and metaphors, through the implications which these set up, to the structure and import of arguments or actions, and the signs, in the discourse, of character, emotion, and action. The meanings to be discovered by our questions are not just any possible meanings we may wish to give to the words but the meanings of the authors. The devices by which these are expressed, and hence the procedures necessary for their recovery, are not essentially different in prose and verse, or in essays, histories, lyrics, dramas, and novels; for meaningful language exists as such and becomes poetic, scientific, or rhetorical only by virtue of the specific uses to which it is put. Diction or style (as I use the term here) is that aspect of discourse which appears when we ask about the kinds of words, among the alternatives available for a given purpose to the writer, which he has selected to convey his meanings, the particular phonetic, rhythmical, and syntactical patterns in which he has chosen to arrange his words, and the devices of imagery, metaphor, antithesis, paradox, and so on, which give to his writing such dynamic quality as it has. We teach an appreciation of diction whenever we call attention by our questions to these things and train our students to make ever more discriminating judgments between appropriate and inappropriate uses by writers of their stylistic resources, and especially between styles that have distinction, no matter of what kind, and styles that have not.

Such an education in the recovery of content and in the perception of dictional devices and qualities may be termed the grammar of literary study. It is an indispensable foundation for whatever else we may attempt to do; and that is why those contemporary critics, in the line of I. A. Richards, who have insisted so constantly on the all-importance of close textual reading are surely right. We need to make one distinction, however. The great virtue of a textbook like *Understanding Poetry* is the exercise it gives in the sensitive grammatical interpretation of texts; its shortcoming is that it superimposes on this a partial and one-sided theory of poetic form, with the result that the student is insensibly conditioned to see only those meanings and stylistic devices in poems which the theory selects as important. Interpretation is one thing, and formal analysis another; it is well, I think, not to allow the first to be controlled by the second, so that our students become adept in finding instances of "ambiguity," "irony," "paradox," "symbol," or "myth" before they are able to say, independently of such notions, what the words and sentences actually mean, what the actions or the arguments are as stated or implied, and how such distinction as the language has is brought about. The criticism of elements, in short, is likely to be most fruitful in education when it is directed by its own special principles, uncontaminated by presuppositions about what the writer, as lyric poet or novelist or historian, *should* be saying; it can then most effectually serve as basis and control in the consideration of questions beyond its scope.

2. The elements and devices of literary works, however, are never there for their own sake merely but ultimately for the sake of what is done with them in the making of concrete literary wholes. Therefore the criticism of elements needs to be completed and reoriented, for any work, by a second kind of criticism—that of structure or form. By form I mean simply the overall principle, whatever it may be, that makes of the materials of a work a single definite thing. It is the aspect of literary works which comes into view when we ask ourselves not simply what the meanings and the dictional devices

are, and what are the immediate effects they produce, but why these meanings and devices and local effects are appropriately in the work (if they do indeed belong) and how, and how well, they function artistically with respect to one another and the whole—the meaning of "Why?" here being relative to the peculiar nature and end of the individual work before us rather than to the general intentions or historical circumstances of its author.

The categories which determine the questions to be asked in such criticism relate, on the one hand, to the structural parts and, on the other hand, to the principle by which the parts, in any work, are synthesized into an artistic whole. The basic structural parts of a literary work are its language and content and whatever these are so shaped as to do. The latter may be the inculcation of an argument of some sort, in which case the other parts are the component premises and devices of proof or persuasion; or it may be the representation of a human experience of some sort, for the sake of its effects on our emotions and the beauty of its rendering, in which case the other parts are such things as thought, character, plot, or whatever corresponds to plot in representational lyrics, and the various technical expedients by which thought, character, emotion, situation, action are brought before us. These can be discussed, up to a certain point, in and for themselves (as when we ask questions about the qualities of character present in a given novel or the special features of its narrative techniques); but our discussions are bound to remain incomplete, and the answers and judgments our questions provoke somewhat arbitrary, until we have considered what the informing principle is that makes of the work a distinctive whole, and how the requirements of this principle have helped to determine the conception and handling of the parts. I have attempted elsewhere, apropos of Fielding's *Tom Jones*, to suggest the types of questions such an inquiry into principles of form involves and how some of them may be answered,[3] and I will merely add now that I think the great need, in this part of our teaching, is for more numerous and more specifically discriminating notions of possible formal principles in literature than we now have. The suggestions contained in *Understanding Poetry* are applicable at best to only one class of poetic works—those designed to embody and give force

[3] Cf. *Critics and Criticism,* pp. 616–47.

to conceptual themes; and, generally speaking, the "new critics" who have concerned themselves with questions of poetic structure have looked for principles of structure, like Cleanth Brooks's "paradox" or "irony," that are common to all poems or at least to all good ones. The analysis of tragic plot form in the *Poetics* approaches more nearly the kind of thing we need, but it would be a mistake to try to fit to Aristotle's formula more than a few of the works we call tragedies; and most of the other common names for classes of literary structures, such as comedy, lyric, or novel, are far too general to be of much practical use. There is some hope, however, that more will be done in the future toward providing the fuller apparatus of distinctions we require for criticism of this kind,[4] and meanwhile we can do something ourselves, as teachers, by continuing to ask, about all sorts of literary works, the basic questions upon which it depends.

3. The criticism of forms is clearly incapable by itself of telling us why a given poem, drama, or novel is a great work of literary art. On the other hand, when sensitively done, it can supply an indispensable foundation—in the appreciation it gives of the enormously varied formal and technical problems faced by writers—for further questions about other aspects of the works we wish to consider. Thus, although literary works, when viewed in and for themselves, are particular syntheses of elements governed immediately by principles of poetic, rhetorical, dialectical, or historical art, they are also, in their origins, the creative acts of men endowed by nature and education with certain qualities of soul or literary personality or "vision," which, as reflected in texts, are capable of stimulating responses not entirely to be accounted for by strictly formal considerations. Here then is another aspect, every bit as important as the others, which can be made the center of a third set of critical questions.

The objects of these are the traits of substance and expression in literary works, taken singly or by authors or schools, which make us feel the presence behind them of a particular kind or degree of genius or sensibility or of a particular way of seeing and ordering the conditions and values of life. We may call this kind of criticism, in distinction from the other two kinds, the criticism of qualities

---

[4] See now Olson's *Tragedy and the Theory of Drama* (Detroit, 1961) for a very full and useful apparatus of such distinctions (with illustrations from ancient and modern tragedy) which can be used in the discussion of works of prose fiction as well as in the criticism of plays.

or of literary personality; it has had a long tradition from Longinus in antiquity, through Dryden, Addison, Pope, Johnson, Coleridge, Hazlitt, Lamb, Sainte-Beuve, Matthew Arnold, Pater, and Bradley, to contemporaries like Benedetto Croce, Middleton Murry, T. S. Eliot, F. R. Leavis, and Wilson Knight. The categories which determine its questions are the general categories, applicable in the discussion of all species of literary works, which Longinus made explicit in his account of the sources of the "sublime"—namely, thought, in the sense of the author's distinctive conceptions of things; emotion, in the sense of the characteristic qualities of his sensibility; and expression, in the sense of all the devices of language by which his thought and emotional responses are realized in his works or particular passages thereof; and the method of procedure is comparative, inasmuch as the only way in which particular literary qualities can be defined is through a consideration, supported by references to other authors and works, of what they are not. The criticism of qualities depends, therefore, to a much greater extent than the first two kinds, upon wide literary experience and developed powers of discrimination and analysis; the very generality of its categories, besides, is a constant invitation to impressionism and irresponsibility. That is no reason, however, for neglecting it in our programs, so long as we do not expect our students to become young Hazlitts or young Eliots at once, and so long as we encourage them to test their qualitative generalizations by reference to what the criticism of elements and of forms has shown them about the same works and to acquire the habit of specifying in the details of texts the particular devices through which the felt qualities of the writer are made manifest.

4. There can be no good teaching of literary history, I think, that does not presuppose and make constant use of the insights into literary works which can be given by the three critical modes already discussed; but these in turn need to be completed by means of the questions appropriate to literary history, or, as we may call it, the criticism of circumstances. The great danger here is, or at least has been in the past, that we will be too ambitious, and think that we have not done our duty by our students—or our degrees— until we have given them a rounded scheme of periods, movements, literary schools, and the like, with definitions of their respective

dominant traits; for to do this is inevitably to implant formulas in our students' heads which they will unfortunately remember but never quite understand. The better way is to try to build up, informally and bit by bit, through our discussions of particular authors and texts, first of all a grasp of essential chronology; then what I should call a sense of period styles (by which I mean an ability to infer from the internal characteristics of texts, without other aids, the generation in which they must have been written); and finally a habit of asking questions about works that will yield such information concerning their occasions, their sources or models, the philosophic "commonplaces" or artistic conventions they use, and the traditions they carry on, as will directly promote our students' understanding and appreciation of them in their aspect as permanently valuable works of art produced at a given time. A useful kind of training in literary history, I have often thought, would be one in which, for instance, we first brought our students to recognize that *Lycidas, An Elegy Written in a Country Churchyard, In Memoriam,* and *The Waste Land* are all works having essentially the same poetic form, and then asked them to consider how far and in what ways the striking differences among the four are to be accounted for by differences in the genius and "vision" of their writers, and how far and in what ways by differences in the conventions of subject matter, language, and technique which depend on the fact that the first poem was published in 1638, the second in 1751, the third in 1850, and the fourth in 1922.

5. With our last set of questions we return from the past to the present. They are the questions that give us what may be called the criticism of moral, social, political, and religious values; and they pertain to that aspect of literary works which is called to mind whenever we consider literature or poetry in the context of education or of the particular goods we are interested in realizing in the society of our time; they are concerned, in short, with the functions of literary works over and above the requirements of formal or qualitative excellence or the satisfaction of contemporary tastes.

In its generalized applications this is the kind of criticism practiced by Plato in his *Republic,* by Aristotle in his *Politics,* by Sidney and Shelley in their defenses of poetry, by Matthew Arnold in his "Function of Criticism" and his "Literature and Science," and by the many later critics who have continued Arnold's line of discussion; here also we may place the criticism of Tolstoi, of the Marxists, of Kenneth Burke. It is surely desirable that our students should be introduced to this great debate about the uses of literature through some of the texts in which it has been carried on; but what I have chiefly in mind here are questions of value in a more limited and particular sense. We cannot read a powerful or vividly convincing author without being influenced in some degree by him in our moral feelings and estimates of things, and we should not try to evade the consequences of this fact in our teaching. We ought to attempt, therefore, to raise questions with our students, and train them to raise questions for themselves, that will lead to discriminating judgments of authors, not only as to the excellences and defects of their art, but also as to the kinds of influence their works are calculated to exert, and more especially as to the relative comprehensiveness or narrowness, complexity or simplicity, humanity or abnormality, truth or falsity of the basic propositions about life and conduct which they set forth or assume. The danger of such criticism of course is its tendency to encourage displays of dogmatic provincialism in morals, politics, and religion, so that we fail, for example, to do justice to the extraordinary breadth and sanity of Shakespeare's moral insights by overemphasis on his undemocratic view of the state. We can do something to guard against this, however, partly by giving priority in our teaching to the other kinds of questions and partly by seeing to it that in discussing questions of this kind our students make clear the assumptions underlying their judgments and relate their statements always to what is really in the text they are reading.

I have presented these five kinds of criticism as so many distinct lines of inquiry into literary works, each with its characteristic questions, presuppositions, and data; and I regard them simply as so many distinct analytical tools at our disposal for making the most of the authors and writings we have to teach. Their distinctness in the account I have given of them, however, does not imply any necessity of keeping them separate in our practice as teachers. If we are at all skillful, indeed, we will move freely among them, with our attention centered not on this or any other scheme of critical topics but on the concrete problems presented by the authors or texts we happen to be dealing with, the scheme operating only as a useful reminder of the varied things we can do. The nature of critical questions and statements is such, moreover, that I should not want to attempt any theoretical defence of the type of scheme I have offered, with its five distinct sets of questions, against the objections of those who prefer to think of criticism as an organic whole that does not lend itself to division into sharply differentiated lines of inquiry. That is clearly a tenable view, since there is an important sense in which all aspects of literature are bound up inextricably with one another, but I should insist that my view is also tenable, since there is another and equally important sense in which they have independent status. The fact is that the two positions are complementary half-truths, the systematic espousal of either one of which necessarily entails leaving out, at least temporarily an essential aspect of literary reality. I do not see how this can be avoided, inasmuch as we can not very well do both things at once. Therefore we are faced with a choice for which the only ground must be the relative utility of the two ways of conceiving criticism for what we want to do; and looking at the matter in these practical terms, I can see important advantages for us as teachers in the style of approach I have adopted. For if we have in mind a reasonably exhaustive inventory of the more clear-cut differences among critical questions and statements, we can the more easily decide, along with other things, whether our program in literature is as complete, in its disciplinary aspects, as it might be, whether we have made a properly varied selection of texts and authors for study, and whether we are doing all that we should do that is appropriate to our place in the total curriculum.

Our success will depend ultimately, however, not only on the kinds of questions we habituate our students to ask of literary works but also on the standards we induce them to apply in deciding upon and testing their answers. This is too complex a subject to permit of more than fragmentary treatment at the end of a discourse like this, and I shall accordingly confine myself to one small part of it.

The five kinds of questions we are concerned with asking are primarily questions about texts, that is, about unique combinations of particular meanings and literary traits; and the general conditions under which a warranted answer to any of them is possible are of two sorts. The first condition I have already touched upon. It is the necessity, simply, that we know what question we are trying to answer before we venture on any statement of our own about a text, or before we accept, or reject, any statement about the same text made by another. "When you say this, just what question do you think you or the critic you are citing or quarreling with is attempting to answer?"—the more often we insist that our students declare themselves in these terms, the more progress we shall make, and the less talking at cross purposes we shall have to endure.

The second condition is more important still, at least on the assumption that we are interested in developing in our students a sense of responsibility in what they say about literary matters rather than merely in giving them uncontrolled exercise in expressing their opinions. There are, as I have argued, various possible and equally legitimate approaches to literary works, and hence, in criticism considered broadly, there is no one type of interpretation or judgment which can be insisted upon as peculiarly "proper" or "right." To say this, however, is not to say that within any one approach, after we are clear about the nature and reference of the questions we are asking, we need subscribe to the now fashionable doctrine of multiple truth. It is possible to attribute to *Oedipus Rex,* for instance, both a tragic plot form in the ordinary sense and also a form resembling that of a primitive religious ritual: the two conclusions are answers to quite different types of questions and have to be argued on the basis of quite different assumptions and evidence; they do not therefore really contradict one another, any more than do the statements that a given pipe is a smoking instrument of such and such a form and that it is a particular concentration of dancing atoms. But the case is clearly altered when we ask a question about this or any other literary work that presupposes a single framework of discussion. Here we may legitimately assume that there can be only one completely true answer to any question we may raise. The doctrine of multiple truth in criticism has arisen, I believe, from a confusion between the two kinds of situations—those in which the conclusions of fundamentally different approaches to the same works are directly opposed to one another and those in which, the questions being essentially of the same order, there is disagreement about what the case really is. And much disagreement of this second sort is of course to be expected in practical criticism, as a consequence of the fact that our objects in such study are always concrete particulars and that our aim is to know and appreciate them as such rather than to treat them simply as data for deriving general scientific laws. Therefore we cannot hope, strictly speaking, to demonstrate anything about literary works, but only to construct hypotheses concerning them which, because they can never be completely adequate to the literary actuality, are always in need of reconsideration or revision.

There are, however—and this is the crux of what I want to say—better and worse ways of going about the making of hypotheses in criticism and literary teaching. And the worse way, unfortunately, is much the commoner. It is what has been called, in science, the method of the favorite or "ruling" hypothesis. What does this passage in this poem or essay mean? Or what is going on in this lyric or this novel or drama? It is easy and natural to come to such questions with the essential formula of the answers already in our minds. We have built up a more or less fixed notion, from our earlier reading or from the study of other critics, of what a given author is characteristically trying to say, either because we have "placed" him as a certain kind of man or because we have assimilated him to a certain age or intellectual tradition. Or we have learned to think of the structure of lyrics or dramas in terms of a certain distinctive pattern of elements, as when we identify the structure of tragedy with the form described in chapter 13 of the *Poetics* or the structure of lyric with the form described, and attributed consistently to all short poems, in *Understanding Poetry*. Our procedure then consists in applying the favorite hypothesis thus obtained directly to the passage or the composition before us and in announcing our recognition, supported by particular references to the text, that it does indeed fit. But after all there is nothing strange or necessarily significant in the fact that, oftener than not, it does fit. For the complexity of all literary texts is such that it is hard to think of any self-consistent hypothesis of meaning or structure under which we cannot subsume enough of the details of a given passage or work to convince ourselves of its truth, so long as the hypothesis in question is the only one we take the trouble to consider. At the worst we can always invent secondary hypotheses, after the fashion of the Ptolemaic epicycles, to get us over the difficult spots.

It would be easy to collect many instances of such malpractice from contemporary and earlier criticism. And there is, I believe, only one available safeguard against it. That is to base our procedure, as consistently as we can, on the principle that the value of any hypothesis is always relative, not merely to the particulars it is intended to explain, but to all the other variant hypotheses which the same particulars might suggest if we gave them a chance: the best hypothesis is simply the best among several possible hypotheses, relevant to the same question about the same work, with which we have actually compared it, and unless we make such comparisons a regular part of our procedure we always court the danger of missing either slightly or fully what the facts really are. This is what has been called, in science, the method of "multiple hypotheses,"[5] and it can be adapted, easily and with great profit, I think, to the situations that constantly arise in our literary teaching.

Let us suppose that we have before us a passage in a poem of which the precise meaning is not obvious at first glance. Instead of asking our students directly what they think the passage means, we can ask them to tell us, first, what are the several different meanings it might possibly have, or that have been imputed to it by different critics, and then to consider, impartially, which one of these conjectures, if any, adequately accounts for its actual wording and arrangement, its distinctive imagery, and its place in the context in which it occurs. Or let us suppose that the question is not one of meaning but of artistic structure: we have before us a short poem concerning which we need to be reasonably sure, before we can talk to any purpose about the functions and qualities of its parts, just what kind of whole its writer has sought to achieve. It will make all the difference, in both our analysis of the poem and our judgment of its success, how we conceive of its overall formal nature—whether we assume it to be that of a simple poetic statement, of the order of epigram, in which the mode of utterance is the chief thing (as, for instance, in Ben Jonson's "Still To Be Neat" or Yeats's "That the Night Come"), or that of an elaborated rhetorical argument (as in Dryden's "Alexander's Feast," Johnson's "Vanity of Human Wishes," or Pope's "Epistle to Dr. Arbuthnot"), or that of a poetically represented human experience, embodied in words for the sake of its emotional values

5 Cf. T. C. Chamberlin, *Journal of Geology*, 39 (1931): 155–65.

and the beauty of the representation; and whether, if the poem appears to be of the last kind, we assume that the form of the represented experience, and hence of the poem, is that of a person in a state of emotion (as in Shelley's "Ode to the West Wind" or Tennyson's "Tears, Idle Tears"), or that of a certain disposition or mode of feeling about things (as in "L'Allegro" or "Il Penseroso"), or that of an internal activity involving either moral choice (as in Gray's "Elegy") or a process of coming to understand (as in Wordsworth's "Intimations" ode or Whitman's "When lilacs last in the dooryard bloomed"), or that of a particularized character manifesting itself in words and actions (as in "The Bishop Orders His Tomb"), or that of an overt act of persuading, threatening, or the like (as in Marvell's "To His Coy Mistress"); and so on through other similarly distinguishable forms of poetic construction.[6] For any given poem we can often eliminate at once some or many of these possible principles, but it is never safe to proceed before we have canvassed explicitly, in our questioning, at least several alternative hypotheses for its form, and excluded all but the one which, after comparison with the others, appears to explain most fully and economically the details of the poem and to do most complete justice to its felt qualities and merits. That is the most we can do, but that is surely much.

And the advantages of such a method go considerably beyond its immediate benefits in a fuller understanding and appreciation of the particular passages or works to which it is applied. There is no better way than this of cultivating critical responsibility in our students and the habit of resisting their all-too-natural tendency to an easy acceptance of ready-made formulas and fashionable opinions. And there is no better way, also—since the very act of comparing hypotheses is bound to make us see more than we would otherwise have seen—of encouraging particularity of observation on texts and hence of sharpening our students' sensitivity to words and meanings, to the variety of forms which literature assumes, to the several ways of thinking and expressing himself which distinguish one writer from another, and similarly to all those other aspects of literary works which our scheme of critical questions, insofar as it is adequate, will bring into view.

[6] Cf. Olson, *Critics and Criticism*, pp. 560, 563–66; Norman Maclean, *ibid.*, pp. 429–36, 448–49.

Every Man His Own Critic

SEVERAL YEARS AGO I came across a sentence of T. S. Eliot's, which has stuck in my memory ever since, and which I want to use as the text of this rather sermon-like essay. There was nothing startling about the sentence; it said simply, in a context which I have forgotten, that "We should *all* try to be critics, and not leave criticism to the fellows who write reviews in the papers"; and I would doubtless have passed it by except that it seemed to crystallize some rather gloomy thoughts of mine at that moment about my own teaching, especially when I extended Eliot's last phrase to include "the fellows, like myself, who teach literature in universities and colleges or write essays on literary subjects for the learned or the critical journals."

It may have been because I had just been reading examinations or term papers; but in any event I had begun to reflect, in no self-flattering mood, on how little I had done, on the whole, to enable my students to stand on their own feet after they left me—every man equipped to be, in a sensible way, his own critic. I thought of those students who had done good work for me, and on whom I believed I had made an impression at the time; and I couldn't help wondering, pessimistically, how many of them, after five or a dozen years, were still able, on their own, to think as well, critically, about a new modern book or an old one they were reading for the first time as they had been able to think about the texts they had discussed under the

Based on a lecture at Indiana University, 1956; not previously published.

194

immediate pressure of my assignments. How many of them, for instance, without the help of some one else's explanation, would not be just as puzzled by Eliot's next important poem as they had been by *Prufrock* or *The Waste Land* before they were initiated into these poems in class? Some of them, of course—mainly among those who are now university teachers of literature—would not be puzzled; but these were too few, as compared with the total number of students I have had, to give me much cheer; and for the best of these, besides, I could not honestly take any decisive credit for what they have since become. I *should* have had many more students of all sorts, it seemed to me, about whom I could feel sure that, in their later dealings with literature, they had become something more than users or victims of the criticism of others, including that which I myself had exposed them to.

I mention these misgivings, which recur from time to time, because I have been led on from them to some more positive thoughts about the kind of education in literature and criticism which, if I could do the job over again, I should wish to aim at, or to aim at more consistently than I have done, in the faith that it would probably help more of my students to be better critics in their own right than the education I have offered them. In setting down these thoughts now, in a somewhat penitentiary spirit, I want to speak first of the general character or direction of the education I have in mind and then of two of its particular ingredients.

The contrast between this kind of education and the kind that I fear I have too often been content with is best illustrated for me in the contrast between two teachers of history I studied with when I was an undergraduate. They were both highly competent men in their fields, but from only one of them did I profit in the manner in which I should like more of my students to have profited from my teaching of literature. It was not that this man was a better teacher in any of the senses in which distinction in teaching is usually thought of. He was commonly supposed, in fact, especially by the Department of Education, not to be a good teacher at all! The difference lay rather in the almost polar opposition between the conceptions of historical teaching which the two men—let me call them Professor A and Professor B—represented.

For Professor A (whom I now remember only as a brilliant and fluent lecturer), the problem of teaching history was simply the problem of communicating effectively a concrete and self-contained subject matter; of putting before us a particular body of facts and generalizations which had presumably been thought about critically and independently by himself and others but which he didn't think about in our presence, and which it was our duty—our whole duty—merely to assimilate and remember as long as we could. It was, in short, what I would call examination-knowledge, presented to us didactically rather than problematically; and being only that, it proved to be a very perishable commodity, leaving no residue, once its particular propositions had faded from my memory, that I could recur to—or ever have recurred to—as a part of my basic historical education. I cannot recall any question in history, in any field, that I have since been able to think about more intelligently, or with any surer grasp of what an answer to it might involve, by virtue of Professor A's teaching.

It was quite the contrary with Professor B. For him too history could not be taught except through the teaching of particular historical subjects that were assumed to be worth knowing as thoroughly as we could know them for their own sake. Such knowledge was an end which he kept firmly in view in all his courses, but it was not, as for Professor A, the final end of what he tried to do for us. He knew that most of it was bound to pass away, sooner or later, after we had ceased to study with him; and I don't believe that this greatly worried him. He was, for one thing, too wise a historian not to be aware of the probable impermanence, for himself and other scholars, as well as for us, of any particular historical interpretations he might offer. But more than this, he was quite consciously concerned with implanting in us, through his analytical mode of lecturing and above all through the independent studies he engaged us in, something over and above his immediate subject matter that might possibly remain with us for the rest of our lives, whether we became historians in a professional sense or not. This something was the discipline of history, which he thought of as a special but universally applicable way of considering human beings and their individual and collective actions, and of getting warranted knowledge concerning them. Whatever we did in later life, he thought, we ought all to be historians in this broader sense of having as a permanent possession the habit of good historical thinking; and it was to the end of helping us to form this habit, in and for ourselves, that he tended consistently to direct his instruction. He was pleased when we answered well the subject-matter questions he set us in quizzes and examinations, but he was far more pleased when we gave some slight evidence, in what we wrote for him, that we were perhaps beginning to learn how to ask good historical questions on our own and to deal with them independently of anything he had told us. That was a sign—and the sign he always took most seriously—that we were actually profiting from his teaching.

I have been greatly influenced by Professor B in my thoughts about education in literature—though much less in my practice, unfortunately! Professor A was a much easier model to follow. It is hard to reduce the difference between the two men to any of the current commonplaces of educational discussion—and certainly not to that most fashionable of current commonplaces, the assumption that there is a necessary opposition between general education, the education that we ought to give to every man, and special or technical education. The kind of education I got in history from Professor B was infinitely better fitted to be of general value to every man than the kind I got from Professor A; and yet Professor B's teaching was much more specialized in its content and technical in its approach than that of his colleague. I have always thought, therefore, that there is something false and dangerous in the antithesis between the general and the special that has played so important a role in modern reforms of undergraduate study, or at any rate that the antithesis is useful only in helping us to think about our ends in education—the good of as many as possible of our students—and has little or no bearing on our consideration of means. The means to a general education, in this sense, may be as specialized and technical as we please, provided we hold fast to two other distinctions which are not so commonly emphasized in the current view.

What I especially admired in the second of my historians as compared with the first was that he taught as a guide rather than as a master, as an inquiring student of history like ourselves, only more advanced, rather than as the equivalent, in his field, of Eliot's professional critics telling the public what to think about the books they read.

He lectured; but always, as I have said, in a problematic rather than a didactic spirit; making explicit to us, as he went along, exactly what he was doing and why, taking us inside the processes of reasoning he brought to bear on his problems and never concealing from us the different degrees of assurance he thought appropriate to his different assertions. Most of the time, however, his teaching consisted only in setting questions for us to work on by ourselves: attempting to make us independent students of history by compelling us to perform personally the various intellectual operations which history involved, on materials for which our only guidance was the general habit of historical thinking we had imbibed not so much from what he told us as from what he did. The first distinction he illustrates for me, in contrast with his colleague, is thus the distinction between teaching as incitement to controlled activity on the student's part in the future and teaching as instruction in the results of activity already performed by the teacher. The fact that many of Professor B's students yearned for more in the way of dogmatically imparted conclusions and formulas concerned him not at all; the best of his students, he knew, were already experiencing as undergraduates the lastingly educative effects, which they might not otherwise have felt until they were well along in their graduate schools, of being treated as students of a subject matter which they could effectively master only by their own efforts rather than as pupils of a teacher who had mastered it for them.

One necessary condition, then, of every man becoming his own critic is that he should be taught literature as far as possible in the manner in which this man taught history. But what he is taught in this manner also makes a great difference; and here again I reproach myself for not having been clearer in my mind all along about a second distinction. I suppose that what I really learned from my second history teacher, and hold with me to the present day, was something extremely simple, and yet something from which, even in his most advanced teaching, he never strayed very far: namely, a set of basic ideas, constituting for him the essential elements of all historical thinking, which he would doubtless have hesitated to expound to his colleagues in the American Historical Association but which he kept constantly recurring to in his dealings with us. He built, in his lectures, more or less elaborate superstructures of historical interpretation, but these were never detached, as in the lectures of my other teacher, from the foundations in primary concepts of human problems, reasons, and actions upon which they were erected.[1] And the longer I have attempted to teach literature to students at all levels, from freshmen to advanced graduates, the more convinced I have become of the wisdom of his procedure. When I began to teach, and for a long time after, forgetting his example, I thought that the basic elements of literary study—the arts by which you read a literary text, for example, and talk fruitfully about how and why it is constituted as it is—could either be taken for granted or confined to introductory teaching; and I busied myself with what seemed to me the much more entertaining complexities of my subject—the latest notions that had occurred to me in critical theory, the most sophisticated views I had acquired of the literary and intellectual currents in my special period. I had many disillusioning experiences from time to time before I really began to see what was wrong: the shock I had one day in a graduate seminar, for example, when no one could tell me what was the conclusion and what were the premises in an easy paragraph by Dr. Johnson, although all the students had elaborate views about the nature of Johnson's thought and its place in the thought of the eighteenth century; or, again, the sudden realization on another occasion that the interpretations of this century which I had expounded a half dozen years before but had since come to distrust were apparently still being imparted as gospel, in all their fancy symmetry, to students in other schools. It finally became evident to me, however, that I had too often encouraged my students to work at a level of complication, both historical and critical, that was beyond even the most advanced of them, and had provided them only inadequately with habits of testing what they heard or read or thought on this high level in the light of the simpler and relatively more permanent principles of logic, common sense, and the literary arts. I have come to believe, therefore, that all teaching of literature, at whatever stage, graduate as well as undergraduate, ought to occupy itself much less than my teaching at least has done with superstructures and much more with foundations.

1 For a much later elaboration of the theory of historical understanding which, in its essence at least, I imbibed from the practice and occasional *obiter dicta* of Professor B, see William Dray, *Laws and Explanation in History* (Oxford, 1957), especially chapter 5. I have tried to express my debt to Professor B more explicitly in the Preface to *The Languages of Criticism and the Structure of Poetry* (Toronto, 1953), pp. xv–xvii.

At any rate, it ought to make a point of constantly reverting to the elementary facts about literary works and their powers and effects which students have to grasp, as much more than verbal formulas, if the superstructures we or others build are to be understood and their validity properly assessed. Only thus, I suspect, can we hope to give our students an education in literature and criticism that has a chance of staying with them through their later years, as a discipline of thinking about literary works and of responding to them, and as a guarantee, to some extent at least, that they will not leave criticism to the people who write in *The New York Times Book Review* or the critical quarterlies.

More teaching, then, in terms of problems to be worked on rather than merely of conclusions to be learned and above all more elementary teaching—these are the two ends I should wish to strive for more persistently than I have done if I could start afresh. I shall not attempt to indicate how they might serve as guiding principles in all of the essential activities that make up a well-rounded literary education—in the teaching of language as this bears particularly on the study of literary works; in the teaching of practical criticism; in the teaching of literary history; in the teaching of literary theory. I shall limit myself to two only of these four major aspects of the problem and dwell particularly, first on literary theory and then on practical criticism.

It is often said nowadays, by critics like F. R. Leavis or some of the reviewers in the *Times Literary Supplement,* that there is little value in attempting to teach anything as abstract as literary theory in an education designed for persons who will never be philosophers of literature but only readers and judges of literary works. Let us by all means, it is said, teach our students how to read and how to respond with their total personalities to what they read; but let us have nothing to do with anything so remote from these concerns as the so-called general principles of literature or criticism. The trouble is that this position is constantly being reduced to absurdity by the very critics and teachers who maintain it most strenuously. For not only is the rejection of theory itself a theory, as philosophers have often pointed out, but the very writers who reject theory in their pronouncements on education themselves make use of theory in all sorts of ways in their discussions of particular books and authors: their essays are full of general propositions and dicta, explicit or implied, which it is incumbent on us to entertain as theoretically valid if we are to make sense of their interpretations or to go along with their judgments. And of course the same thing is true of all other writings on concrete questions in literary history or literary criticism: theoretical commitments of one kind or another underlie them all. It is true even of the term papers of our least advanced and philosophically most innocent students. When they write about what they suppose to be the defects of Jane Austen's "plotting" and narrative technique or about the alleged symbolism in Shakespeare's later plays or about the "philosophy" in the poems of Wallace Stevens, their statements rest on presuppositions about the nature of literary works, however vague, and are couched in a set of general terms, however confused, which have quite as much to do with determining what they say or leave unsaid as their direct observations of the texts. We ask them to write from their firsthand experience with the works, and to give us their own judgments; but both the experience and the judgments are shaped or distorted, before they come to us, by critical commonplaces and dogmas of various kinds which these students have managed somehow to absorb without knowing what is happening to them. It is an inevitable result, since no one can think or speak or write about literary works except through the medium of *some* set of general concepts—be they adequate or inadequate, well or ill understood—which constitutes for him his literary theory, whether he is consciously aware of its influence on him or not.

The problem of theory in the teaching of literature is therefore not one that can be solved by doing nothing about it. Theory of some sort will be there, in the minds of our students, in any case; and hence we have a responsibility to see to it that the general notions about literature and its values which they will inevitably absorb in the course of their studies are such as will promote rather than retard their development as independent readers and judges of writers and works. For there are two ways in which critical theory of any kind may function in our literary reading and appreciation. It may function positively as a stimulus to observations and judgments which, without the concepts and distinctions it provides, we might have been unable to make; or it may function negatively, in the form of "doctrinal adhesions," as I. A. Richards called them, to restrict what we will allow ourselves to see and to prejudice our valuations. I can think of no literary theories, from antiquity to our own day, that are not capable of producing the first of these effects, and I can think of none also that has not in fact, for many readers, led to effects of the second kind. It all depends on how we possess our theories; and here again there are two possibilities. We may possess them as unexamined dogmas which we are under some kind of compulsion to apply to whatever we read, or we may possess them as useful but necessarily limited hypotheses that may or may not be relevant to any particular case. We may say therefore that the essential problem of teaching literary theory is the problem of emancipating our students as completely as we can from the first of these attitudes—the attitude, unfortunately, they seem prone to take—and of winning them over to the other.

And here, once more, it seems to me, the only lastingly effective solution consists in a constant return to the foundations. Every particular critical doctrine depends for its meaning, its scope of application, and its validity upon a twofold reference to things which are more basic than the doctrine itself. The first and more immediate reference is to the underlying principles and the controlling method of the theoretical discourse in which the doctrine is asserted. Take, for example, the various doctrines about the nature and importance of the plot, in works of drama or fiction, that have been set forth by critics from Aristotle to the present day. Looked at merely as isolated doctrines, they appear to be in hopeless contradiction: Aristotle, on the one hand, exalting plot as the first principle, or soul, of tragedy and epic; many moderns, on the other hand, depreciating plot as something useful merely to hold together, in a novel or play, the more important elements of character and thought. And so long as we look at the doctrines in this way, there is little we can do about the matter except to take sides, as between the two positions, in terms of purely arbitrary preferences. But the truth is that neither in Aristotle nor in these moderns is the conception of what they both call plot an isolated doctrine which we can judge to be meaningful or meaningless, true or false, in the light of itself alone. For behind the particular discussions of plot, in both periods, lie many other much more general and basic propositions, about literature and the method of studying it, which make up the characteristic critical philosophies of the two groups of critics; and once we have recovered these, as the foundations on which they have built, it might well turn out—indeed, I think it would—that Aristotle and these modern theorists were really not contradicting one another but were talking, under the same name, about quite different things. We may still prefer to discuss plot in the language of Aristotle or in that of the moderns, or we may use the two languages on different occasions; but in any case we are proceeding no longer as passive victims of one or the other doctrine but as intelligent users of it for whatever practical purposes it will serve.[2] It seems to me, therefore, that our primary task in teaching the history of criticism ought to be to raise questions about all the doctrines we come across that would direct our students' minds back from the doctrines themselves to the premises and reasons that make their assertions intelligible and determine the conditions under which they do and do not make useful sense.

The foundations of critical theory, however, are not merely philosophical; there can be no full understanding of any literary doctrine or proper judgment of its validity or the limits of its relevance without a second reference to something more basic than itself, a reference beyond the doctrine or the theoretical system in which it has been elaborated to the direct practical knowledge of literary things which we all possess in some measure if we have read at all widely or have attempted even the simpler forms of writing. This commonsense knowledge of literary principles would still exist if the development of critical theory had never come about; it is enshrined in the practical understanding of the literary arts which is handed down, independently of doctrine, from one generation of writers to another; it is enshrined also in the ability of ordinary readers or theatergoers to react to what they read or see, now and then at least or in the long run, more or less appropriately. There is an important sense in which the data of literary theory, unlike the data of the natural sciences in their modern development, are accessible to everyone: the effects aimed at in literary works are effects of a kind that all men, in some measure, must be able to feel; and the causes of these effects, or at any rate the most powerful of them, are likewise within the comprehen-

2 Since this was written, Elder Olson has developed much the same point more fully in his *Tragedy and the Theory of Drama* (Detroit, 1961), pp. 71–81.

sion of any one who has ever tried to tell a comic or tragic story or to give expression to his feelings in a letter to a friend. To dwell on the reality and extent of this common-sense literary knowledge is not of course to disparage the theorists of literature who have attempted, in Pope's words, to reduce it to method—to refine and elaborate upon it, to rid it of its confusions, to formulate general principles by which its fragmentary insights might be justified philosophically. Common sense, we must all agree, is not enough, and indeed much of what we think of as common-sense understanding of literature now is the result of generations of conditioning at the hands of theoretically minded critics and schoolmasters. But on the other hand, it is equally important to keep in mind two things. In the first place, just as our common-sense practical knowledge of the moral life, as we engage in it from day to day, is obviously much broader at any time than the theorized knowledge of morals contained in any aggregate of contemporary ethical writings, so it is with our common-sense practical knowledge of the literary life: we always know many things, as readers or writers, which the favorite methods and principles of the literary theorists we read will not allow them to talk about, but which are not on that account any less essential to know. And, in the second place, literary theorists in all ages have tended, for various reasons, to assert their doctrines in much more unqualified terms than they had a right to do and have thus brought themselves into direct collision with the practical insights of common sense.

Of all the great critics, the one who saw most clearly these restrictive tendencies in literary theory, and pointed most emphatically to the means of guarding against them, was Dr. Johnson. It is sometimes said of Johnson that he himself had no principles in criticism *except* those of common sense. This is not true, I think, as several recent studies of Johnson have made evident. What is true of him is rather that his theorizing about literature was founded on premises of a kind that allowed him to appeal constantly to what every man is aware of in literary matters against the dogmas of theorists who had based themselves, in his phrase, on "narrower principles." It is thus that he proceeds in his famous defense of Shakespeare for having, as he says, "united the powers of exciting laughter and sorrow not only in one mind, but in one composition," so that most of his plays "are divided between serious and ludicrous characters, and, in the successive evolutions of the design, sometimes produce seriousness and sorrow, and sometimes levity and laughter." Johnson admits that this is a practice "contrary to the rules of criticism." But so what? he says in effect; for, as he puts it, "there is always an appeal open from criticism to nature"; and he goes on to make such an appeal, by calling in the authority of common sense against the doctrinaire theorists in criticism who have held that the "mingled drama" cannot possibly have the "power to move, which constitutes the perfection of dramatic poetry." "This reasoning," he says, "is so specious, that it is received as true even by those who in daily experience feel it to be false. The interchanges of mingled scenes seldom fail to produce the intended vicissitudes of passion. Fiction cannot move so much, but that the attention may be easily transferred; and though it must be allowed that pleasing melancholy be sometimes interrupted by unwelcome levity, yet let it be considered likewise, that melancholy is not always pleasing, and that the disturbance of one man may be the relief of another; that different auditors have different habitudes; and that, upon the whole, all pleasure consists in variety."

"There is always an appeal open from criticism to nature": we might do well to take this maxim of Johnson's as a guiding principle in our attempts to educate our students in the elements of literary theory. This would mean, in the first place, trying to carry them beyond the philosophical understanding of doctrines I have spoken of to what might be called a practical understanding: encouraging them to look for equivalents in their own experience of writing and reading for the problems the theorists they read are dealing with; inducing them to translate the abstract statements of the critics into concrete operations with words, thoughts, and incidents such as they might perform in compositions of their own. Most of the great doctrines in criticism—Aristotle's "imitation" or Coleridge's "reconciliation of opposites" or James's "rendering"—can with a little effort be made to take on this kind of common-sense practical intelligibility; and it is only when this has happened, indeed, that we can expect them to have any permanent educational value, or to remain in our students' minds as anything more than vaguely remembered verbal formulas, which we might just as well not have taught them.

But the appeal from criticism to common sense would also have another function, very much like that for which Johnson used it in his examination of the various neoclassical dogmas about drama and other forms of literature that had become sacred commonplaces of critical opinion in his time. The trouble with the critical rules which he attacked, as he saw it, was not that they had no basis at all in reason and nature but that they had been given a false universality of application by being separated from the specific practical ends in writing which they had originally been designed to serve, and so had become merely obstacles both to new invention in literature and to a full appreciation of the literary works in which they were not observed. At best they were half-truths, in relation to which it was necessary, he thought, to restore the other half by reverting to the foundations of critical principles in the common precritical knowledge of readers and writers.

We are no longer bothered, as Johnson's generation was, by the three unities or the proscription of "mingled drama" or most of the other neoclassical dogmas he concerned himself with. But that is not to say that contemporary criticism—the criticism our students are most likely to absorb and use uncritically—is without rules of its own, essentially similar, in their claims to universality and exclusive validity, to those of the eighteenth century, and hence calling constantly for the same kind of common-sense reexamination that Johnson undertook. One of the great spheres of such rules nowadays is the theory of the novel, especially as this theory took form, during the past half-century, as a codification of the technical changes in novel writing that separate prose fiction after Flaubert and more particularly after Henry James from the fiction of earlier periods. The results have been highly useful in helping us to see more clearly what these particular modern novelists and their disciples have been trying to do. They get in our way, however, when they come to be erected into an orthodoxy of procedure for the novel in general, and hence into a body of precepts to which it is assumed that all novelists, past and present, ought to have conformed irrespective of the particular effects they were aiming at—irrespective indeed of the success with which these effects were often achieved by means contrary to those specified by the precepts. And that is what has happened not only in latter-day textbooks on the art of fiction but in the minds of many of our students. It is always bad art in the novel, they think, to violate consistency of point of view; it is always a fault when the author or his narrator intrudes into the story, after the manner of Fielding, Thackeray, and so many others; there is something wrong when a crucial event is given to us in summary, however charged with the right emotion, rather than dramatically through conversation; it is a point against a character in a novel that it is of the "flat" rather than the "rounded" type; it is a sign of crudity whenever a writer delineates one of his characters analytically rather than by allowing him to dawn on us in gradual stages, according to the rules for their own practice set down by Conrad and Ford Madox Ford. I have often encountered these dicta and others like them in the term papers and discussions of my courses; and the only proper response to them, surely, is to remind one's students, in the name of literary common sense, that no rules of technique can have universal validity; that devices in literature can never be judged good or bad in themselves but only relative to what they enable a writer to do in a particular work or passage; and that what look like faults when viewed in the light of critical dogma may actually be the most appropriate and powerful means available for producing the desired effect.[3]

What has been called "practical criticism" as distinguished from critical theory—the criticism, that is, which concentrates on the meanings, structures, and values of individual works—has taken on, in the last twenty or thirty years, an immensely greater prominence in literary education than it had when I was a student, at least in English and the other modern literatures. It was a rare thing then for professors of these subjects to descend from the heights of literary history or biography to the detailed consideration of texts; nowadays, on the other hand, thanks to various influences, including the "new criticism" and the "Great Books" movement, the situation is largely reversed, and most of us devote much time to initiating students into the difficult mysteries of reading closely and discussing critically particular poems, dramas, short stories, and novels. I have no doubt that this widespread "return to the text" has been a good thing. It is a necessary condition of any teaching that would give first place to those basic and relatively permanent elements in literary study which

[3] Wayne Booth has recently argued this position with great cogency and particularity in *The Rhetoric of Fiction* (Chicago, 1961), especially, but not exclusively, in chapters 2–5 of part I.

our students must master if they are to become critics in their own right. It is, however, a necessary condition only, and not a sufficient one: we can teach texts after all on various levels of sophistication; and there is no guarantee in such teaching by itself that we will not neglect the fundamentals of literary analysis and judgment in our naturally keener interest in the higher things.

I want to speak particularly of one kind of practical criticism of literary works which seems to me more basic than many of the other kinds now in vogue and to which, for that reason, I should wish to give an especially prominent place in the critical education of every man.[4]

I began this essay with a sentence of T. S. Eliot, and I shall introduce this final section of it with another sentence of his, which sums up rather well the special concern of the criticism I have in mind and the grounds of its priority. "No artist," he says, "produces great art by a deliberate attempt to express his personality. He expresses his personality indirectly through concentrating on a task which is a task in the same sense as the making of an efficient engine or the turning of a jug or a table leg." He might have added to "his personality" several other things and said that no artist produces great art by a deliberate attempt to express his philosophy, his vision of the world, his place in his age, or his participation in the archetypal experiences of his cultural tradition or of mankind in general. All these causes lie behind and are reflected in any individual work a writer may compose; and there can plainly be no full understanding or appreciation of the work—no adequate criticism of it—that does not take them into account. But Eliot is surely right in saying that these things are expressed in a given work only indirectly, the extent and character of the expression being always qualified by something much more immediate, which is the particular artistic task the writer is concentrating upon. He is engaged in making an individual work of literary art of a certain kind; and this always presents him with problems of various sorts, in the constitution of its subject as a whole and in the invention, disposition, and proportioning of its parts, which are

---

4 It presupposes, of course, other still more elementary questions about texts, especially questions concerning vocabulary and syntax and those which Olson groups under "hermeneutics" in his recent essay in *Modern Philology* 61 (1964): 225–37. But these are, strictly speaking, precritical rather than critical questions, which is not to say that any good teacher of criticism can safely neglect them.

problems more or less peculiar to this individual work, and which allow him only a certain range of choices if they are to be appropriately solved. What he can reveal to us of his personality, his philosophy, his age, his depth psychology is thus necessarily conditioned by the literary exigencies of the work he is making. He cannot say everything he may wish to say or be capable of saying because of the kind of man he is, but only what he *can* say as an artist in the working out of his particular task. It would seem therefore that the first business of practical criticism, in dealing with a given work, must be to ask what were the *literary* problems the writer was faced with, why these were problems for him in relation to his overall *literary* task, and what *literary* reasons or justifications may be found for what he actually did in solving them. We can then go on to look for reasons or causes beyond the literary, and we obviously need to do this. But there is always a danger that in concentrating on these without first considering the specifically literary rationale of a literary work, we may come out with explanations or judgments either wholly or partly beside the point: psychological, philosophical, or historical constructions on the work that will appear unnecessary or far-fetched when we descend to the simpler level of the writer's literary task.[5]

I shall try to illustrate what I have just been saying by giving two examples from recent criticism in which the concept of what I call the writer's immediate literary task is left out of account and suggesting briefly some of the more obvious consequences of bringing it in.

I take the first example from a work which has been widely discussed in the last few years in what seems to me much too fancy a way. The question concerns Swift's depiction of the Yahoos in the last Voyage of *Gulliver's Travels,* and especially what we are to make of all the vivid and highly repulsive imagery in which he renders "their strange disposition," as Gulliver calls it, "to nastiness and filth," in their persons, their actions, and their tastes in food. Many

[5] I have attempted this sort of problematic and functional analysis in an essay on the plot of *Tom Jones* (*Critics and Criticism*, pp. 616–47), in a brief discussion of *Macbeth* (*The Languages of Criticism*, pp. 169–73), and in some essays at the end of the present volume. See also Olson, *Tragedy* . . . , pp. 171–94 (*Agamemnon*), 195–215 (*King Lear*), 217–36 (*Phèdre*); Norman Friedman and Charles A. McLaughlin, *Poetry: An Introduction to Its Form and Art* (New York, 1961); Booth, *The Rhetoric of Fiction*, pp. 243–66 (*Emma*) and his "Shakespeare's Tragic Villain," in *Shakespeare's Tragedies*, edited by Laurence Lerner (Penguin Books, 1963), pp. 180–90 (*Macbeth*); Bernard Weinberg, *The Art of Jean Racine* (Chicago, 1963).

of Swift's recent critics have thought it necessary to find special reasons for both the character and the quantity of this imagery; and, almost without exception, they have assumed that the explanation must
involve reasons not directly deducible from the fourth Voyage itself,
when this is read simply as a literary composition. The extraordinary
"nastiness and filth" of the Yahoos, we are told by some critics, is
obviously a sign of something abnormal in Swift himself—a morbid
giving in to that supposed personal obsession with cleanliness and
the nastier bodily functions which has been detected in some of his
other works. This is one line of explanation; and it is sometimes
joined with another explanation, derived not from Swift's psychology
but from what are taken to be his secret theological intentions in
writing the fourth Voyage. He wanted to represent in the Yahoos, we
are told,[6] the condition into which man had been brought by original sin; and he consequently dwelt as elaborately as he did on their
physical characteristics and their filth and deformity and their shocking tastes in food because these were among the most frequent images
by which moral corruption had been metaphorically described not
only in parts of the Bible but in many of the homiletic writings of the
Anglican tradition to which Swift belonged.

Now either or both of these hypotheses about the Yahoos may have
some truth in them. I should be more impressed with them, however,
if I thought that either one was necessary in order to make sense of
the text. But I can see little if anything in the conception and depiction of the Yahoos that cannot be adequately accounted for in much
simpler *literary* terms. Whatever else the fourth Voyage may be, it is
first of all a highly circumstantial account of the experiences through
which Gulliver, instructed by the Houyhnhnms, came eventually to
entertain the same feelings for mankind in the mass as he had for the
Yahoos when he first encountered them in chapter 1. "Upon the
whole," he says in that chapter, "I never beheld in all my travels so
disagreeable an animal, nor one against which I naturally conceived
so strong an antipathy." And a little later he remarks that "although
there were few greater lovers of mankind, at that time, than myself,
yet I confess I never saw any sensitive being so detestable on all accounts"; "and the more I came near them, the more hateful they

---

[6] See especially Roland M. Frye, "Swift's Yahoo and the Christian Symbols for Sin,"
Journal of the History of Ideas, 15 (1954): 201–15.

grew, while I stayed in that country." This initial and continuing re-sponse of Gulliver to the Yahoos, then, was one of the basic *données* of the fable, and it presented Swift with a clear problem merely as an artist in narrative. If the story was to be imaginatively convincing as a vehicle for his satirical thesis, he had obviously to find imagery with which to depict the Yahoos that would justify as completely and forci-bly as possible *for the reader* the extreme abhorrence and disgust which their appearance, actions, and habits immediately aroused in Gulliver. No one can say, I suppose, that he made the only possible choice of imagery under the circumstances; but it is not easy to think of any other imagery that would be better calculated to produce the required effect than the accumulated details of the Yahoos' "deform-ity and filth" which he elaborates so vividly in the first half of the Voyage. But if this is true, then there are surely good and sufficient *literary* reasons, inherent in the nature of Swift's immediate artistic task, for his having done what he does with the Yahoos; and it seems that no interpretation of the Voyage can be solidly grounded that does not take explicit account of these reasons as a necessary first step in understanding and evaluation, after which—but not before—we can assess intelligently the relevance of other non-literary reasons.

My second example I take from the recent criticism of Jane Aus-ten, which has been peculiarly rich in judgments that point the same moral. It has to do with the little episode in chapters 6 and 8 of *Per-suasion* which concerns the dead son of Anne Elliot's friend Mrs. Musgrove. "The real circumstances of this pathetic piece of family history," the narrator explains at the outset, when "poor Dick" is first alluded to, "were that the Musgroves had had the ill fortune of a very troublesome, hopeless son; and the good fortune to lose him before his twentieth year; that he had been sent to sea because he was stupid and unmanageable on shore; that he had been little cared for at any time by his family . . . ; seldom heard of, and scarcely at all re-gretted, when intelligence of his death abroad had worked its way to Uppercross, two years before." What brings him into the story is the fact that his mother's thoughts of him are revived when she hears of the impending return to the neighborhood of Anne's former fiancé, from whom she is now estranged, Captain Wentworth, and then sud-denly remembers that Captain Wentworth had been her son's supe-rior officer, had been kind to him, and had indeed been responsible for "the only two disinterested letters" the boy had ever written home. This chance sentimental memory throws Mrs. Musgrove "into greater grief for him than she had known on first hearing of his death"; and not long afterwards she expresses her feelings somewhat overobtrusively to Wentworth himself at a large evening party following his return. "There was," we are told, "a momentary expression in Captain Wentworth's face at this speech, a certain glance of his bright eye, and curl of his handsome mouth, which convinced Anne, that instead of sharing in Mrs. Musgrove's kind wishes, as to her son, he had probably been at some pains to get rid of him . . . [by getting him transferred to another ship]." But "in another moment [Wentworth] was entirely collected and serious; and almost instantly afterwards coming up to the sofa, on which [Anne] and Mrs. Musgrove were sitting, took a place by the latter, and entered into conversation with her, in a low voice, about her son, doing it with so much sympathy and natural grace, as shewed the kindest consideration for all that was real and unabsurd in the parent's feelings."

It is no doubt possible, taking this episode by itself, and looking for a deep explanation, to see in it an expression of something rather peculiar in Jane Austen's attitude toward certain kinds of people; and one recent critic has set forth precisely this view. "Why," he asks, "are Mrs. Musgrove and her son so ill-treated?" and he goes on to say that "Jane Austen . . . has never shown much tolerance toward the dead; but she shows none at all, nothing indeed but a fierce personal distaste, toward Dick Musgrove. . . ." And "this savage caricature—without pretext itself—serves as an excuse for abusing Mrs. Musgrove." The only explanation this critic can find is that Jane Austen the woman had a very queer sense of humor. And so, he concludes, "Dick Musgrove is exhumed from his undeserved sanctification, and Mrs. Musgrove engages Jane Austen's sense of humor; but neither Mrs. Musgrove nor her son illustrates anything except the author's exasperation with both."[7]

But would a critic be likely to write in this way if he had asked himself seriously beforehand just what was Jane Austen's problem as a novelist—her *literary* problem—at the point in *Persuasion* where this episode occurs? I think not; for though the business of Mrs.

---

[7] See Marvin Mudrick, *Jane Austen: Irony as Defense and Discovery* (Princeton, 1952), pp. 211–13.

Musgrove and Dick may not have been in itself a very happy invention, it was certainly not an invention without a "pretext" or, in other words, a definite artistic function. That function, as an attentive reader of the text unprejudiced by theories of Jane Austen's personal psychology can easily see, has to do not primarily with Mrs. Musgrove or her son but with Captain Wentworth: the point of the episode is the impression it gives us of Wentworth's quick intelligence and goodness of heart; and that point would obviously not have been nearly so clear if there had been anything *really* "pathetic" about Dick's loss: he had therefore to be the worthless kind of boy he was and his mother had to sentimentalize him unduly. But why is the incident necessary or desirable at all at just this stage of the action, immediately preceding and immediately following Wentworth's first painful meeting with Anne, eight years after she has been persuaded by Lady Russell and her own sense of duty to break her engagement to him? The answer is that it is essential to the plot Jane Austen is developing in *Persuasion,* with its emotional climax in the final reunion of the lovers after Wentworth's long estrangement from Anne, that we should take Anne's unbroken attachment to Wentworth as seriously as she does, sharing sympathetically her pain and depression during the separation and her happiness in the reunion and, more than that, feeling that both are justified by his intrinsic merits. We must be made somehow, therefore, to see these merits for ourselves, independently of her belief in them; and this posed a difficult problem for Jane Austen, partly because she had chosen, for good reasons, I think, to tell the story almost entirely from Anne's point of view, thus precluding any full inside appreciation of Wentworth's thoughts and motives at this stage, but mainly because the plot required that Wentworth should act, for some time after his return, in a manner contrary to Anne's wishes and ours: in his "angry pride" treating her coolly as a mere indifferent acquaintance, accepting uncritically and irresponsibly the attentions of the Musgrove girls, becoming entangled with Louisa Musgrove, so obviously inferior to Anne, without being really in love with her. Something clearly had to be done, and as early as possible, to convince the reader that Wentworth actually had other and better capabilities of feeling and action than his continuing resentment at Anne's earlier rejection of him allowed him to manifest in his dealings with her. Jane Austen was too good an artist to miss seeing the problem or to be willing to evade it; and it is as her first attempt to solve it, I suggest, that she introduces the episode of Dick Musgrove and his mother and of Captain Wentworth's gratuitous kindness to both and gives it the emphasis it has, just at the moment, after the awful first meeting with Anne, when we need especially to think well of him.[8]

There is much more to this kind of problematic practical criticism, in terms of the writer's immediate literary task, than this example, with its deliberate emphasis on the more obvious possibilities, can hope to make clear. It is a kind of criticism that is capable, I think, of indefinite development and refinement, within the limits of its basic point of view, once that point has been firmly grasped, not as an abstract principle, but as a habit of everyday thinking about the novels, poems, and dramas we read or see. But the point of view itself is extremely simple; it is one of those primary concepts in criticism which everyone can be led to comprehend and work with who has ever written anything himself, even a series of term papers. A good deal of leading, indeed, is required; it is much easier for students to approach literary works in terms of the greatly more complicated notions that underlie most of the other currently fashionable critical modes. There are relatively few students, however, who cannot be taught, with some sustained effort on our part, to understand even so simple a set of fundamental ideas as are here involved and, more than that, to make them a part of their habitual thinking. And the effort, it seems to me, is abundantly worth making—and making more strenuously than I at least have made it. For although much more than this is entailed in helping our students to become their own critics, I cannot help believing that they will be all the better critics in the end—all the more independent of their former professors and of the fellows who write reviews in the papers—if they have acquired the habit of reading literary works in the light of their specifically *literary* ends, problems, and reasons which a training in the kind of practical criticism I have been talking about can give them.

8 It serves also, of course, the minor function of hastening the first meeting of Anne and Wentworth after their long estrangement.

Varieties of Dramatic Criticism

A SENTENCE in Arthur Mizener's preface to Volume I of the *Carleton Drama Bulletin* may serve to point the direction of my remarks. It is our ambition, he says, "to pull together the drama as a thing alive on the stage and the drama as a thing read, contemplated, and discussed"—in other words, to conjoin drama in the concrete, as presented to our eyes, ears, and emotion by producers and actors, with drama in the abstract, as brought to our minds through the concepts and reasonings of dramatic critics. Mizener's chief concern was properly with the kinds of plays that would best promote a union of the living stage and the stage as a formulated art. My concern, on the other hand, will be with the second element in the combination: namely, with the conditions under which, in such a program, the reading and study of dramatic criticism may help to advance rather than to hinder the realization of its double aim.

For it is surely better to remain innocent of dramatic criticism than to read even a great deal of it in the expectation that it will automatically make us more competent judges of the plays we see. The effect, indeed, may be just the opposite. There is always a temptation, when we come upon an especially clear-cut and per-

A lecture at Carleton College, 1953; here reprinted with permission of the college, from the *Carleton Drama Review*, Vol. I (1955–56). I have not attempted to revise the text in order to account accurately for the dramatic theory set forth in the first six chapters of Elder Olson's recent *Tragedy and the Theory of Drama* (Detroit, 1961), which seem to me to constitute an original contribution not to be adequately described in the terms of any of the categories used in my essay.

suasively argued statement of doctrine about the drama, to attach ourselves to it in a kind of exclusive faith, and so close our minds to those characteristics and values in plays for which our favorite theory makes no provision, in the manner so abundantly illustrated in the history of Shakespearean criticism from Thomas Rymer and Voltaire to William Archer and Wilson Knight. And the results are little better when as an alternative to such discipleship, we try to eke out a critical education in the drama by picking and choosing among pieces of the various theories we meet in our reading: we are able, in that case, to say more things about any play, but at the cost of not knowing very clearly why we say them.

What is lacking in both of these uses of dramatic criticism is a critical view of that criticism itself. It is the business of critics of the drama to make propositions about plays or about the art of which plays are products, and it is our business, as students of the drama, to utilize these propositions to the end of improving our capacity for contemplating and discussing the plays we read or see. But we cannot do this intelligently or fruitfully if we are content to concentrate merely upon what is explicitly said about this or that topic. For the propositions of critics, or at least of those most likely to repay our study, are never either fully intelligible or completely verifiable in themselves as independent judgments or statements of doctrine. They are not propositions simply but reasoned propositions, and as reasoned propositions they derive their meaning and validity not only from their relations to the objective dramatic things they refer to, but, more immediately, from their place in a network of other propositions, not all of them expressed, which serve both to fix their terms and to provide a warrant for their assertion. If we are really to profit, therefore, from our study of critical writings about the drama, we must form the habit of reading them with a view not merely to what they say about a given subject but to why they say this, whatever it may be, rather than something else. We must consider, that is, not only the doctrines and judgments of critics but the basic reasons, or, as Dryden puts it in his essay on tragedy, the "grounds of criticism," upon which these rest.

Why is it, for instance, that, although no important critics in the seventeenth century ever thought of making a sharp separation between poetry and drama, such a separation is to be met with on all sides in the criticism of our time? Or why is it that Aristotle can make plot "the first principle and as it were the soul" of tragedy, with character second, whereas, for William Archer, the "noblest part" of drama—that which makes it live—is not action but character? The history of dramatic criticism is full of such conflicts of doctrine, which can never be satisfactorily resolved without taking into account something more fundamental to the positions of the various critics than appears on the surface of their statements or than can be discovered by a direct appeal to facts or to changing fashions in taste.

That thing may be called the "necessity" of the critic's principles. It is the more or less impersonal compulsion, with respect to what a critic is able to say, or will find it appropriate and relevant to say, on any question, which comes from the fact that he has chosen, however undeliberately, to set up his problems in terms of one rather than any other of the many distinct aspects or relationships in which drama may be viewed, and to solve them by one rather than any other of the several possible methods of critical inquiry. For what Etienne Gilson says of philosophers is no less true of dramatic critics: they "are free to lay down their own sets of principles, but once this is done, they can no longer think as they wish—they think as they can." We ought therefore to examine the nature and variety of the compulsions by which dramatic critics are led to say the kinds of things they do and not to say the kinds of things other critics say— critics who are ostensibly discussing the same subjects, but under the compulsion of different principles. Only by doing this can we make something more of the dramatic criticism of the past than a collection of arbitrary dogmas or statements of personal opinion and put ourselves in a position to utilize it sensibly toward the improvement of our powers of judgment. It is all a matter of grasping the basic reasons of what we read; and I have thought that I could best illustrate what that means by taking as my subject the major varieties of dramatic criticism which have been developed, between the time of the Greeks and our own time, as a result of the choice by different critics of different sets of compulsive first principles.

It will make a very great difference, in the first place, to a critic of the drama, whether, on the one hand, he assumes that the drama can be adequately discussed in terms of principles peculiar to the drama itself, as a distinctive form of art, or, on the other hand, holds that the truth about the drama must be deduced from the truth about something else, to which the drama is related as a part or a means. Of these two fundamentally different ways of considering the drama, the great early representative of the first was Aristotle, of the second Plato; and the two modes of discussion have persisted as more or less distinct traditions, though often borrowing elements from one another, throughout the subsequent history of dramatic criticism.

The criticism in the "Platonic" tradition, in spite of the great variety of forms it has taken and the many conflicting views of the drama to which it has given currency, can be identified by one common characteristic. It is essentially a criticism that looks upon the drama as an activity or function in the context of other human activities or functions, and hence is governed by principles that signify or point to some larger good than that of the drama itself, a good which the drama ought to serve if it is to become what it can be or if it is even to be tolerated in society. The larger good may be so conceived that the activities of dramatists in bringing on the stage actors who mimic many characters, good and bad, and excite the passions of audiences are bound to seem a perpetual threat to its realization. This of course is the line taken by Plato himself, with fairly negative results: in *The Republic* drama is condemned in the light of the final good, an ideally just state ruled by philosopher-kings; in *The Laws* the drama is allowed a place in the second-best state depicted in that work, but under heavy censorship. The extreme negativism of *The Republic* had its later counterpart in the Puritan attacks on the stage, such as Sidney undertook to answer in his *Apology for Poetry*, whereas the somewhat more tolerant position of *The Laws* has descended to us both in the numerous efforts of moralists, like Jeremy Collier and Rousseau, to expose the ethical imperfections and dangers of the existing stage and to direct it to more innocent ends, and in the attempts of politicians, such as the present rulers of Russia, to assimilate the drama, in its themes and techniques, to the governing ideology of the regime.

But there is nothing in the "Platonic" approach as such that prevents its being turned to more positive uses in the criticism of the drama. All that one needs for this purpose is a conviction that the drama as it is, collectively, is imperfect, and a set of ideas, embodying some conception of the good of society or of human conduct or knowledge or of art in relation to these, by means of which one can argue to what the drama at its best ought to be. This is so natural a pattern of argument, indeed, that one is embarrassed to know which illustrations of it to select out of the many that come to mind. Here is Bernard Shaw, writing of that high conception of the uses of the theater which had guided him as a weekly critic of plays for the *Saturday Review*. "Only the ablest critics," he says, "believe that the theatre is really important: in my time none of them would claim for it, as I claimed for it, that it is as important as the Church was in the Middle Ages and much more than the Church was in London in the years under review." Hence the Church, he goes on, "is giving way to that older and greater Church to which I belong: the Church where the oftener you laugh the better, because by laughter only can you destroy evil without malice, and affirm good fellowship without mawkishness." And this would be a very good thing "if the theatre took itself seriously as a factory of thought, a prompter of conscience, an elucidator of social conduct, an armory against despair and dullness, and a temple of the Ascent of Man. I took it seriously in that way, and preached about it instead of merely chronicling its news and alternately petting and snubbing it as a licentious but privileged form of public entertainment."

And here is T. S. Eliot, concluding a lecture on how he has attempted in his own plays to bring poetry back into the drama with an eloquent suggestion of an ideal end to be served by poetic drama beyond anything he has been able to achieve: "I should not like to close . . . without attempting to set before myself and, if I can, before you, though only in dim outline, the ideal towards which it seems to me that poetic drama should strive. It is an unattainable ideal: and that is why it interests me, for it provides an incentive towards further experiment and exploration, beyond any goal which there is prospect of attaining. It is a function of all art to give us some perception of an order in life, by imposing order upon it. . . . To go as far in this direction as it is possible to go, without losing that contact with the ordinary everyday world with which the drama must come to terms, seems to me the proper aim of dramatic poetry.

For it is ultimately the function of art, in imposing a credible order upon ordinary reality, and thereby eliciting some perception of an order *in* reality, to bring us to a condition of serenity, stillness, and reconciliation; and then leave us, as Virgil left Dante, to proceed toward a region where that guide can avail us no further."

And here is Christopher Fry, arguing the superiority of "the theatre of poetry" over "the theatre of prose" from a distinction between two orders of perception: a lower order in which human existence is taken for granted and a higher order in which human existence is an incredible and fantastic surprise. The first is the sphere of the ordinary prose drama, and of that we have perhaps had enough. But the language "in which man explores his own amazement" is poetry, and a shift to the poetic theater could "help us to see ourselves and the world freshly, as though we had just rounded the corner into life. . . . This change of viewpoint would be no escapism or fantasy. Nothing could be so wildly, perilously, incomprehensibly fantastic as reality itself, and we may as well dare to look at it, and like it."

I will mention one more contemporary example of this approach. It is Francis Fergusson's *The Idea of a Theater,* the very title of which betrays its intellectual origins. The main intention of the book is to exhibit the drama as it is, in its best forms, today, in the light of "the perennial idea" of a drama devoted to the "imitation" of human life and action in the most comprehensive sense; a theater "formed at the center of the culture of its time, and at the center of the life and awareness of the community, . . . focusing all the available insights—historical, ethical, religious—upon 'two boards and a passion.' " Fergusson's "idea of a theater" is thus a kind of Platonic paradigm, which, however, has come close to realization in two dramatists of the past, Sophocles and Shakespeare, and is embodied most usefully for us, outside the drama, in *The Divine Comedy,* which is "the very pattern of the imitation of action—mirroring the greatest height and depth of human experience, as Eliot says—in the most comprehensive scene-of-human-life to be found in our tradition." Needless to say, we have no such theater now, nor has one existed since Shakespeare: the whole modern age has been one of limited realizations and "partial perspectives," and it is hard to see how it can be otherwise in the future. "But we need the 'Idea of a

Theater,' " Fergusson says, "both to understand the masterpieces of drama at its best, and to get our bearings in our own time."

By contrast with the approach represented in these writers, we can identify the dramatic criticism in the "Aristotelian" tradition, not only by its relative indifference to the exalted views and eloquent language of the "Platonic" critics, but, more significantly, by its insistence on finding principles that are dictated in some sense by the peculiar nature of the drama as an art or craft. It is essentially a criticism of forms and techniques, and it seeks to establish criteria for these by considering not so much the social or moral functions of drama as the necessities and possibilities determined for the dramatic artist by such things as the character of his medium, the nature of his subjects, the psychology of his audience, or the standards set by earlier practitioners of his art. In the long history of this criticism from Aristotle to the present day, we can distinguish two principal phases, which differ rather clearly from one another according to which of two aspects of the drama is taken as the central object of attention. The distinction is suggested by Aristotle himself in chapter 3 of the *Poetics,* where, after summarizing the three respects in which poetic "imitations" may differ—namely, in their means, in their objects, and in their manner—he goes on to remark that "as an imitator Sophocles will be on one side [that is, with respect to the quality of the objects imitated] akin to Homer, both portraying good men; and on another [that is, with respect to the manner of imitating] to Aristophanes, since both present their personages as acting and doing. This in fact, according to some, is the reason for plays being called dramas, because in a play the personages act the story." It is possible, in other words, to discuss the art of drama either by emphasizing the particular poetic forms such as tragedy and comedy, which it embodies dramatically or by emphasizing its general character as dramatic representation and the requirements and opportunities which this defines for the playwright regardless of his more specific formal aims.

There can be no question which of the two was primary for Aristotle himself. We cannot read the *Poetics,* to be sure, without becoming convinced of his strong interest in the theater and his great respect for the drama as a mode of literary art. Out of the twenty-six

chapters of the treatise as it has come down to us, seventeen are devoted to tragedy and only two to epic, and the treatise ends with
an argument for the superiority of the dramatic method of representation characteristic of tragedy over the narrative method characteristic of epic. The culminating stage, moreover, in the history
of poetry outlined in chapters 4 and 5, is the emergence of drama,
in its two extreme forms of tragedy and comedy, out of the epic;
and here and elsewhere the great praise of Homer is that he knew
how to give a "dramatic" quality to his imitations of both serious
and comic actions by keeping himself out of sight as far as possible
and letting his characters act and speak his story. Little wonder that
the *Poetics* has always been hailed as the great classic of dramatic
criticism in our tradition.

And yet, in a very significant sense, it is this only incidentally.
The nature of dramatic representation is a principle in the argument, but a secondary one. Inferences can indeed be drawn from it,
as when Aristotle distinguishes between the shorter actions proper
to plays and the longer actions possible in epic, or as when he discusses the difficulty of making the marvelous seem credible on the
stage. But when we look at the context of these remarks, we see
that they belong to an inquiry in which tragedy and comedy are
being considered primarily, not as kinds of drama but as forms of
imitative poetry, the notion of drama, in the sense of dramatic
manner, being one of the differentia merely, though an important
one, rather than the controlling genus of the discussion.

Nor could it well be otherwise, given the special subject matter
and aims of poetic science as Aristotle conceived them. For the
task of poetic science, in the view he took of it, is to inquire into the
art, in the sense of the habits of correct artistic reasoning, which
poets must possess (along with poetic genius) if they are to make
poems that have a maximum of excellence in their respective kinds.
The science must start, therefore, by distinguishing the various
species of poetry that now exist, since these obviously present to the
poet quite different problems of artistic construction. It must attempt, moreover, to formulate the peculiar nature of each kind in
its concrete wholeness, as it appears in completed individual poems,
since without a clear intuition of the whole to be constructed in any
given case the poet would be unable to reason to what he ought to

do in any of its parts, if the poem is to be beautiful. The kinds of poems Aristotle proposes to deal with are those—including tragedy, epic, and comedy—which happen, as he says, to be "imitations," that is to say, artistic productions using speech as their medium which achieve their effects by bringing before us interesting or moving semblances of human actions, characters, and passions. Hence it is primarily as "imitations" that they must be considered; and the wholeness of any of them will involve the combination of four things: the moral quality of the action imitated (as serious or ludicrous, for example), the specific character of the means used (as merely verse or verse with music), the manner of the imitation (as dramatic, narrative, or mixed), and the peculiar emotional "working or power" to which everything is directed in a good poem. The first principles of poetics, accordingly, will be definitions of poetic forms or species in which all four of these variables are specified in proper correlation, with the object of imitation primary, as in the definition of tragedy in chapter 6. Nothing short of this will serve the practical needs of poetics in Aristotle's meaning of the term, inasmuch as the wholes which any poet seeks to construct can be brought into existence successfully only if he has acquired the total art of using a certain means and a certain manner of imitating to body forth a certain object in such a way as to yield a certain definite effect. Hence it is that the generic art of drama is subordinated in Aristotle, as merely one kind of poetic manner, to the specific arts of making tragedies or comedies. For no dramatist ever writes drama merely, but always tragedy or comedy or something else of a similarly formal sort: with respect to this form mastery of dramatic manner is only one condition of artistic excellence and is subordinate to the more distinctively poetic mastery required by the peculiar natures of the objects to be represented and of the emotional effects to be achieved.

Poetry and the forms of poetry are thus the primary considerations in Aristotle's dealings with the drama. The same thing, however, can be said of a good many later critics, and if we are to grasp what is special in the approach to dramatic criticism exemplified in the *Poetics,* we must take note of two further points, the first of which has to do with Aristotle's conception of poetry and the second with his conception of poetic forms.

Now for Aristotle poetry in the most distinctive sense is the art of constructing wholes of which the matter is language, used either simply or as embellished with meter and music, and the organizing form is the pattern of some kind of human action or passion such as can be made credible and emotionally effective for us in the words and rhythms of the completed work. The poet must therefore be one skilled in language and meter, and also, if he writes plays, in the techniques of the dramatic manner; but these are only necessary conditions: he becomes a poet, essentially, by reason of his ability to imitate, that is, to construct wholes in which everything that he does with his words and rhythms, and with his techniques of representation, is made to contribute to the beauty and peculiar "power" of the represented action. Hence poetry, for Aristotle, is not what it has commonly been for later critics. It is not the art or faculty of writing verse as distinct from the art or faculty of writing prose, nor is it a certain quality of language or thought or sensibility which ought to be present, but is not always, in writings conventionally called poems. Poetry is a character, rather, that belongs to all imitations in words—and to these as wholes—by virtue simply of the fact that they are imitations. And this means that the great modern problem, which I shall touch upon later, of the relations between "drama" and "poetry" does not exist for him. The drama, in the sense of the forms of tragedy and comedy (or whatever other forms employ a dramatic manner), *is* poetry, and the makers of such works *are* poets, by definition; and the only question we can sensibly ask is how good, in its kind, and irrespective of the verbal medium (verse or prose) that happens to be used, any given dramatic work is.

This view which Aristotle took of the nature of poetic, and hence of dramatic, forms is clearly discernible in his analysis of tragedy, and here again he stands in sharp contrast to the majority of later critics who have concerned themselves with this question. The analysis begins, as we all know, with the definition of a class of poetic works, called "tragedy," the essential nature of which, as induced from an inspection of existing plays, is the imitation in embellished language of a serious action (that is, an action in which good men are confronted with issues of life-and-death import) which is complete and of a certain extent; the imitation being effected dramatically rather than narratively, and so conducted that its peculiar "power" is the bringing about, through incidents arousing pity and fear for the protagonist, of a catharsis or resolution of these and other painful emotions excited by the plot. And this definition is followed by an elaborate deduction of its consequences for the ways in which the constituent parts of such a work—especially its plot in the two aspects of plot and tragic plot, its rendering of character, its thought, and its diction—ought to be conceived and handled if the work is to embody the tragic form with a maximum of poetic beauty and emotional power. Now what I should especially like to emphasize here is the character of the reasoning underlying this whole procedure. We can imagine Aristotle saying to himself something like this: "There does now actually exist in our theaters, as a result of the successive efforts of many earlier poets, trying to improve on what their predecessors had discovered, a class of productions called tragedies, which appear, when I examine them analytically, to be imitations of complete and extended serious actions, in embellished language, that gain their effects through dialogue and acting; and I observe further that the most powerful and most prized of these are so constructed as to excite and resolve emotions which I would identify roughly as pity and fear. I will concentrate, therefore, on this form and try to make evident the artistic reasoning which the best achievement of it must presuppose, and in doing this I will not consider whether or not tragedy is now fully developed in all its possible species, but simply what, if future poets should want to write works of the special existing kind I have isolated, are the essential causes of success and failure, artistically speaking, in such an effort." Tragedy, in short—and the same thing holds true of comedy—is for Aristotle merely a particular species of literary art that exists and has the characteristics he assigns to it solely because poets have happened to write dramatic works possessing these characteristics. It does, indeed, have a natural basis, both in the instinctive delight which all men take in imitation and in the capacity of men to respond emotionally in certain ways to the crimes and sufferings of other men. But it is not in itself a natural form, or the embodiment of a natural form, in any sense that requires us, in judging of particular tragedies, to refer for our criteria to some Platonic "idea" of tragedy or to some doctrine as to what is and is not essentially "tragic" in life.

There is a strong contrast between Aristotle's conception of the forms of drama and the conceptions of these forms to be found in most of the later criticism of the drama which has given a primary place to distinctions of dramatic form. The decisive cause of the change was undoubtedly the disappearance of Aristotle's method of definition. Had this been revived in the Renaissance along with the doctrines about tragedy and comedy it was used to state, the consequence might well have been the recognition and analysis, in a scientific and undogmatic spirit, of many possible forms of serious drama besides the one species of tragedy Aristotle talks about, and the development, similarly, of a poetics of comedy and the intermediate forms of drama more nearly adequate to modern achievements in these forms than anything we now have. But the method was not revived, with the result that the criticism of dramatic forms which has been built upon the *Poetics* since the sixteenth century, while it has retained the traditional names of "tragedy" and "comedy," and added others like "tragicomedy," has tended to treat the nature of the realities signified by these names in a quite un-Aristotelian way.

It is the difference between a criticism that would have asked about Arthur Miller's *Death of a Salesman*, for instance, What, precisely, is the form, old or new, being aimed at in this play, and how fully are its possibilities realized? and a criticism that asks of Miller's drama, Is it or is it not a tragedy in the true sense of that word? The modern method, in short, has not been one that proceeds typically by induction from what dramatists have done, on the assumption that the forms of drama are determined merely by differences in the artistic principles that happen to govern the making of existing plays; it is a method, rather, in which the nature of any dramatic form is deduced from principles more general than drama or even art itself, on the assumption that the common name of any such form must necessarily correspond to some more or less fixed, unitary idea or essence which can be defined dialectically in relation to other literary ideas or essences and, as so defined, be made to yield rules to direct poets in constructing plays and criteria to guide critics in analyzing and judging them. The result has been to confer a kind of ideal and invariant character upon the entities designated by such words as "tragedy" and "comedy." They are still forms, but forms in the sense of quasi-Platonic patterns or models rather than in that of particular animating principles of concrete artistic wholeness; and they can be defined, therefore, in abstraction from the works in which they are embodied, in much the way in which we define the concepts of mathematics; as when we are told, for example, without any indication of what works the critic has in mind, that "tragedy shares with comedy its concern with man's limitations, but differs from it, in one respect at least, in presenting these limitations as both disastrous and part of the ultimate configuration of life itself; tragedy, at its best and as distinct from mere pathos or melodrama, rests upon and implies a universal import in the structure of man's situation in the world."

As the nature of the method might lead one to expect, the history of this later mode of discussing the forms of drama has been marked, since its emergence in the Renaissance, by a tendency toward ever more general and comprehensive definitions of these forms and toward definitions increasingly remote from the actual conditions of artistic production. For many if not most of the critics of the neoclassical period, the governing assumption continued to be that which Horace had stated when he advised poets to let each peculiar species of writing fill with decorum its proper place. It was primarily a question, that is, of what actions, what characters, what sentiments, what forms of language, what moral and emotional effects are proper to, or appropriately go with, the idea of comedy as distinct from that of farce or tragedy, the idea of tragedy as distinct from that of epic, and so on. For examples see Dryden's dramatic essays or, for more extreme specimens, the comments of Rymer and Voltaire on Shakespeare. The ideas of comedy, tragedy, tragicomedy, farce, and the like, in this criticism, were still, for the most part, rather limited ideas, of which the reference was bounded by the sphere of art; when these critics talked about comedy and the comic or tragedy and the tragic, they had in view forms and qualities which owed their existence to the contrivances of poets rather than to the nature of things or of the human mind, however often they might appeal to moral or psychological principles in support of their conclusions as to what comic and tragic poets ought to do.

The definitions of these neoclassical critics were more general than anything Aristotle had thought worth attempting, but the definitions developed in the nineteenth century, under the influence of idealist philosophy, were more general still. The discussion of dramatic

forms, it was now widely assumed, must start from something fundamental in the nature of human existence or thought that can be
taken as the basic tragic or comic "fact" or the basic tragic or comic
"view of life"; it must then proceed to draw out deductively the consequences of this hypothesis for what dramatic poets have done or
should do. Thus for August Wilhelm Schlegel the basis of tragedy
is "that longing for the infinite which is inherent in our being" and
which is "baffled by the limits of our finite existence. . . . This is
the tragic tone of mind; and when the thought of the possible issues
out of the mind as a living reality, when this tone pervades and ani-
mates a visible representation of the most striking instances of violent
revolutions in a man's fortunes, either prostrating his mental energies
or calling forth the most heroic endurance—then the result is *Tragic
Poetry*. We thus see how this kind of poetry has its foundation in
our nature." For Hegel the "essentially tragic fact" is something still
more abstract: it is "the self-division and intestinal warfare of the
ethical substance, not so much the war of good with evil as the war
of good with good"—for example, the conflicting claims of the family
and the state in *Antigone,* of love and honor in Corneille's *Le Cid*—
and the end of the conflict is the denial of both exclusive claims.
For Andrew Bradley, whose paraphrase of Hegel's definition I quote,
this is true as far as it goes, but the definition needs to be generalized
still further if it is to give us "the common essence of all tragedies";
and he proposes a more inclusive formula, according to which *"any
spiritual conflict involving spiritual waste is tragic"* provided the
conflicting values are sufficiently great.

We are still largely under the influence of this characteristic
nineteenth-century desire for maximum generality in the definitions
of literary forms. Idealist metaphysics, however, is much less to our
taste nowadays than analytical psychology and cultural anthropology;
and the latest phase in the long series of modern attempts to give to
the traditional distinctions among dramatic forms a fixed and natural
basis in some kind of dialectic of universal essences has been dominated by concepts deriving from the speculations of anthropologists
like Sir James Frazer and Jane Harrison and of psychologists like
Sigmund Freud and C. G. Jung. The common ambition of the critics
who have taken this line has been to renew our understanding of the
existing forms of artistic drama by exploring the broad analogies be-

tween them and the more general forms of primitive religious ritual and myth, or of the unconscious operations of the psyche, from which they must be supposed to have emerged; as, for example, in the writings of Gilbert Murray and F. M. Cornford on Greek tragedy and comedy, in Maud Bodkin's Jungian discussion of the universal "tragic pattern" in her *Archetypal Patterns in Poetry,* and in parts of Francis Fergusson's *The Idea of a Theater.* I shall not dwell here on the results of these efforts except to say that the criticism of dramatic forms seems now to have moved a long way from its original starting point in Aristotle's inductive definitions of tragedy and comedy as highly particularized forms of developed art.

There remains the second major variety of dramatic criticism in the "Aristotelian" line, the variety that results when critics take as the special object of their concern not the various species of drama but the drama as such, and talk primarily of those principles which constitute tragedies, comedies, tragicomedies, farces, and the like, simply as plays rather than as kinds of poetry in dramatic form. The possibility of such a criticism, as I have said before, is clearly indicated in the *Poetics* itself, where it remains, however, a subordinate mode of consideration. Its chief representative in antiquity was Horace in the *Ars Poetica,* but the full development of its potentialities has come only in modern times. We can see it taking form, first of all, perhaps, in Castelvetro, with his radical substitution of the character of the theatrical audience for the nature of tragedy or comedy as the first principle of dramatic criticism, and then, more clearly still, in such works of the mid–seventeenth century as the Abbé d'Aubignac's *La Pratique du théâtre* (translated under the significant title of *The Whole Art of the Stage*), Corneille's *Discours,* and Dryden's *Essay of Dramatic Poesy.* It was the characteristic approach, in the eighteenth century, of writers like Johnson, Diderot, and Lessing; but the great flourishing period of the method has been in the century and a half since 1800, when it has become probably the most widely accepted frame of reference for writers on the dramatic arts—the controlling concept of works as diverse in other respects as August Wilhelm Schlegel's *Lectures on Dramatic Art and Literature,* Gustav Freytag's *Technique of the Drama,* Francisque Sarcey's *Theory of the Theater,* Ferdinand Brunetière's "Law of the Drama," Brander Matthews' *Study of the Drama* and *Principles of Play Making,* William Archer's *Play-Making* and *The Old Drama and the New,* and George Pierce Baker's *Dramatic Technique,* to mention a few of the more familiar titles.

The most obvious feature of most of these writings, as well as of the earlier ones I have mentioned, is their preoccupation, in a thoroughly practical spirit, with questions of dramatic manner in Aristotle's sense, as determined by the common requirements of literary composition for the stage irrespective of the particular forms which that composition takes. How should plays, of whatever kind, be written if they are to be actable in theaters to the satisfaction of spectators?—that is the simple form to which the dramatic theorists in this tradition have tended to reduce their problems, as a consequence of their decision to theorize to practical ends about the drama as such. The collective result has been a large body of more or less useful advice to playwrights concerning a great variety of technical topics, ranging from the question of how to get ideas for plays and what stories can and cannot be put on the stage, through questions of general dramatic construction (for example, the shaping of the theatrical action through its stages of exposition, rising action, climax, falling action, dénouement; the functions of the successive acts; the unities of place and time), to more particular questions of probability, foreshadowing, suspense and surprise, the better and worse ways of beginning and ending plays, the structure and connection of scenes, the delineation of character, the writing of dialogue, the use of choric devices, the relative advantages of blank verse and rhyme or of verse and prose, and so on.

If we ask how such advice can be validated, the answer is that it can be validated, in the first place, by arguments from example: the critic can point to earlier or contemporary plays in which the procedure he is recommending has achieved brilliant or at least successful results; and of arguments of this kind there are innumerable instances in the critical works we are considering. If the rules of dramaturgy, however, are to be put on a really firm foundation, something more general and basic is obviously needed than a mere appeal to precedent; and it is clear that such ultimate reasons cannot be found where Aristotle found them—namely, in principles of specific form; they must be looked for in the common character of all play-writing as an art which issues in public performances in theaters. For the great majority of these modern critics, therefore, the first principle of dramatic criticism has been that principle which received its classic statement in Dr. Johnson's "The drama's laws the drama's patrons give." It is a principle that permits of a wide range of interpretations, from the merest box-office expediency to the idealism expressed by Dryden when he identified the proper audience for the dramatic poet with those spectators whose taste has been formed on Virgil. But in one formulation or another it has been the starting point from which most of the generalizing critics of the drama have reasoned, from Horace in antiquity and Castelvetro in the sixteenth century to the present day.

"It is an indisputable fact," Francisque Sarcey wrote in 1876, "that a dramatic work, whatever it may be, is designed to be listened to by a number of persons united and forming an audience. . . . No audience, no play. The audience is the necessary and inevitable condition to which dramatic art must accommodate its means. I emphasize this point because it is the point of departure, because from this simple fact we can derive all the laws of the theater without a single exception." And here, closer to our time, is William Archer: "The art of theatrical story-telling," he says, "is necessarily relative to the audience to whom the story is to be told. One must assume an audience of a certain status and characteristics before one can rationally discuss the best methods of appealing to its intelligence and sympathies. . . . The painter may paint, the sculptor model, the lyric poet sing, simply to please himself, but the drama has no meaning except in relation to an audience. It is a portrayal of life by means of a mechanism so devised as to bring it home to a considerable number of people assembled in a given place." All of which means that the whole art of the drama, for the critics who thus take the satisfaction of the audience as a first principle rather than merely as a necessary condition of dramatic production, inevitably assumes the character of a kind of rhetoric (the dramatic poet's occupation, said Schlegel, "coincides with that of the orator"), all the special problems involved in the making of plays being assimilated to the central problem of how "as promptly as possible to win the attention of the audience" and how "to hold that interest steady, or, better, to increase it till the final curtain falls." And the task of the dramatic theorist is to discover and sort out the commonplace devices available to playwrights for exciting and sustaining interest in any kind of play, producing conviction or illusion, and eliciting emotional responses. In this context distinctions among the specific forms of drama may still be recognized, but only as subordinate principles qualifying the applicability of particular general rules; and questions of better and worse in drama tend to become questions primarily either of the playwright's genius or seriousness of purpose or of the quality of the audience he is attempting to please—for example, as more or less intelligent or "adult."

Not all the critics in this tradition, however, have been content to view drama merely as a manner or technique or "mechanism," with rules determined by the character of theatrical audiences. It is natural for theorists in any special field to want to give their ruling concepts as much territory to rule over as they can; and once the concept of "drama" had been taken as the controlling theme of dramatic criticism, it was doubtless to be expected that its original scope of meaning would sooner or later be considerably enlarged. This at any rate is what happened in the nineteenth century, and under the influence of the same philosophical spirit in criticism to which we owe those extreme generalizations of the concepts of "tragedy" and "comedy" I have already spoken of. It was at this time that drama began to be discussed, not as a technique merely, but as a comprehensive form of art, coordinate with the two other great literary arts of lyric poetry and epic (the latter including the modern novel), but distinct from these in its essential nature. It became necessary, therefore, to define that essential nature; and so it was that the question, What is dramatic? came to be of burning interest to a long line of theorists through the nineteenth century and into the twentieth. It was answered, of course, in a good many different ways, but nearly always in terms that involved, in the first place, a comparison of drama with lyric poetry and with the epic or novel and, in the second place, an insistence on finding the essence of drama, not merely in its character as a mode of representation, but in some attribute common to all the human experiences or actions which drama may represent, that is to say, in the least common denominator of all properly dramatic plots. The method and the kind of results it could yield are well illustrated in what became perhaps the most famous and influential of all these attempts, Brunetière's essay on "the law of the drama."

"Will any argument, however ingenious," he asks, "alter the fact that all poetry is either lyric, epic, or dramatic? Certainly not." And does it not follow, if such-and-such tragedies, comedies, farces are admittedly dramatic, that "all these works, so different, must nevertheless have not merely a few points of contact or vague resemblance, but an essential characteristic in common? What is this characteristic?" Brunetière's answer is simply that the essence of drama is "the spectacle of a *will* striving towards a goal, and conscious of the means which it employs." This is what separates drama from lyric poetry and from the epic or novel (which is indeed the contrary of drama inasmuch as it represents men not as willing particular ends but as being acted upon by external conditions); and Brunetière goes on to show how this principle may be used to distinguish the various essential species of the drama and to illuminate the history of the drama in relation to the spiritual conditions of the different ages in which it has either flourished or declined.

The predictable result of all these attempts to declare the independence of the drama as a complete art form in its own right has been to raise the question, which was not a question at all for Aristotle or the "neo-Aristotelian" critics of the early modern period, of how the concept of "drama," as thus enlarged, is related to the concept of "poetry." I want to touch on this matter briefly by way of conclusion because the very fact that we ask the question at all illustrates rather vividly, I think, the main thesis I have been trying to expound, the necessary relativity of the problems and doctrines of dramatic criticism to the nature of the principles upon which that criticism, at any given time or in any given critic, happens to be based. For I suggest that we should never have thought of using the term "poetic drama," as we nearly all do, in a specialized and exclusive sense, or of writing, as T. S. Eliot has done, about "Poetry and Drama," or of distinguishing, as Christopher Fry has done, between "the theatre of poetry" and "the theatre of prose," had it not been for two major developments in critical theory during the past one hundred and fifty years. One of these is the change of fashions in the principles of dramatic criticism itself which I have just been speaking of. The other is a parallel change in the criticism of poetry, which has brought it about that, for most critics since at least the end of the eighteenth century, the term "poetry" no longer signifies the art of imitating human actions in appropriate speech but stands for something much more general than that—a certain quality of expression, commonly identified with verse rather than with prose, a certain way of feeling or conceiving things, a certain power of unifying experience imaginatively.

Thus both of our terms have been radically redefined and, as a consequence, made to refer to two entities that need have no intimate relation with one another. Drama, that is to say, may or may not be also poetry, as the terms "poetry" and "drama" are now conceived; and a new problem is thereby generated for critics, of making up their minds whether the two ought or ought not to be united in one composite whole. The orthodox answer, down almost to our own time, has been an affirmative one. A dramatic work, wrote Schlegel, may be regarded from a double point of view—how far it is *poetical,* and how far it is *theatrical.* "The two," he adds, "are by no means inseparable," but his own position is that there can be no good drama in which a "poetical" element is not present, in the sense not of metrical language necessarily but of a certain "spirit and design" in a play which may exist in as high a degree when the medium is prose as when it is verse; and he identifies this "higher excellence" with the mirroring in the play of "thoughts and feelings which in their character are necessary and eternally true, and soar above this earthly life." There were few critics, during the next hundred years, who would have quarreled with this, however differently they might define the essence of "poetry." But then at last came William Archer. Dramatic criticism has not yet completely recovered from the shock that it was administered, in the early twenties of the present century, by his famous book on *The Old Drama and the New.* For what Archer did, in effect, was to take the current notion that drama at its best is a combination of two distinct things, drama and poetry, and to oppose to this a conception of "pure" or "unmixed" drama, that can come to exist only when the essence of drama—which for Archer is the faithful "imitation" of life as we know it—is freed from the "poetical" or "lyrical" elements, including verse, which had been imposed upon it by its religious origins; the thesis of his book is that the history of English drama has been a progress, culminating in the realistic prose plays of Pinero, Galsworthy, and Granville-Barker, from a "mixed and heterogeneous art" to "a pure and logical art form." Archer saw the whole matter, in short, in the framework of terms already adopted by Schlegel and many others; he merely insisted on separating sharply what they had kept joined. And the same thing has been true of most of those who have pleaded the cause of "poetic drama" since his book appeared. He has been answered many times, but nearly always, I think, by critics who have been content to accept, without question, the principles he used in stating his case for "the theatre of prose"— the antithesis of "poetry" and "drama" and the opposition of "pure" and "mixed" forms—and who, accordingly, have had no way of refuting him except by turning his scale of values upside down (so that the "drama" in Shakespeare, for instance, is said to be less important than the "poetry," and *Macbeth* is praised as a "poem" of the order of *The Waste Land*), or else by arguing that since each element in the combination of "drama" and "poetry" is incomplete by itself, the best drama must be such a union of the two elements as that envisaged in the theories, among many others, of T. S. Eliot and Christopher Fry.

I dwell on this as one final instance of that compulsive influence of principles in dramatic criticism which critics can never escape, however unaware they may be of what is happening to them, and which we, as readers of such criticism, would do well to take constantly into account, lest, by not grasping clearly why different critics are impelled to say the things they do, we fail to profit as much as we might from what the many varied critical approaches to the drama, ancient and modern, have to tell us about the nature and possibilities of that art.

On Hypotheses in "Historical Criticism": Apropos of Certain Contemporary Medievalists

IN READING the publications of D. W. Robertson, Jr., and of others in the same school of American medievalists, I have been struck by what seems to me a serious confusion over the proper use of hypotheses in the historical interpretation of texts. The same confusion is apparent in many other fields of literary study, as the essay immediately following this one will show, and it may be worthwhile, therefore, to consider what it involves. I begin with some remarks on hypotheses in general.[1]

Suppose—to take an example from a poem on which several of these scholars have written commentaries—that the text to be interpreted is the well-known passage toward the beginning of *Piers Plow-*

A revision and expansion, mainly for use in a graduate seminar on problems of interpretation, of a much shorter paper read before a Conference on Symbolism and Allegory in the Middle Ages and Renaissance at the 1961 meeting of the Modern Language Association. Now first published.

1 I am especially indebted for suggestions in the preparation of this paper to T. C. Chamberlin's "The Method of Multiple Working Hypotheses," *Journal of Geology*, 39 (1931): 155–65; the various writings of Sir Karl Popper on the logic of hypotheses in the natural sciences and history, including, besides those mentioned later, his *The Logic of Scientific Discovery* (London, 1959); E. D. Hirsch's "Objective Interpretation," *PMLA*, 75 (1960): 463–79 and his forthcoming book, *Validity in Interpretation* (which I have read in manuscript); and Elder Olson's "Hamlet and the Hermeneutics of Drama," *Modern Philology*, 61 (1964): 225–37. I owe much also to conversations with Professor Olson and with three other Chicago friends, Professors Herbert Lamm, Theodore Silverstein, and Warner Wick.

man in which the speaker, asleep in the Malvern Hills, dreams that
he sees

> . . . a towr on a toft, trieliche ymaked,
> A deep dale benethe, a dungeon thereinne
> With deep diches and derke, and dredful of sighte.
> A fair feeld of folk foond I therbitweene
> Of al manere of men. . . .

The problem is to discover the poet's intention in giving us these
images of the tower and the dungeon and of the field full of people
between them; and since his intention is not immediately obvious
from the lines themselves, clear as these are in a simple grammatical
sense, the interpreter can proceed only by guessing at what it might
have been and then criticizing his guesses in the light of whatever
facts within the poem or outside it may be relevant.[2] The process of
interpretation, here and elsewhere, thus involves two distinct operations: first we have to guess and then we have to test our guesses.
The guesses are hypotheses; I will call them particular hypotheses
because, unlike the general hypotheses I shall speak of later, their
reference is only to the text we are trying to understand. With respect to this, they are, before they have been tested, merely tentative
answers to the question. Is it possible that the writer composed the
text as he did in order to convey such-and-such a meaning? For
example (to stay with the passage in *Piers Plowman*), could the
poet have intended his images to be taken literally, as elements
in a simple landscape setting for what was to come later in the poem?
Or did he mean them to be understood symbolically, as substitutes
for ideas beyond themselves? And if the latter, what were the particular concepts he meant them to stand for? Is it possible that his
design was to represent the two ways of life open to men on earth:
the one, governed by truth and charity, that would lead upward
to heaven and God; the other, dominated by falsehood and self-
seeking, that would lead downward toward hell and the Devil?
Or did he have in mind, as the symbolic point of the lines, the
patristic and medieval contrast between the two cities of Jerusalem
and Babylon, with the various levels of spiritual meaning associated

---

[2] I am aware that explicit meanings are assigned to these images later in the poem.
Cf. the speech of Lady Holy Church at the beginning of Passus I. But the latter passage
in turn, of course, raises questions of interpretation.

with each of them and with the implied conception of human life as ideally a pilgrimage from the second city to the first? Or are there still other possibilities that ought to be considered in subjecting these conjectures to critical examination?

Now there are two closely related and widely prevalent assumptions about particular interpretative hypotheses and their verification which are clearly at odds with what I have just been saying. Neither assumption, so far as I know, has ever been explicitly stated and defended, but both of them have governed, however unconsciously, a considerable part of the modern literature of "interpretation."

The first is the assumption that certain hypotheses, or kinds of hypotheses, contain in themselves, by virtue of their nature or origin and quite apart from the immediate facts of the case, a greater likelihood of proving correct than other hypotheses relative to the same text. For example, it might be held that it is antecedently more probable that the poet of *Piers Plowman* intended the landscape in his opening vision to be understood symbolically rather than literally and that I would be justified in presuming this even if I had never read more of the poem than the lines in question. Let us call this assumption the doctrine of the privileged hypothesis and ask ourselves what warrant, if any, it has.

Frequently, it must be said, the only discoverable warrant is the force of critical fashion; and on this we need not dwell—no one could sensibly argue that a hypothesis attributing "Christ images" to a work void of any signs of a religious intention is nevertheless made plausible by the fact that interpretations of this sort happen to enjoy nowadays a special vogue. A more respectable reason, however, can be given for thinking some hypotheses better than others prior to any critical scrutiny of their relevance to a particular work. It is an obvious fact that the more we know of the ideas and literary practices of a given period or author the better able we are to frame hypotheses about one of the productions of this period or author which have a chance of surviving our subsequent tests. And this seems to justify us in assuming that a given hypothesis has a greater antecedent chance of being correct than any others pertaining to the same problem merely because it accords more completely with what our previous conceptions of the writer and his age have led us to expect.

Here, I think, a distinction needs to be made. We very often rule out hypotheses, which we might otherwise have been willing to entertain, as far-fetched or even impossible in the light of our general historical or literary knowledge apart from any special study of the text; and the greater this knowledge the greater is our warrant for doing this. Even the least learned student would laugh if it were suggested that the writer of *Piers Plowman* meant his "towr on a toft" and his "dungeon" to stand for the opposed principles of "Marxism-Leninism" and "Imperialism"; for this presupposes a background of ideas completely foreign, so far as anyone knows, to the Middle Ages, and he would reject it out of hand because he could not imagine the existence of any evidence in its favor. Not all cases in which we make such negative a priori judgments are as clear as this; the imputation of anachronism to a certain hypothesis may be merely a sign of the incompleteness of our general knowledge. Subject to due caution in its application, however, the principle is sound enough: the task of the interpreter is to choose among possible explanations of his texts without wasting his time on explanations patently impossible. Now the hypotheses concerning the lines in *Piers Plowman* listed above are clearly of the former type. They all have some possibility of being true, in the sense that they contradict no known facts about medieval ways of thinking or writing and that some evidence for all of them may at least conceivably exist. The problem, accordingly, is whether we can make positive a priori judgments of their comparative explanatory value with respect to our text. Can we say, on the basis merely of our general knowledge of the Middle Ages aside from *Piers Plowman* itself, that any one of them has a greater chance of accounting adequately for the poet's intention in writing the lines than any of the others? I think not, and for reasons which should be fairly easy to see.

It cannot be a question here of invoking some universal law from which the favored particular hypothesis can be shown to be a necessary deduction; for history, unfortunately, knows of no such thing. At first sight, however, there seems to be another possibility. In any period of history, for all the diversity which it presents to specialists if not to the writers and readers of textbooks, historians with sufficiently wide learning can be trusted to discriminate between those collective developments which engaged the interest of many writers or thinkers and those other developments which affected only a few. And this appears to justify us in expecting more in advance from a hypothesis about a particular work or passage that reflects a widespread contemporary mode of thought or writing than from one that reflects only a minor trend. Thus in reading the vision literature of the Middle Ages I find many more occurrences of obviously symbolic landscapes than of obviously literal ones; and I think it only natural to infer from this that the second of my two main hypotheses about the passage in *Piers Plowman* has a greater antecedent probability than the first.

Now in one sense of "probability" this is so. Just as there are more chances of death within the next ten years for a man of seventy than for a man of thirty-five, so there are more chances that a landscape in a medieval vision poem will require a symbolic reading than that it will permit a merely literal one. But this kind of probability is merely statistical; it applies only to classes of things and never to individuals within those classes. Although such probabilities are useful in inventing hypotheses, they cannot properly be given any deciding weight in our inquiries into particular matters of fact in history or literary criticism; these have to do wholly with individual happenings and productions—with the actual dates of death of John Peter (aged 35) and Peter Thomas (aged 70) or with the actual intention reflected in the landscape at the beginning of *Piers Plowman;* and for all such inquiries the only safe guiding maxim is Hume's "What is most probable [statistically speaking] in human affairs, is not always true." We can of course assign varying degrees of probability to our conclusions after we have weighed the relevant evidence; but this is particular historical probability and is relative only to the facts of the text we are studying; it cannot inhere in the hypotheses which facilitated our search for the facts. For unless we can say (as we never can) that all vision poets in the Middle Ages necessarily intended all their descriptions of landscape to be understood symbolically, it is indifferent whether we say that this was true of most of them or of many of them or of some of them or of only a few of them; there is no power in any of these propositions to give us the slightest advance assurance that it was true of this particular landscape in this particular vision poem by this particular poet—only the evidence of the poem can decide that. It is fairly clear, I think, that the landscape in *Piers Plowman* was intended symbolically, but I say this for reasons quite independent of the high statistical probability of my hypothesis. No hypothesis can increase the probability of a conclusion of fact reached with its aid, and, conversely, any solidly established conclusion of fact can destroy the antecedent statistical probability of any hypothesis incompatible with it. We know, thus, that the patristic cliché of the two symbolic cities and the symbolic pilgrimage from one to the other was unquestionably familiar to most educated people in the Middle Ages; we are therefore predisposed to think that the poet of *Piers Plowman* probably intended to evoke the same traditional religious meanings in his description of the tower, the dungeon, and the field full of folk. But suppose now that we were to discover irrefutable proof that he actually intended nothing of the sort. What would then become of the superior probability we had ascribed to our hypothesis? The moral is that we should cease to attribute higher or lower degrees of probability to hypotheses as such, as if they were principles or premises of proof, and be content to think of them only as expendable guesses—necessary means of getting ahead in our inquiries, but with no capacity in themselves for affecting the results.

The second common assumption about hypotheses is a corollary of the first, since it treats a hypothesis as, in effect, an already partly established thesis and conceives of the remaining stage in the inquiry as a search for further confirmation of its truth rather than as a critical examination of its claims. I have never seen this view expounded by any respectable logician or theorist of method, but it patently governs the practice of many literary scholars and of perhaps a majority of those who publish "interpretations" of texts. We may call it the doctrine of the sufficiency of positive corroboration. A hypothesis is thought to be "confirmed" if particulars can be found within the text or outside it which either harmonize with it or can be construed to harmonize with it; and the more such particulars the interpreter can discover, the greater his assurance that his case is "proved." In this respect he resembles a lawyer intent only on finding such evidence as will support his brief; in both cases, though for different reasons, the guiding principle is a will to believe.

How inconsistent this is with the view of hypotheses I have argued for above can be readily seen: if a hypothesis in interpretation is only a tentative guess at one possible meaning or form of a given text, with no advance guarantee that it will provide a more accurate or adequate explanation of the text than any alternative guess, it is clearly inadmissible for a critic to rest the case for his own preferred guess merely on the fact that some or even many of the details in the text appear to lend it credence. For this is true also of any alternative hypothesis that another critic might advance; without at least some apparent support in the details of the passage or work he would hardly have ventured to put his guess into print. There have been many widely variant or even contradictory interpretations of *Hamlet,* for example; but I know of none, however absurd I may think it to be, for which the writer has not been able to find an ample body of according evidence in Shakespeare's text. And the reason is very simple. All literary texts are ambiguous in the sense that more than one cause or intention, and hence more than one meaning, can be attributed with greater or less plausibility to them, from particular sentences or passages up to the overall combination of these. There will thus be for any text a plurality of entertainable hypotheses about its writer's intentions, for all of which their proponents can adduce confirmatory indications, more or less abundant. From this it follows, not that one interpretation is as good as any other, but merely that something more than positive evidence is required to establish any one of them as superior in explanatory power to its rivals. Positive evidence is obviously necessary, but by itself, unchecked by a consideration of alternative possibilities, it can never suffice.

But not only is the prevalent faith in the adequacy of positive evidence unfounded, it tends also to obscure, in the minds of critics who cherish it, the all-important distinction between interpretation and fact. The will to believe is a dreadfully insidious thing; and when the belief is in something of our own making, such as the new explanation we have just thought of for a difficult and much controverted text, the temptation to find as much confirmatory evidence for it as possible is hard to resist. There will usually be particulars in our text which are hard to bring into line, and these we will either pass over in silence or rule out as irrelevant. But very commonly there will likewise be other particulars which, though useless to us given only the literal sense which their immediate context dictates, can yet with a little construction be made to fit our hypothesis; and with respect to these, our natural impulse, if we are true believers, will be to give the hypothesis the benefit of the doubt. A good example is the maxim of Gulliver's Houyhnhnm master in Part IV of the *Travels:* "reason alone is sufficient to govern a rational creature" (chapter 7). The literal sense of "reason alone" in this context is unmistakably "reason" unaided in its operations by the external directives and controls of laws and government. This is the objective fact, about which all disinterested interpreters of Swift's text must agree. But the phrase "reason alone," taken by itself, can also be construed as meaning "reason without revelation;" and it can be argued—and in fact has been argued by several recent critics—that if, as they are convinced, Swift's main intention in creating the Houyhnhnms was to denigrate the deists, he would undoubtedly have wanted his readers to understand the phrase in this religious sense. Thus interpreted the phrase can be used as confirmatory evidence for their hypothesis, but clearly at the cost of a vicious circularity in the argument: the fact becomes evidence for the hypothesis only by virtue of an interpretation the sole warrant for which is the hypothesis it is then used to support. And it is hard to see how such circularity can be avoided so long as critics think it sufficient to look only for confirmatory evidence and have a stronger desire to preserve their hypotheses than to account completely and convincingly for the facts. The literature of "interpretation" abounds, alas, with arguments in which it has not been avoided. (For more on this matter apropos of Swift, see *PQ*, 40 [1961]: 427–30.)

From all this two main inferences can be drawn about the proper conduct of our interpretative inquiries. The first follows from the character of hypotheses as merely expendable conjectures, whose only use is to facilitate understanding of the literary facts. We will be skeptical of any conclusion that presupposes the truth of the hypothesis which has led to its discovery, and we will admit as supporting evidence, accordingly, only such particulars within the text or outside it as do not depend in any way on the exigencies of our theory for the meanings we attribute to them. In other words, we will look upon any of our inquiries as a process of first setting up hypotheses and then of emancipating ourselves as completely as we can from their tyranny. For most of us such emancipation is not easy. What it demands is the contrary of the common attitude mentioned above; namely, a strong will to *dis*believe our own as well as other peoples' conjectures until, after a serious independent examination of the facts, that disbelief is no longer rationally possible. We need to assume, in short, that the correct interpretation is more likely to be one forced on us against our initial expectations or hopes than the one our original hypothesis envisaged. This may not be so; our first guess may turn out to be right; but the working presumption that it has a better than even chance of being wrong is our best assurance that we will not accept it as right merely because it is ours. By "right" I do not mean "proved" in any strict sense; there can be no such thing as certainty in the interpretation of texts; demonstration is out of the question; the most we can hope for, if we are lucky, is a high degree of probability. But we can at least aim at conclusions which other scholars will find hard to dismiss as merely hypothetical impositions on the texts.

The second inference follows from the fact that, as we have seen, there are very few texts so unambiguous as not to permit alternative interpretations, for all of which at least some positive evidence can be found. Our problem, accordingly, is to determine which one of these—or what combination of compatible conjectures—best represents the author's actual intention (that is, his effective intention in the sense of the principle governing what he wrote). How can we do this? The ideal is to be able to say—and to say convincingly to both ourselves and other scholars—about any interpretation of a given text, not merely that *if* its author's intention was such-and-such, he might very well have written as he did—that is still only hypothesis—but that *only if* his intention was such-and-such would he in all probability have written as he did. We can seldom hope to be able to say this, but the formula may still serve as a criterion for judging our own and others' arguments, and it can help us to see what is involved in any successful attempt to move, in interpretation, from tentative hypotheses to substantiated conclusions. The process is commonly referred to as one of confirmation, verification, or proof, but these are misleading words when understood in their ordinary acceptations, for they then inevitably suggest the erroneous identification of hypotheses with partly established theses which I discussed above and hence tend to blind the interpreter to the possibility of other hypotheses that may be as deserving of consideration as his own. Moreover, if confirmation, in this positive sense, is his aim, he will seldom fail in achieving it, whatever the actual case may be. We need to view the process, therefore, rather as one of critical examination or testing, in which the emphasis, as in good medical diagnosis, is on the discovery of facts or other considerations which, if they exist, would have the effect of invalidating our hypothesis or forcing us to modify it more or less radically. Only if we fail in this self-denying effort can we have any justified confidence in our conclusions.

To avoid failing prematurely, we need to do two things, which together constitute the technique of critical testing. One is to treat any alternative hypotheses as if they were of our own devising, and marshal as much evidence as we can find in support of each of them: even if it turns out eventually that our own theory explains more of the relevant facts and is open to fewer objections, we shall, by doing this, be better able to assess justly its comparative powers and limitations. The other part of the procedure is the opposite of this: we here treat our own hypothesis as if it had been proposed by some one else and do our best to refute or qualify it by looking for relevant facts with which it is inconsistent wholly or in part. The chances are we will find some, but even if none can be found, we will be a step farther along the road away from hypothesis and toward fact.

There is an excellent brief statement of this view of "proof" in Sir Karl Popper's *The Poverty of Historicism* (London, 1957), pp. 133–34; see also his *Conjectures and Refutations* (London, 1963); it is no less pertinent to literary interpretation than to the empirical sciences which Popper had chiefly in view:

> The result of tests is the *selection* of hypotheses which have stood up to tests, or the *elimination* of those hypotheses which have not stood up to them, and are therefore rejected. It is important to realize the consequences of this view. They are these: all tests can be interpreted as attempts to weed out false theories—to find the weak points of a theory in order to reject it if it is falsified by the test. This view is sometimes considered paradoxical; our aim, it is said, is to establish theories, not to eliminate false ones. But just because it is our aim to establish theories as well as we can, we must test them as severely as we can; that is, we must try to find fault with them, we must try to falsify them. Only if we cannot falsify them in spite of our best efforts can we say that they have stood up to severe tests. This is the reason why the discovery of instances which confirm a theory means very little if we have not tried, and failed, to discover refutations. For if we are uncritical we shall

always find what we want; we shall look for, and find, confirmations, and we shall look away from, and not see, whatever might be dangerous to our pet theories. In this way it is only too easy to obtain what appears to be overwhelming evidence in favour of a theory which, if approached critically, would have been refuted. In order to make the method of selection by elimination work, and to ensure that only the fittest theories survive, their struggle for life must be made severe.

This may seem a counsel of perfection, but it is actually only a summary of what happens in the history of successful inquiry on a given problem. A scholar proposes and argues for a certain hypothesis; objections are brought against it by other scholars on the basis of new evidence or old evidence ignored or misconstrued in the original argument; still other alternative or supplementary hypotheses are put forward and criticized in the same way; finally, perhaps, a consensus is reached on the questions at issue, at least for the time being. The life of scholarship, in other words, is the perpetual making of guesses followed by the perpetual criticizing of them; and the ideal scholar is he who reproduces this sequence most completely in his own practice.

I now want to apply these general considerations about hypotheses to the Robertson school of medievalists. But first let me make explicit the general assumption about the nature of interpretation which underlies what I have been saying. I have been taking for granted, first, that interpretative hypotheses are hypotheses of historical fact and, second, that they presuppose an individual designing intellect (the historically conditioned author) as the sole proximate cause of the meanings to be ascribed to the words of a text, so that the prime task of the interpreter is to distinguish between those meanings which are more and those which are less likely to have been what the writer wanted to convey. This is of course the traditional scholarly view; it explains why no scholar would take seriously the Marxist gloss on the lines of *Piers Plowman* mentioned earlier. It is not the only possible view, however, or the view most commonly to be met with nowadays among critics. The current tendency is rather to define "meaning" in literature in ways that separate it, more or less completely, from the directing aims of individual writers: it is "what the author's contemporaries would ideally have construed, what the ideal present-day reader construes, what the norms of language permit the text to mean, what the best critics conceive to be the best meaning, and so on" (E. D. Hirsch, Jr., in *PMLA*, 75 [1960]: 466; the article is an admirably reasoned defense of the conception of interpretation I am presupposing here). Now it makes no sense to argue that either of these views is more nearly correct than the other; they are merely different, the first conceiving of meaning in literature as something created and expressed by writers, the second as something received and more or less recreated by readers (as, for instance, "meaning for us"); and who is to say that a text does not have these two aspects of meaning? Yet one or the other view must be assumed in any given inquiry if our interpretation of a text is to be logically coherent. We may call this assumption, which may or may not be made explicit, a general hypothesis of method: it determines in no way the content of our particular hypotheses, but merely the character and range of the questions we will ask in framing them and hence the kinds of evidence required in testing our preliminary answers.

I dwell on this point because it would be obviously unfair to criticize the "Robertsonian" medievalists by standards alien to their own. As it happens, however, their basic methodological assumption is the same as that presupposed in this discussion: they too conceive of interpretation as a matter-of-fact, causal inquiry into the effective intentions of writers as conditioned by the circumstances of their times. What I find reprehensible in them is simply that their characteristic use of hypotheses is incompatible with a successful working out of this controlling conception.

I will start by making another distinction, suggested by the word most commonly used to describe the collective effort of these scholars. The word is "approach"; they have given us, it is said, a new "approach" to the study of medieval literature. The term occurs frequently in their own writings: Robertson and Huppé, in the Preface to their *Piers Plowman and the Scriptural Tradition*, speak of the "basic ideas and attitudes underlying our approach"; Robertson elsewhere refers to "the approach advocated here"; and there are repeated uses of the word, along with such synonyms as "method," "kind of criticism," and "discipline," in R. E. Kaske's defense of the school in the recent English Institute symposium on *Critical Approaches to Medieval Literature*.

Now by itself this manner of speaking doesn't tell one very much beyond the fact that what is being alluded to is some kind of specialization. The important question is what kind; and there are two radically different possibilities, to both of which the term "approach" has come to be applied in current scholarly slang.

To say of a scholar that he is primarily a textual critic or primarily a formal or technical critic or primarily a literary historian is to define his peculiar "approach" merely in terms of the special aspect of literary works that he is habitually most interested in investigating and explaining; the difference between the two points of view in interpretation referred to above is likewise a difference of "approach" in this first sense. Such specialization predetermines only the kind of problems the scholar will normally prefer to deal with; it leaves completely open the question of what particular hypotheses he will find most useful in solving them; and it involves him in no theoretical opposition to other "approaches" of the same sort.

To say, however, that some one is a Freudian or archetypal or "myth" critic or a Marxist literary historian is to define his "approach" in a very different way: in terms not of a preferred set of problems but of a preferred principle of explanation—the special order of causes or theory about these which he will habitually invoke, to the exclusion of others, in formulating and justifying his conclusions. Such specialization is much more narrowly determinative of results than the other kind, for as long as the scholar remains loyal to his favorite explanatory principle, he will be disposed to frame all his particular hypotheses in harmony with it; his "approach" to that extent is a closed one (the convinced Freudian interpreter may eventually lose his faith, but until he does we can almost always predict the sort of thing he will say). What then of the "Robertsonians"? It is significant that the adjectives which both they and their critics have most often used to describe their special interests are all specifications not of problems or objects of study but of principles of explanation: "patristic," "exegetical," "symbolic," "pan-allegorical." Their "approach" thus seems to be of the second type; and this is borne out by the two most explicit manifestos of the school: Robertson and Huppé's chapter on "The Method" in their book on *Piers Plowman* and Robertson's essay on "Historical Criticism" in *English Institute*

Essays, 1950. It will be well to look somewhat closely at what they say there.

"Historical criticism," according to Robertson, is a rather new thing; in actual practice not a great deal of it has been written. It is to be distinguished not only from non-historical criticism (with its context of modern notions) but from literary history and the history of ideas. It differs from the former in being concerned with "intellectual" rather than "purely literary" traditions and from the latter in aspiring to go beyond a concentration on particular concepts and patterns of ideas. It is "that kind of literary analysis which seeks to reconstruct the intellectual attitudes and the cultural ideals of a period in order to reach a fuller understanding of its literature." The "historical critic" attempts to form "a workable conception of the intellectual background of a period as a whole, so that the various ideas he has to deal with may be considered in perspective." Such knowledge, he assumes, will "contribute to a better understanding" of the literary productions of that period.

All this looks innocent enough until we read the rest of Robertson's essay and the opening chapter of his and Huppé's work on *Piers Plowman* and observe what is said there about the "intellectual background" of the Middle Ages "as a whole" and the bearing of this on the interpretation of medieval poetic texts. The argument runs as follows. The central fact in the intellectual and literary life of this period was "the dominance of the Church" and its teaching; and the primary and almost exclusive end of this teaching was "the promotion of *caritas,* the love of God and of one's neighbor," and by the same token the discouragement of *cupiditas,* the love of one's self. This was the "most fundamental doctrine of medieval Christianity"; and since the Bible was universally held to teach nothing but charity and to condemn nothing but cupidity, the interpretation of the Bible in this all-important sense continued to be the absorbing preoccupation of learned men throughout the Middle Ages. The prevailing mode of this exegesis had been fixed in the patristic period. It had been recognized very early that large portions of the Scriptures, in the Old Testament especially, set forth the message of charity in very obscure terms, so that many people tended to doubt that it was there at all. In all such cases its presence in the sacred text had to be demonstrated by a technique of interpretation designed to penetrate beneath the *cortex,* or surface meaning of the text, to its *nucleus,* or hidden spiritual meaning; and for this purpose there was introduced the notion of three levels of meaning, or devices of interpretation, besides the literal—the allegorical, tropological, and anagogical. In the course of the Middle Ages, this type of exegesis was extended to other writings besides the Scriptures and was regularly taught and practiced in the schools, to the extent at least that all students were instructed to look beyond the words and their literal meanings of the books they read to the *sententia,* or higher meaning, simple or complex, which these concealed.

Now it is only reasonable to expect (so the argument concludes) that these developments in the religious teaching of the Middle Ages would have had a decisive influence in shaping the substance and method of medieval Christian poetry (in the sense of poetry, whether religious or secular, written by authors who were Christians). It is only natural to suppose that, having been taught to look for a higher level or levels of meaning in what they read, poets would deliberately compose their works in a way calling for the same kind of allegorical or symbolic interpretation. It is natural to suppose also that, being Christians, they would write, literally or allegorically, on only one great theme—the Christian message of charity; and finally, that in doing so they would almost certainly avail themselves of the great storehouse of symbolic or "spiritual" meanings for persons, places, objects, and actions provided by the rich tradition of Scriptural exegesis, with its controlling assumption that all references to such things (for example, to the cities of Babylon and Jerusalem) must be understood as signifying either a positive or a negative aspect of the central Christian truth.

The nature of "historical criticism," as Robertson conceives it, should now perhaps be clear. What he gives us, as "a workable conception of the intellectual background" of the Middle Ages "as a whole," is no inventory of the many different "intellectual" traditions at work in that period which the student of its literature ought to know about, but a formula assigning to one such tradition—the "Scriptural," "patristic," "exegetical" tradition—an architectonic status with respect to all particular intellectual and literary developments of the age. This, he seems to imply, if only by his silence concerning anything else that happened during these many centuries, *is* the Middle Ages, at least so far as the critic of medieval literary texts is concerned. The historian Etienne Gilson is reported to have remarked once in a lecture that there were as many distinct major medieval philosophies as there were major medieval philosophers; but there is little or nothing of this differentiating spirit among the "Robertsonians," who seldom hesitate to talk of such entities as *"the* Christian doctrine of charity," *"the* medieval conception of allegory," and especially *"the* medieval poem." This last Robertson has defined as follows: "It had a lying surface meaning (*cortex*) covering an inner truth (*nucleus*). The surface meaning (*cortex* or *sensus*) might be interpreted to reveal a doctrinal truth (*sententia*) which was, in Christian poetry, always an aspect of charity" (*SP,* 48 [1951]: 691).

The ultimate concern of the "historical critic," however, is "a fuller understanding" of particular literary texts, and the essence of the new "method" Robertson has proposed is the assumption that such understanding will be greatly facilitated if the critic brings to his texts the kind of unified formulation of the thought of his period "as a whole" which Robertson himself has devised for the Middle Ages. "When the method is applied," he says, "literary works which have hitherto seemed incoherent or meaningless become consistent, meaningful, and artistically attractive." And again: "a Christian poem may contain a description of a garden based on signs taken from both Genesis and the Canticum and dressed up to suit the literary tastes of the poet's own audience. The result is a *pictura* which is fundamentally Biblical, but which does not resemble any Biblical scene and does not contain any Biblical phrases. There are gardens of this kind in Old English literature, in the romances, in the *Roman de la Rose,* in Chaucer, in *Piers Plowman,* and in a great many other places, but it is impossible to detect their presence except by the methods of historical criticism" (that is, the application to these texts of the propositions about medieval poetry and its background summarized above). And we can know in the same way that the pilgrims to Canterbury "are actually pilgrims to Jerusalem, except for the Pardoner."

Thus the "workable conception" of medieval thought "as a whole" which the historical critic must attempt to form becomes for him a principle of explanation applicable to all medieval poetic texts, to be used as other contemporary critics have used the scientific or pseudo-scientific concepts they have taken over from Freud, Jung, Frazer, or Marx. The difference is that here there is no science or even pseudo-science to borrow from; the interpretative principles of "historical criticism" are not general laws but particular constructs, varying in content from period to period and arrived at by assigning to a certain sequence or pattern of happenings in a given period, such as the tradition of scriptural exegesis in the Middle Ages, a greater explanatory value with respect to its literature than to any of the others. But the logical model is the same, the model of the "privileged hypothesis": given his principle, the "historical critic" can then predict what is more likely than not to be the case with any individual literary productions of his period he may be about to study for the first time. He can assume, thus, that he has a general warrant for approaching all medieval poems in terms of Robertson's paradigm for "the medieval poem" cited above, or something similar to that; that he is justified accordingly in treating the "surface" or literal meanings of all of them not as ends in themselves but as means to the expression of other "hidden" or "allegorical" meanings which reflect the "real" intentions of their authors; that he is not likely to err if he interprets these deeper meanings as assertions of "the message of charity or some corollary of it"; and that he can safely construe the signs by which they are expressed by looking for parallels in the literature of biblical exegesis from Augustine on.

What I have said thus far about the "exegetical approach" is based on statements, mainly by Robertson himself, written a decade or more ago. Since then this "approach" has been subjected to rather severe scrutiny by a number of competent medievalists, including Morton Bloomfield, Talbot Donaldson, Robert Frank, Charles Donahue, Theodore Silverstein, and John Lawlor. Their criticism has been directed in part against particular applications of the "method," notably to texts in Chaucer and *Piers Plowman,* but it has also done much to damage one of its original presuppositions by showing that Robertson and others had greatly underestimated the concern of biblical exegetes in the Middle Ages for the literal meanings of scriptural texts and had greatly exaggerated the vogue of the so-called "four-fold" technique of interpretation even for the Bible and certainly for writings of a merely human inspiration.

It is hard for me to assess the effects of these objections on those already committed to the "approach"; I can see little evidence, however, that they have led to any radical conversions. R. E. Kaske's recent English Institute essay "in defense" of the school (in *Critical Approaches to Medieval Literature*) is indeed rather more restrained in its claims than the earlier statements cited above. He leaves open, for example, the "large problem" of the extent to which medieval writers employed "creatively the famous 'four levels' of biblical exegesis." And he lays down criteria for judging whether "exegetical meanings" are actually present in medieval poems which are unexceptionable as far as they go. On the other hand, his program for future research on the influence of the "exegetical tradition" is clearly based on a conviction, no less strong than Robertson's, that its influence is there to be found and in more abundant measure than has so far been suspected. He acknowledges, for example, that there are faults in Robertson and Huppé's book on *Piers Plowman* but attributes them mainly to the fact that theirs was a pioneer effort. "An interpretation of *Piers Plowman,* supported by whatever is most relevant from the immense and still imperfectly conquered exegetical tradition, is hardly a task to be begun *ex nihilo* by two scholars and brought to perfection within the covers of a single book; if it were, the book would be one we might all have to get a year's grant to read. ... It seems less accurate, then, to say that the approach to *Piers Plowman* by way of the exegetical tradition has failed, than that it has not yet been painstakingly tried." (Is he here implying that if it were "painstakingly tried," it would *not* fail?) "What we need first," he says in another passage, "is a really prodigious amount of minute, systematic research centered on individual medieval works, *with the immediate aim of showing* the precise contributions made by the exegetical tradition to the meaning of descriptive details, figures of speech, characters, limited passages, and so on" (italics mine). The essence of the "approach"—its commitment to a special principle of explanation—thus remains intact; and I will not, therefore, be merely caviling about a position no longer held if I venture to add to the technical criticisms currently being made of the findings of these scholars a more general criticism of their "method" itself, especially as this determines their conception and use of hypotheses in the historical interpretation of texts.

The main point to be considered here is the logical status of the contention which distinguishes them as a school—that knowledge of the allegorical tradition of biblical exegesis is indispensable to a full understanding of medieval poetry in both its doctrinal and its technical aspects. Taken by itself, apart from the use it has been put to in arguments about particular poems, this is clearly a hypothesis of the sort described in the first part of this paper; that is to say, a tentative guess, suggested by a limited body of observations, about something that may possibly be true of poems not yet examined; a warrant, in short, for looking to see whether this is the case or not. In the present state of detailed research in the field, it can hardly be more than that. What differentiates it from the interpretative hypotheses discussed earlier is simply the fact that it is general or collective rather than particular in its reference, constructed with a view to explaining not one poem but many in terms of a cause—the "exegetical tradition"— capable of producing widely disseminated effects.

Viewed in this light, the contention of the Robertsonians is comparable to many other proposals for new lines of literary inquiry, in this and other periods, which have been put forward by scholars during the present century: the hypothesis of the Celtic origins of Arthurian romance, for example, or Bédier's theory of the *chansons de geste*, or the ideas of Croll and Williamson about the development of seventeenth-century prose style, or the pioneer work of Lovejoy on the "great chain of being" and other ruling notions in European literature since 1600. Some of the many initiatives of this sort have proved less fruitful than others; many of them have led only to dead ends; and most of them, as research has proceeded, have suffered modification in more or less radical ways. But of all such hypotheses, and whatever their fate, it must be said that we are the better off for their having been proposed; at the very least they have been challenges to inquiry and critical thought. It is always better, as Augustus De Morgan said, to have a bad hypothesis than no hypothesis at all, for in the latter case no research is possible, whereas in the former, if we are critical-minded enough, the hypothesis, however wild in itself, may lead us to discoveries we would otherwise have missed.

When we consider the "exegetical approach" to medieval literature from this point of view—as a general working hypothesis or exploratory hunch, to be used, along with other similar leading ideas, for what it may turn out to be worth—I think we can only welcome it. It is certainly a good thing to have had our attention called so vigorously to the potential value for the study of medieval poetry of the rich store of symbolic materials contained in the writings of the biblical exegetes.

This is not quite the way, however—if we may judge by what they have written—that the Robertsonians themselves look upon their central hypothesis or would encourage their pupils to look upon it. It is hard to detect much scholarly tentativeness either in their general statements of the "method" or in their applications of it to poems. They have not been content with saying merely that knowledge of the "exegetical tradition" promises to cast much fresh light on the meanings of many medieval poems and hence that the texts embodying this tradition deserve far closer study by literary scholars than they have received so far. This would have been a general historical hypothesis of a properly heuristic kind, suggesting many particular interpretative hypotheses about individual poems that might not otherwise have occurred to students, but leaving open the question of their relevance and explanatory power in any given case. The actual claim of the Robertsonians, however, has been considerably less modest, as I think must be clear from what has been said already about the "basic ideas and attitudes underlying" their "approach." On the one hand, they have presented the "exegetical tradition" not simply as one important and neglected element in the general "intellectual background" of medieval poetry but as, in effect, the one "background" essential for understanding that poetry, thus giving it priority over other possible sources of literary inspiration in this period. On the other hand, they have assumed its relevance, as the essential explanatory principle, not merely to many medieval poems, but to "all serious poetry" of the Middle Ages "written by Christian authors, even that usually called 'secular'" (Robertson, in *English Institute Essays* [1950]). They have thus transformed what is at most only a general working hypothesis— one capable of suggesting particular hypotheses about the possible meanings and devices of medieval poems, which then have to be tested independently—into a ruling hypothesis, or what my colleague, Elder Olson, has called a subsumptive hypothesis. Any particular reading of a given text, if it is found to harmonize with the ruling hypothesis, will have conferred upon it a privileged status. Although it may require, as a particular hypothesis, some support in the form of evidence from the text, it will not seem to require the kind of testing that will be applied, as a matter of course, to all interpretations—that is, to particular hypotheses—that are not easily subsumed under the general view. And since, as we have seen, supporting evidence is almost always available, every work will seem to validate, when read "properly," the interpreter's ruling hypothesis.

This subsumptive procedure, which of course is not peculiar to the Robertsonians, is made all the more necessary for them by one article of their historical faith which I have alluded to earlier. This is the doctrine summed up in Robertson's description of the medieval Christian poem as a composition having "a lying surface meaning" (its *cortex*) "covering an inner truth" (its *nucleus*), which was always an aspect of *caritas;* this inner truth may be an explicit part of the surface meaning, in which case there is no problem for the critic, or it may be hidden beneath the surface meaning, in which case it must be discovered by allegorical interpretation guided by knowledge of the spiritual senses which the various concrete objects and persons in the *cortex* of the poem had been given in the tradition of scriptural exegesis. The modern interpreter of medieval poetry *must* be provided with such a general rule if he is, in the first place, to be sure that a hidden spiritual meaning is actually embodied in, say, this romance of chivalric adventure and, in the second place, to be able to construe the allegory correctly with respect to the particular aspect of charity it is concerned with. But given the rule, the problem is largely solved for him. It is impossible, as Robertson says in a passage quoted above, to detect the hidden spiritual meanings of the various gardens to be met with in many medieval poems of different genres "except by the methods of historical criticism," but once the poems are read with these methods in mind, he implies, the truth becomes clear. And so similarly with this statement that the pilgrimage to Canterbury is "actually" a pilgrimage to Jerusalem; this interpretation is clearly not forced on us by the "lying surface" of Chaucer's text; we can know it to be correct, and a literal hypothesis about the poet's meaning wrong, only—here again—"by the methods of historical criticism." In both instances, that is to say, any compulsion we may feel to accept the "exegetical" interpretations comes not from the facts of the case but from the hypothesis by which our understanding of those facts is to be governed. This we must believe —given the postulated nature of "medieval poetry"—before we can think ourselves competent interpreters of any medieval poems we may be interested in studying. Some such necessity as this, I think, is inseparable from any "approach" to the interpretation of texts that can be described, as this has been described, as "symbolic" or "pan-allegorical." But the inevitable consequence is to emancipate the practitioners of all such "approaches" from the ordinary obligations of scholarly proof. For no hypothesis of fact is capable of being "proved" if it is so conceived as to make "disproof" impossible even when the facts are against it. How can any hypothesis be refuted by an appeal to facts when, as here, the facts we have to appeal to— namely, the literal statements of the text, its *cortex*—are by definition irrelevant to a determination of its "real" meaning, which is hidden from the eyes of all except "historical critics" in the Robertsonian sense of that word?

It may be objected that I am overlooking an important considera- tion. It is certainly true that there have been many general hypotheses —Darwin's on the origin of species is one of them—which, though at first only venturesome guesses requiring a vast amount of subsequent testing, have nevertheless in the course of time, and after undergoing various modifications, achieved the status of accepted theories to which investigators can appeal as a warrant for preferring certain explanations of newly observed facts to others. Why may not some- thing like this be in store for the Robertsonian hypothesis about medieval poetry and its causation, as it is applied successfully to more and more individual poems? This is clearly the expectation behind the proposals for further research outlined by R. E. Kaske in his re- cent essay. I reply that whereas the Darwinian hypothesis was of a kind that permitted falsification and hence genuine testing, this hy- pothesis is not. There is no way of showing it to be wrong with re- spect to any individual poem to which it is applicable, that is, any serious poem of the Middle Ages written by a Christian author. That is precluded by the assumption that if the message of charity is not explicitly present in a given poem of this class, it, or "some corollary of it," will be present allegorically, that is, "by interpretation" ac- cording to rules laid down in the hypothesis itself. I may, for example, argue that I can see no compelling evidence in the text of Chaucer for construing the very worldly pilgrimage to Canterbury as an allegory of the spiritual pilgrimage to Jerusalem; but I must expect to be told in rejoinder, "That shows that you don't really understand the nature of the Middle Ages or its poetry." And so the "method" moves on irresistibly from triumph to triumph.

I referred in the beginning to the "confusion" over the proper use of interpretative hypotheses which seems to me to characterize this school of medievalists. I also said that the same confusion was apparent in other fields of literary study. It is not my intention here to develop the latter point (for examples from recent studies of the eighteenth century, see *Reason and the Imagination: Studies in the History of Ideas, 1600–1800* [New York and London, 1962], pp. 231–42, and *PQ*, 40 [1961]: 427–30); but I should like to add one general remark on the nature of the confusion itself and its bearing on the practice of historical criticism.

For this purpose let me borrow, and use somewhat freely, Kant's distinction between "determinant" and "reflective" judgments. What is fundamentally wrong with the Robertsonians and all other schools of interpretation that approach texts from the vantage point of a single preferred principle of explanation is their unconscious craving for "determinant" judgments in a field where only "reflective" judgments are possible by reason of the contingent and unpredictable nature of the subject matter. A "determinant" judgment, according to Kant, is one in which the universal (the rule, the principle, the law, whatever it may be) is given and the particulars to be explained are then subsumed under it. A "reflective" judgment, on the other hand, is one in which only the particulars to be explained are given and the explanation has to be found by critical inquiry— by making many guesses and trying to rule out all those that do not fit. There is little enough critical inquiry of this sort in the work of the scholars we have been considering, and their principle of explanation is "given" only in the sense that they have assumed it.

What is the bearing of all this on the practice of what Robertson has called "historical criticism"? I mean by this essentially what he means, namely, a use of propositions about the cultural "milieu" or "background" of a literary work as a basis of inferences concerning its intentions and devices. I am as convinced as he is of the importance of such knowledge in literary interpretation. To say this, however, is not to say very much, for everything depends on how the problem of "background" is conceived and on how one goes about determining what is and is not the relevant "background" of a given work or writer. And here there are two opposed possibilities, which correspond roughly to Kant's "determinant" and "reflective" judgments. In the first view, the "background" the critic needs to study is something that he can know and make statements about without prior knowledge of the writer or work he proposes to interpret in the light of it, inasmuch as it represents influences and forces that operate on the writer from the outside, so to speak: his "age," his "society," his "cultural environment," his "tradition." We are all familiar with this conception of "background" in the general chapters on the intellectual, religious, social, and artistic environment of writers which many literary historians think it necessary or useful to prefix to their period surveys (as in several volumes of the Oxford History). There is usually little discernible relation between what is said in these "background" chapters and what is said about particular authors and works in the chapters that follow. But that need not be the case: a "background" conceived in the same way but normally emphasizing some one major development or conflict of ideas in a period may be constructed by the historian and then used by him in the interpretation of individual texts. The procedure of the Robertsonians is of this order, as is also that of Kathleen Williams in her recent book on *Jonathan Swift and the Age of Compromise* (where the last words of the title suggest what she is doing); and many other examples could be given. In all these cases the relevance of the chosen background to the writers and works it is used to explain is assumed in advance on the basis of considerations which have nothing to do except accidentally with the texts it is then applied to. It may be called for that reason a "postulated background"; and any particular interpretation of a text resulting from its use will be a "determinant" judgment arrived at by means of a subsumptive hypothesis.

The alternative possibility is exemplified in another recent book on Swift the title of which seems at first sight to imply a procedure similar to that of Miss Williams: Phillip Harth's *Swift and Anglican Rationalism*. But only at first sight: actually Harth's procedure is the reverse of Miss Williams'. His subject is the satire on "corruptions in religion" in *A Tale of a Tub;* and he starts not by positing "Anglican rationalism" in some abstract sense as the "proper" key to an understanding of this but by analyzing the text in its own terms, both grammatical and artistic, independently of any assumed background and then asking what possible antecedent or contemporary developments in the Church of England would explain most adequately the targets of Swift's attack, the assumptions motivating the attack, and the rhetorical devices by which it was elaborated. His inquiry led him to the hypothesis that the immediate effective background of this part of the *Tale* (but not of the other part on "corruptions in learning") was the propaganda of a particular group of Anglican divines of the mid-seventeenth century whom he decided to call, somewhat misleadingly perhaps, the "Anglican rationalists." In other words, the background he uses to interpret Swift's text is not one imposed on it a priori but one inferred from it a posteriori after an independent consideration of what in it calls for historical explanation: it is a discovered rather than a postulated background, and its discovery and use in interpretation involves the making only of "reflective" judgments arrived at by framing and testing hypotheses in the ordinary way. This is the direction I would be happy to see all historical criticism take.

The Houyhnhnms, the Yahoos, and
the History of Ideas

I SHALL BE CONCERNED in this essay with two ways of using the history of ideas—or, in the case of the first of them, as I shall argue, misusing it—in the historical interpretation of literary works. The particular issue I have in mind is forced on one in an unusually clear-cut manner, I think, by what has been said of the "Voyage to the Country of the Houyhnhnms" in the criticism of the past few decades; and for this reason, and also because I wish to add a theory of my own about Swift's satirical argument in that work to the theories now current, I base the discussion that follows almost exclusively on it.

1

With a very few exceptions (the latest being George Sherburn)[1] since the 1920's, and especially since the later 1930's, writers on the fourth Voyage have been mainly dominated by a single pre-

A paper read, in a somewhat different text, at Wadham College, Oxford, in April, 1959, before the Annual Conference of Non-professorial University Teachers of English of the British Isles. Published in *Reason and the Imagination: Essays in the History of Ideas, 1600–1800*, edited by Joseph R. Mazzeo (New York and London, 1962); reprinted by permission of the publishers, Columbia University Press and Routledge and Kegan Paul.

[1] See his "Errors Concerning the Houyhnhnms," *MP*, 56 (1958): 92–97. To this may now be added Edward Rosenheim, Jr.'s "The Fifth Voyage of Lemuel Gulliver: A Footnote," *MP*, 60 (1962): 103–19, and his *Swift and the Satirist's Art* (Chicago, 1963), *passim.*

occupation.[2] They have sought to correct the misunderstanding of Swift's purpose in the Voyage which had vitiated, in their opinion, most earlier criticism of it and, in particular, to defend Swift from the charge of all-out misanthropy that had been leveled against him so often in the past—by Thackeray, for example, but many others also—on the strength of Gulliver's wholesale identification of men with the Yahoos and his unqualified worship of the Houyhnhnms.

It is easy to see what this task would require them to do. It would require them to show that what Gulliver is made to say about human nature in the Voyage, which is certainly misanthropic enough, and what Swift wanted his readers to believe about human nature are, in certain crucial respects at any rate, two different and incompatible things. It would require them, that is, to draw a clear line between what is both Swift and Gulliver and what is only Gulliver in a text in which Gulliver alone is allowed to speak to us.

The resulting new interpretations have differed considerably in emphasis and detail from critic to critic, but they have been generally in accord on the following propositions: The attitudes of Swift and his hero do indeed coincide up to a certain point, it being true for Swift no less than for Gulliver that men in the mass are terrifyingly close to the Yahoos in disposition and behavior, and true for both of them also that the Houyhnhnms are in some of their qualities—their abhorrence of falsehood, for instance—proper models for human emulation. That, however, is about as far as the agreement goes: it is to Gulliver alone and not to Swift that we must impute the radical

2 The list of writings that reflect this preoccupation is now a fairly long one; in the present essay I have had in view chiefly the following: Ernest Bernbaum, "The Significance of 'Gulliver's Travels,'" in his edition of that work (New York, 1920); T. O. Wedel, "On the Philosophical Background of *Gulliver's Travels*," *SP*, 23 (1926): 434–50; John F. Ross, "The Final Comedy of Lemuel Gulliver," in *Studies in the Comic* (University of California Publications in English, Vol. VIII, No. 2, 1941), pp. 175–96; Robert B. Heilman, Introduction to his edition of *Gulliver's Travels* (New York, 1950), especially pp. xii–xxii; Ernest Tuveson, "Swift: The Dean as Satirist," *University of Toronto Quarterly*, 22 (1953): 368–75; Roland M. Frye, "Swift's Yahoo and the Christian Symbols for Sin," *JHI*, 15 (1954): 201–15; W. A. Murray's supplementary note to Frye, *ibid.*, pp. 596–601; Samuel H. Monk, "The Pride of Lemuel Gulliver," *Sewanee Review*, 63 (1955): 48–71; Irvin Ehrenpreis, "The Origins of *Gulliver's Travels*," *PMLA*, 72 (1957): 880–99 (reprinted with some revisions in his *The Personality of Jonathan Swift* [London, 1958]); Kathleen Williams, *Jonathan Swift and the Age of Compromise* (Lawrence, Kansas, 1958); Calhoun Winton, "Conversion on the Road to Houyhnhnmland," *Sewanee Review*, 68 (1960): 20–33; Martin Kallich, "Three Ways of Looking at a Horse: Jonathan Swift's 'Voyage to the Houyhnhnms' Again," *Criticism*, 2 (1960): 107–24.

pessimism of the final chapters—it is he and not Swift who reduces men literally to Yahoos; it is he and not Swift who despairs of men because they cannot or will not lead the wholly rational life of the Houyhnhnms. Gulliver, in other words, is only in part a reliable spokesman of his creator's satire; he is also, and decisively at the end, one of the targets of that satire—a character designed to convince us, through his obviously infatuated actions, of the absurdity both of any view of man's nature that denies the capacity of at least some men for rational and virtuous conduct, however limited this capacity may be, and of any view of the best existence for man that makes it consist in taking "reason alone" as a guide. What, in short, Swift offers us, as the ultimate moral of the Voyage, is a compromise between these extremist opinions of Gulliver: human nature, he is saying, is bad enough, but it is not altogether hopeless; reason is a good thing, but a life of pure reason is no desirable end for man.

Now it is evident that however appealing this interpretation may be to those who want to think well of Swift and to rescue him from his nineteenth-century maligners, it is not a merely obvious exegesis of the "Voyage to the Country of the Houyhnhnms," or one that most common readers, past or present, have spontaneously arrived at. It is not an exegesis, either, that goes at all comfortably with that famous letter of Swift's in 1725 in which he told Pope that his chief aim was "to vex the world rather than divert it" and that he never would have peace of mind until "all honest men" were of his opinion. For there is nothing particularly vexing in the at least partly reassuring moral now being attributed to the Voyage or anything which "honest men" in 1726 would have had much hesitation in accepting. And again, although we must surely agree that there is a significant difference between Gulliver and Swift, why must we suppose that the difference has to be one of basic doctrine? Why could it not be simply the difference between a person who has just discovered a deeply disturbing truth about man and is consequently, like Socrates' prisoner in the myth of the cave, considerably upset and one who, like Socrates himself, has known this truth all along and can therefore write of his hero's discovery of it calmly and with humor?

I introduce these points here not as decisive objections to the new interpretation but rather as signs that it is not the kind of interpretation which (in Johnson's phrase), upon its first production, must be acknowledged to be just. Confirmatory arguments are plainly needed; and a consideration of the arguments that have in fact been offered in support of it will bring us rather quickly to the special problem I wish to discuss.

A good deal has been made, to begin with, of what are thought to be clear indications in the Voyage itself that Swift wanted his readers to take a much more critical view than Gulliver does of "the virtues and ideas of those exalted Houyhnhnms" and a much less negative view of human possibilities. If he had designed the Houyhnhnms to be for us what they are for Gulliver, namely, the "perfection of nature" and hence an acceptable standard for judging of man, he would surely, it is argued, have endowed them with more humanly engaging qualities than they have; he would surely not have created them as the "remote, unsympathetic, and in the end profoundly unsatisfying" creatures so many of his readers nowadays find them to be. We must therefore see in Gulliver's worship of the rational horses a plain evidence of the extremist error into which he has fallen. And similarly, if Swift had expected us to go the whole way with Gulliver in his identification of men with the Yahoos, he would hardly have depicted the human characters in his story—especially the admirable Portuguese captain, Don Pedro de Mendez, and his crew—in the conspicuously favorable light in which they appear to us. They are bound to strike us as notable exceptions to the despairing estimate of "human kind" to which Gulliver has been led by his Houyhnhnm master; and we can only conclude that Gulliver's failure to look upon them as other than Yahoos, whom at best he can only "tolerate," is meant as still another sign to us of the false extremism of his attitude.

All this looks at first sight convincing—until we begin to think of other possible intentions that Swift might have had in the Voyage with which these signs would be equally compatible. Suppose that his primary purpose was indeed to "vex the world" by administering as severe a shock as he could to the cherished belief that man is par excellence a "rational creature," and suppose that he chose to do this, in part at least, by forcing his readers to dwell on the unbridgeable gap between what is involved in being a truly "rational creature" and what not only the worse but also the better sort of men actually are. It is plain what he would have had to do in working out such a design. He would have had to give to his wholly rational beings precisely those "unhuman" characteristics that have been noted, to their disadvantage, in the Houyhnhnms; to have made them creatures such as we would normally like or sympathize with would have been to destroy their value as a transcendent standard of comparison. And it would have been no less essential to introduce characters, like Don Pedro, or, for that matter, Gulliver himself, who, in terms of ordinary human judgments, would impress us as unmistakably good; otherwise he would have exempted too many of his readers from the shock to their pride in being men which, on this hypothesis, he was trying to produce. He would have had to do, in short, all those things in the Voyage that have been taken as indications of a purpose very different from the one I am now supposing, and much less misanthropic. Clearly, then, some other kind of proof is needed than these ambiguous internal signs before the current view of Swift's meaning can be thought of as more than one possibility among other competing ones.

A good many defenders of this view, especially during the past decade, have attempted to supply such proof by relating the Voyage to its presumed background in the intellectual and religious concerns of Swift and his age; and it is their manner of doing this—of using hypotheses based on the history of ideas in the determination of their author's meaning—that I want to examine in what immediately follows.

They have been fairly well agreed on these three points: in the first place, that Swift's main design in the Voyage was to uphold what they describe as the traditional and orthodox conception of human nature, classical and Christian alike, that "recognizes in man an inseparable complex of good and evil," reason and passion, spiritual soul and animal body; secondly, that he conceived the Houyhnhnms and the Yahoos, primarily at least, as allegorical embodiments of these two parts of man's constitution taken in abstraction the one from the other; and thirdly, that he developed his defense of the orthodox view by directing his satire against those contemporary doctrines, on the one hand, that tended to exalt the Houyhnhnm side of man in forgetfulness of how Yahoo-like man really is, and those doctrines, on the other hand, that tended to see man only as a Yahoo in forgetfulness of his Houyhnhnm possibilities, limited though these are. All this has been more or less common doctrine among critics of the Voyage at least since Ernest Bernbaum in 1920; there has been rather less agreement on the identity of the contemporary movements of ideas which Swift had in view as objects of attack. It was usual in the earlier phases of the discussion to say simply, as Bernbaum does, that he was thinking, at the one extreme, of the "sentimental optimism" of writers like Shaftesbury and, at the other, of the pessimism or cynicism of writers like Hobbes and Mandeville. Since then, however, other identifications have been added to the list, as relevant especially to his conception of the Houyhnhnms; we have been told, thus, that he "obviously" intended to embody in the principles and mode of life of these creatures, along with certain admittedly admirable qualities, the rationalistic errors of the neo-Stoics, the Cartesians, and the deists—some or all of these, depending upon the critic.

Now if we could feel sure that what was in Swift's mind when he conceived the fourth Voyage is even approximately represented by these statements, we should have little reason for not going along with the interpretation of his design they have been used to support. For if he was indeed engaged in vindicating the "Christian humanist" view of human nature against those contemporary extremists who made either too much or too little of man's capacity for reason and virtue, the current view of Gulliver as partly a vehicle and partly an object of the satire is surely correct. Everything depends, therefore, on how much relevance to what he was trying to do in the Voyage this particular historical hypothesis can be shown to have.

Its proponents have offered it as relevant beyond reasonable doubt; which suggests to me that some special assumptions about the application of intellectual history to the exegesis of literary works must be involved here. For they would find it difficult, I think, to justify their confidence in terms merely of the ordinary canons of proof in this as well as other historical fields.

They can indeed show that the hypothesis is a possible one, in the sense that it is consistent with some of the things we know about Swift apart from the Voyage. We know that he was a humanistically educated Anglican divine, with traditionalist inclinations in many matters; that he looked upon man's nature as deeply corrupted by the Fall but thought that self-love and the passions could be made, with the help of religion, to yield a positive though limited kind of virtue; that he held reason in high esteem as a God-given possession of man but distrusted any exclusive reliance on it in practice or belief, ridiculing the Stoics and Cartesians and making war on the deists; and that he tended, especially in his political writings, to find the useful truth in a medium between extremes. A man of whom these things can be said might very well have conceived the "Voyage to the Country of the Houyhnhnms" in the terms in which, on the present theory, Swift is supposed to have conceived it. And beyond this, it is possible to point to various characteristics in the Voyage itself which, *if* the hypothesis is correct, can be interpreted as likely consequences of it. *If* Swift had in fact intended to symbolize, in the sustained opposition of Houyhnhnms and Yahoos, the deep division and conflict within man between his rational and his animal natures, he would undoubtedly have depicted these two sets of creatures, in essentials at least, much as they are depicted in the text (although this would hardly account for his choice of horses as symbols of rationality). So too with the supposition that we were meant to see in the Houyhnhnms, among other things, a powerful reminder of how inadequate and dangerous, for weak and sinful human nature, is any such one-sided exaltation of reason as was being inculcated at the time by the deists, the neo-Stoics, and the Cartesians: it would not be surprising, if that were actually Swift's intention, to find Gulliver saying of "those exalted quadrupeds," as he does, that they consider "reason alone sufficient to govern a rational creature," that they neither affirm nor deny anything of which they are not certain, and that they keep their passions under firm control, practice "universal friendship and benevolence," and are immune to fear of death and grief for the death of others.

Now all this is to the good, to the extent at least that without such considerations as these about both Swift and the fourth Voyage there would be no reason for entertaining the hypothesis at all. But can we say anything more than this—so long, that is, as we judge the question by the ordinary standards of historical criticism? In other words, do the considerations I have just summarized tend in any decisive way to establish the hypothesis as fact? The answer must surely be that they do not, and for the simple reason that they are all merely positive and favoring considerations, such as can almost always be adduced in support of almost any hypothesis in scholarship or common life, however irrelevant or false it may turn out to be. It is a basic maxim of scholarly criticism, therefore, that the probability of a given hypothesis is proportionate not to our ability to substantiate it by confirmatory evidence (although there obviously must be confirmatory evidence) but to our inability—after serious trial—to rule it out in favor of some other hypothesis that would explain more completely and simply the particulars it is concerned with. We have to start, in short, with the assumption that our hypothesis may very well be false and then permit ourselves to look upon it as fact only when, having impartially considered all the counter-possibilities we can think of, we find disbelief in it more difficult to maintain than belief. This is a rule which few of us consistently live up to (otherwise we would not publish as much as we do); but there are varying degrees of departure from it; and I can see few signs that its requirements are even approximated in the current historical discussions of the fourth Voyage. It would be a different matter if these critics had been able to show statements by Swift himself about *Gulliver's Travels* that defy reasonable interpretation except as references to the particular issues and doctrines which the hypothesis supposes were in his mind when he wrote the Voyage. But they have not succeeded in doing this; and they have given no attention at all to the possibility that there were other traditions of thought about human nature in Swift's time (I can think of one such, as will appear later) with which he can be shown to have been familiar—traditions which they ought to have considered and then, if possible, excluded as irrelevant before their hypothesis can be said, on ordinary scholarly grounds, to be confirmed.

What then are the special assumptions about interpretative method on which, in view of all this, their confidence must be presumed to rest? Their problem has naturally led them, as it would any historian, to make propositions about Swift's thought apart from *Gulliver* and about the thought of Swift's age: what is distinctive is the character of these propositions and the use they are put to in the interpretation of the Voyage. In the eyes of the ordinary historian of ideas inquiring into the intellectual antecedents and constituents of this work, the thought of Swift as expressed in his other writings is simply an aggregate of particular statements and arguments, some of which may well turn out to be relevant to an understanding of its meaning; for any of them, however, this is merely a possibility to be tested, not a presumption to be argued from. It is the same, too, with the thought of Swift's age: this, again, in the eyes of the ordinary historian, is nothing more determinate than the sum of things that were being written in the later seventeenth and early eighteenth centuries, from varying points of view and in varying traditions of analysis, on the general theme of human nature. Some of these, once more, may well be relevant to the argument developed in the Voyage, but the historian can know what they are only after an unprejudiced inquiry that presupposes no prior limitation of the ideas Swift might have been influenced by or have felt impelled to attack in constructing it. For the ordinary historian, in short, the fact that the "Voyage to the Country of the Houyhnhnms" was written by Swift at a particular moment in the general history of thought about man has only this methodological significance: that it defines the region which he may most hopefully look for the intellectual stimuli and materials that helped to shape the Voyage; it gives him, so to speak, his working reading list; it can never tell him—only an independent analysis of the Voyage can do that—how to use the list.

That the critics we are concerned with have taken a different view of the matter from this is suggested by the title of the book in which the current historical theory of Swift's intentions in the Voyage is argued most fully and ingeniously—Kathleen Williams' *Jonathan Swift and the Age of Compromise.* For to think of a period in intellectual history in this way—as the age *of* something or other, where the something or other is designated by an abstract term like "compromise"—is obviously no longer to consider it as an indefinite aggregate of happenings; it is to consider it rather as a definite system of happenings; something like the plot of a novel in which a great many diverse characters and episodes are unified, more or less completely, by a principal action or theme. It is to assume, moreover, not only that the historian can determine what was the central problem, the basic conflict or tension, the dominant world view of a century or generation, either in general or in some particular department of thought, but that he can legitimately use his formula for this as a confirmatory premise in arguing the meanings and causes of individual works produced in that age. It is to suppose that there is a kind of probative force in his preferred formula for the period which can confer a priori a privileged if not unique relevance upon one particular hypothesis about a given work of that period as against other hypotheses that are less easily brought under the terms of the formula, so that little more is required by way of further proof than a demonstration, which is never hard to give, that the work makes sense when it is "read" as the hypothesis dictates.

These are, I think, the basic assumptions which underlie most of the recent historical discussions of the fourth Voyage and which go far toward explaining the confidence their authors have felt in the correctness of their conclusions. It would be hard, otherwise, to understand why they should think it important to introduce propositions about what was central and unifying in the moral thought of Swift's age; the reason must be that they have hoped, by so doing, to establish some kind of antecedent limitation on the intentions he could be expected to have had in writing the Voyage. And that, indeed, is the almost unavoidable effect of the argument for any reader who closes his mind, momentarily, to the nature of the presuppositions on which it rests. For suppose we agree with these critics that the dominant and most significant issue in the moral speculation of the later seventeenth and early eighteenth centuries was a conflict between the three fundamentally different views of man's nature represented by the orthodox "classical-Christian" dualism in the middle and, at opposite extremes, the newer doctrines of the rationalists and benevolists on the one side and of the materialists and cynics on the other. Since this is presented as an exhaustive scheme of classification, it will be easy for us to believe that the view of man asserted in the Voyage must have been one of these three. And then suppose we agree to think of Swift as a man predisposed by his humanist education and his convictions as an Anglican divine to adhere to the traditional and compromising view as against either of the modern extremisms. It will be difficult for us now to avoid believing that the "Voyage to the Country of the Houyhnhnms" was therefore more probably than not an assertion of this middle view against its contemporary enemies, and it will be harder than it would be without such an argument from the age to the author to the work, to resist any interpretations of its details that may be necessary to make them accord with that theory of Swift's intentions.

This is likely to be our reaction, at any rate, until we reflect on the peculiar character of the argument we have been persuaded to go along with. There are many arguments like it in the writings of modern critics and historians of ideas in other fields (those who have interpreted Shakespeare in the light of "the Elizabethan world picture," for instance); but they all betray, I think, a fundamental confusion in method. The objection is not that they rest on a false conception of historical periods. There is nothing intrinsically illegitimate in the mode of historical writing that organizes the intellectual happenings of different ages in terms of their controlling "climates of opinion," dominant tendencies, or ruling oppositions of attitude or belief; and the results of such synthesizing efforts are sometimes—as in A. O. Lovejoy, for example—illuminating in a high degree. The objection is rather to the further assumption, clearly implicit in these arguments, that the unifying principles of histories of this type have something like the force of empirically established universal laws, and can therefore be used as guarantees of the probable correctness of any interpretations of individual writings that bring the writings into harmony with their requirements. That this is sheer illusion can be easily seen if we consider what these principles really amount to. Some of them amount simply to assertions that there was a tendency among the writers of a particular time to concentrate on such and such problems and to solve them in such and such ways. There is no implication here that this trend affected all writers or any individual writer at all times: whether a given work of the age did or did not conform to the trend remains therefore an open question, to be answered only by independent inquiry unbiased by the merely statistical probabilities affirmed in the historian's generalization. But there are also principles of a rather different sort, among which we must include, I think, the formula of Swift's critics for the dominant conflict about human nature in his time. These are best described as dialectical constructs, since they organize the doctrinal facts they refer to by imposing on them abstract schemes of logical relationships among ideas which may or may not be identical with any of the various classifications and oppositions of doctrines influential at the time. Thus our critics' characterization of Swift's age and of Swift himself as a part of that age derives its apparent exhaustiveness from a pattern of general terms—the concept of "Christian humanism" and the two contraries of this—which these critics clearly owe to the ethical and historical speculations of Irving Babbitt and his school. Now it may be that this scheme represents accurately enough the distinctions Swift had in mind when he conceived the fourth Voyage; but that would be something of a coincidence, and it is just as reasonable to suppose that he may have been thinking quite outside the particular framework of notions which this retro-spective scheme provides. We must conclude, then, that this whole way of using the history of ideas in literary interpretation is miscon-ceived. From the generalizations and schematisms of the synthesizing historians we can very often get suggestions for new working hy-potheses with which to approach the exegesis of individual works. What we cannot get from them is any assurance whatever that any of these hypotheses are more likely to be correct than any others that we have hit upon without their aid.

I should now like to invite the reader's criticism, in the light of what I have been saying, on another view of the intellectual back-ground and import of the fourth Voyage (or a considerable part of it at least) which I shall attempt to argue on the basis merely of ordinary historical evidence, independently of any general postulates about Swift or his age.

2

Whatever else may be true of the Voyage, it will doubtless be agreed that one question is kept uppermost in it from the begin-ning, for both Gulliver and the reader. This is the question of what sort of animal man, as a species, really is; and the point of departure in the argument is the answer to this question which Gulliver brings with him into Houyhnhnmland and which is also, we are reminded more than once, the answer which men in general tend, complacently, to give to it. Neither he nor they have any doubt that only man, among "sensitive" creatures, can be properly called "rational"; all the rest—whether wild or tame, detestable or, like that "most comely and generous" animal, the horse, the reverse of that—being merely "brutes," not "endued with reason." The cen-tral issue, in other words, is primarily one of definition: is man, or is he not, correctly defined as a "rational creature"? It is significant that Gulliver's misanthropy at the end is not the result of any increase in his knowledge of human beings in the concrete over what he has had before; it is he after all who expounds to his Houyhnhnm master all those melancholy facts about men's "actions and passions" that play so large a part in their conversations; he has known these facts all along, and has still been able to call himself a "lover of mankind." The thing that changes his love into antipathy is the recognition that is now forced upon him that these facts are wholly incompatible with the formula for man's nature which he has hitherto taken for granted—are compatible, indeed, only with a formula, infinitely more humiliating to human pride, which pushes man nearly if not quite over to the opposite pole of the animal world.

What brings about the recognition is, in the first place, the deeply disturbing spectacle of the Houyhnhnms and the Yahoos. I can find nothing in the text that forces us to look on these two sets of strange creatures in any other light than that in which Gulliver sees them— not, that is, as personified abstractions, but simply as two concrete species of animals: existent species for Gulliver, hypothetical species for us. The contrast he draws between them involves the same pair of antithetical terms (the one positive, the other privative) that he has been accustomed to use in contrasting men and the other animals. The essential character of the Houyhnhnms, he tells us, is that they are creatures "wholly governed by reason"; the essential character of the Yahoos is that "they are the most unteachable of brutes," without "the least tincture of reason." The world of animals in Houyhnhnmland, in other words, is divided by the same basic difference as the world of animals in Europe. Only, of course—and it is the shock of this that prepares Gulliver for his ultimate abandonment of the definition of man he has started with—it is a world in which the normal distribution of species between "rational creatures" and irrational "brutes" is sharply inverted, with horses, which he cannot help admiring, in the natural place of men, and manlike creatures, which he cannot help abhorring, in the natural place of horses.

This is enough in itself to cause Gulliver to view his original formula for his own species, as he says, "in a very different light." But he is pushed much further in the same misanthropic direction by the questions and comments of his Houyhnhnm master, acting as a kind of Socrates. What thus develops is partly a reduction to absurdity of man's "pretensions to the character of a rational creature" and partly a demonstration of the complete parity in essential nature between men and the Houyhnhnmland Yahoos. There is of course one difference—unlike the Yahoos, men are after all possessed of at least a "small proportion," a "small pittance" of reason, some in greater degree than others. But I can see no clear signs in the text that this qualification is intended to set men apart as a third, or intermediate, species for either Gulliver or the reader. For what is basic in the new definition of man as a merely more "civilized" variety of Yahoo is the fundamentally irrational "disposition" which motivates his habitual behavior; and in relation to that his "capacity for reason" is only an acquired attribute which he is always in danger of losing and of which, as Gulliver says, he makes no other use, generally speaking, than "to improve and multiply those vices" whereof his "brethren [in Houyhnhnmland] had only the share that nature allotted them."

It is clear what a satisfactory historical explanation of this line of argument in the Voyage would have to do. It would have to account for Swift's patent assumption that there would be a high degree of satirical force, for readers in 1726, in a fable which began with the notion that man is preeminently a "rational creature" and then proceeded to turn this notion violently upside down, and which, in doing so, based itself on a division of animal species into the extremes of "rational creatures" and irrational "brutes" and on the paradoxical identification of the former with horses and of the latter with beings closely resembling men. Was there perhaps a body of teaching, not so far brought into the discussion of the Voyage but widely familiar at the time, that could have supplied Swift with the particular scheme of ideas he was exploiting here? I suggest that there was, and also that there is nothing strange in the fact that it has been hitherto overlooked by Swift's critics. For one principal medium through which these ideas could have come to Swift and his readers—the only one, in fact, I know of that could have given him all of them—was a body of writings, mainly in Latin, which students of literature in our day quite naturally shy away from reading: namely, the old-fashioned textbooks in logic that still dominated the teaching of that subject in British universities during the later seventeenth and early eighteenth centuries.[3]

[3] There are useful descriptions of many, though by no means all, of these in Wilbur Samuel Howell, *Logic and Rhetoric in England, 1500–1700* (Princeton, 1956).

It is impossible not to be impressed, in the first place, by the prominence in these textbooks of the particular definition of man which the Voyage sought to discredit. *Homo est animal rationale:* no one could study elementary logic anywhere in the British Isles in the generation before *Gulliver* without encountering this formula or variations of it *(Nullus homo est irrationalis)* in his manuals and the lectures he heard. It appears as the standard example of essential definition in the great majority of logics in use during these years at Oxford, Cambridge, and Dublin; and in most of those in which it occurs, it is given without comment or explanation as the obviously correct formula for man's distinctive nature, as if no one would ever question that man is, uniquely and above all, a rational creature. It is frequently brought in many times over, in various contexts, in individual textbooks: I have counted a dozen or so occurrences of it in Milton's *Art of Logic,* and many times that number in the *Institutionum logicarum . . . libri duo* of Franco Burgersdijck (or Burgersdicius), which was one of the most widely used, and also one of the longest lived, of all these writings—it appeared in 1626 and was still prescribed at Dublin when Edmund Burke went there as a Junior Freshman in 1744.[4] I shall have some more to say of Burgersdicius, or "Burgy" as Burke called him, presently; but it is worth noting that he provides us, in one passage, with the very question on which much of the fourth Voyage was to turn and with the answer Swift was *not* to give to it: "Quaerenti enim, Quale animal est homo? appositè respondetur, Rationale."

Not only, however, was the definition omnipresent in these books, but there is some evidence that it was thought of, in Swift's time, as the special property of the academic logicians. Locke, for instance, calls it in his *Essay* "the ordinary Definition of the Schools," the "sacred Definition of *Animal Rationale*" of "the learned Divine and Lawyer"; it goes, he implies, with "this whole *Mystery* of *Genera* and *Species,* which make such a noise in the Schools, and are, with Justice, so little regarded out of them" (III.iii.10; vi.26; iii.9). And there are other later testimonies to the same effect; among them these opening lines of an anonymous poem of the period after *Gulliver,* once ascribed to Swift—"The Logicians Refuted":

---

[4] *The Correspondence of Edmund Burke,* edited by Thomas W. Copeland, I (Cambridge and Chicago, 1958), 4, 7–9, 21, 28.

Logicians have but ill defin'd
As rational, the human kind;
Reason, they say, belongs to man,
But let them prove it if they can.
Wise Aristotle and Smiglesius,
By ratiocinations specious,
Have strove to prove with great precision,
With definition and division,
Homo est ratione preditum;
But for my soul I cannot credit 'em.[5]

But the logicians had more to offer Swift than the great authority which they undoubtedly conferred on the definition "rational animal." They could have suggested to him also the basic principle on which the inverted animal world of Houyhnhnmland was constructed, and consequently the disjunction that operated as major premise in his argument about man. Whoever it was, among the Greeks, that first divided the genus "animal" by the differentiae "rational" and "irrational," there is much evidence that this antithesis had become a commonplace in the Greco-Roman schools long before it was taken up by the writer who did more than any one else to determine the context in which the definition *animal rationale* was chiefly familiar to Englishmen of Swift's time. This writer was the Neoplatonist Porphyry of the third century, whose little treatise, the *Isagoge*, or introduction to the categories of Aristotle, became, as is well known, one of the great sources of logical theorizing and teaching from the time of Boethius until well beyond the end of the seventeenth century. There is no point in going into the details of Porphyry's doctrine: what is important for our purpose here is the new sanction he gave to the older division of animal species through his incorporation of it into the general scheme of differentiae for the category of substance which was later known as the *arbor porphyriana* or Porphyry's tree, especially in the diagrams of it that became a regular feature of the more elementary textbooks. Here it is, set forth discursively, in the crabbed prose of Burgersdicius (I quote the English version of 1697, but the Latin is no better). In seeking the definition of man, he writes, we must first observe that

5 *The Busy Body,* No. 5, October 18, 1759. Both the ascription to Swift, which occurs in a note prefixed to this first known printing of the poem, and the later ascription to Goldsmith seem to me highly dubious.

Man is a Substance; but because an Angel is also a Substance; *That it may appear how Man differs from an Angel,* Substance ought to be divided into Corporeal and Incorporeal. A Man is a *Body,* an Angel *without a Body:* But a Stone also is a *Body:* That therefore a Man may be distinguished from a Stone, divide Bodily or Corporeal Substance into Animate and Inanimate, that is, *with or without a Soul.* Man is a Corporeal Substance Animate, Stone Inanimate. But Plants are also *Animate:* Let us divide therefore again Corporeal Substance Animate into *Feeling and void of Feeling.* Man feels, a Plant not: But a Horse *also feels,* and likewise other Beasts. Divide we therefore Animate Corporeal Feeling Substance into Rational and Irrational. Here therefore *are we to stand,* since it appears that every, and only Man *is Rational.*[6]

And there was, finally, one other thing in these logics that could have helped to shape Swift's invention in the fourth Voyage. In opposing man as the only species of "rational animal" to the brutes, Porphyry obviously needed a specific instance, parallel to man, of an "irrational" creature; and the instance he chose—there were earlier precedents for the choice[7]—was the horse. The proportion "rational" is to "irrational" as man is to horse occurs more than once in the *Isagoge;* and the juxtaposition, in the same context, of *homo* and *equus* was a frequently recurring cliché in his seventeenth-century followers, as in the passage in Burgersdicius just quoted: other species of brutes were occasionally mentioned, but none of them nearly so often. And anyone who studied these books could hardly fail to remember a further point—that the distinguishing "property" of this favorite brute was invariably given as whinnying (*facultas hinniendi*); *equus,* it was said again and again, *est animal hinnibile.*

To most Englishmen of Swift's time who had read logic in their youth—and this would include nearly all generally educated men—these commonplaces of Porphyry's tree, as I may call them for short, were as familiar as the Freudian commonplaces are to generally educated people today, and they were accepted, for the most part, in an even less questioning spirit, so that it might well have occurred to a

[6] *Monitio logica: or, An Abstract and Translation of Burgersdicius His Logick* (London, 1697), pp. 13–14 (second pagination).

[7] E.g., Quintilian, *Institutio oratoria,* VII.iii.3, 24. For the contrast of man and horse in Porphyry see especially Migne, *PL,* 64, col. 128 (Boethius' translation): "Differentia est quod est aptum natum dividere ea quae sub eodem genere sunt: rationale enim et irrational, hominem et equum quae sub eodem genere sunt animali dividunt."

clever satirist then, that he could produce a fine shock to his readers'
complacency as human beings by inventing a world in which horses
appeared where the logicians had put men and men where they had
put horses, and by elaborating, through this, an argument designed
to shift the position of man as a species from the *animal rationale*
branch of the tree, where he had always been proudly placed, as far as
possible over toward the *animal irrationale* branch, with its enormously less flattering connotations. But have we any warrant for
thinking that this, or something like it, was what Swift actually had
in mind? It is clearly possible to describe the Voyage as, in considerable part at least, an anti-Porphyrian satire[8] in the genre of the poem
I quoted from earlier, "The Logicians Refuted." But is there any
evidence that Swift planned it as such?

That the Porphyrian commonplaces had been known to him in
their full extent from his days at Trinity College in the early 1680's

[8] Since this essay was first printed, my colleague Edward Rosenheim has pointed out
(*MP*, 60: 109–10; cf. his *Swift and the Satirist's Art*, p. 100 n.) that this description of
the fourth Voyage as an "anti-Porphyrian satire" needs some clarification. How, he
asks, "are our own opinions changed by Swift's discrediting the definition of man to be
found in such texts on logic as that of Narcissus Marsh? Is the reader's skepticism being
chiefly directed against the texts themselves? (Crane's phrase, 'anti-Porphyrian satire'
suggests that he may think so.) Or, on the other hand, is the satire directed against the
substance of the proposition itself without particular concern for the contexts in which
it has appeared?"

My phrase, I must acknowledge, clearly invites the construction Rosenheim puts on
it. It does seem to imply that just as the targets of Swift's satire in Part III of *Gulliver*
were the experimenters and projectors of the Royal Society, so, in much the same sense,
his targets in Part IV were the academic logicians of the Porphyrian school. My actual
view of the relation between the Voyage and these logicians, however, is quite different
from this and much closer to the view Rosenheim himself expounds in the latter part
of his essay. Like him, I regard the fourth Voyage, not as an attack on either logicians or
logic (low as was his opinion of this subject), but as a satirical "homily" directed against
a much more nearly universal object—namely, that form of human pride which the late
Arthur O. Lovejoy once called "the generic pride of man as such" (*Essays in the History
of Ideas*, p. 63), the pride that springs from the imagined superiority of man as a species
over all other living creatures in some major aspect of his nature.

For Swift in the fourth Voyage, the chief foundation of this pride was the almost
universally prevalent conviction, which the academic logicians in the tradition of
Porphyry and his Greek and Roman predecessors did so much to keep alive, that the
essence of man—and hence of all men—is contained in "that definition *animal rationale*."
He had only to prove the falsity of this, and he had knocked out one of the great supports—perhaps the greatest support—of man's pretension to unique eminence in the
animate world. This—I think Rosenheim would agree with me—was the major task
he set himself in contriving his fable of Gulliver among the Houyhnhnms and the
Yahoos, to the end of shocking his readers into that attitude of philosophic misanthropy
("not in Timon's manner") which consisted in thinking less exaltedly of themselves
and expecting less of virtue and sense from their fellow creatures.

we can hardly doubt in view of the kind of education in logic he was exposed to there. Among the books which all Junior Freshmen at Dublin in those years were required to study or hear lectures on, we know of three in which the Porphyrian apparatus and examples had a prominent place: the *Isagoge* itself (which was prescribed by the statutes of the College to be read twice over during the year), the older logic of Burgersdicius, and the newer *Institutio logicae* of Narcissus Marsh. It is true that Swift, according to his own later statement, detested this part of the curriculum, and it is true that on one examination in the "philosophy" course (specifically Physica), in his last year, his mark was *Male* (he had a *Bene* in Greek and Latin). But this was an examination in a more advanced part of the Aristotelian system, and it is likely that he had fared better in the earlier examination in logic, since he had evidently been allowed to proceed with his class. It is possible, moreover, to infer from his occasional use of logical terms in his later writings that, abhorrent as the subject was to him, the time he had been compelled to spend on it as a Junior Freshman was not a total loss. He at least remembered enough of it to allude familiarly in different places to such things as a "long sorites," "the first proposition of a hypothetical syllogism," and the fallacy of two middle terms in a single syllogism;[9] and if this was possible, there is good reason to suppose that he had not forgotten the much simpler Porphyrian points about genera, species, and definition, "rational" versus "irrational" animals, men and horses which he had been introduced to at the same time.

The crucial question, however, is whether he had these notions of the logicians actively in mind when, in the 1720's, he conceived and wrote the "Voyage to the Country of the Houyhnhnms." And here it will be well to take a fresh look at the two much-quoted letters about *Gulliver's Travels* which he sent to Pope in 1725, just after that work was completed. In the first of these, that of September 29, after having told Pope that his chief aim is "to vex the world rather than divert it" and that he hates and detests "that animal called man," he goes on to remark: "I have got materials towards a treatise proving the falsity of that definition *animal rationale,* and to show it should be only *ra-*

---

[9] See John M. Bullitt, *Jonathan Swift and the Anatomy of Satire* (Cambridge, Mass., 1953), p. 73. Cf. also Swift, "A Preface to the B——p of S——m's Introduction," in *Works,* edited by Temple Scott, III, 150.

tionis capax. Upon this great foundation of misanthropy, though not in Timon's manner, the whole building of my Travels is erected; and I never will have peace of mind till all honest men are of my opinion." In the second letter, that of November 26, he desires that Pope and "all my friends" will "take a special care that my disaffection to the world may not be imputed to my age, for I have credible witnesses . . . that it has never varied from the twenty-first to the f——ty-eighth year of my life." He then adds a passage which has been read as a retraction of the judgment on humanity expressed in the first letter, although the final sentence makes clear, I think, that it was not so intended: "I tell you after all, that I do not hate mankind; it is *vous autres* [Pope and Bolingbroke] who hate them, because you would have them reasonable animals, and are angry for being disappointed. I have always rejected that definition, and made another of my own. I am no more angry with ——— than I am with the kite that last week flew away with one of my chickens; and yet I was glad when one of my servants shot him two days after."

The casual references in both letters to "that definition"—*animal rationale*" and "reasonable animals"—which Swift tells Pope he has "always rejected" have usually been interpreted by his modern critics as allusions to such contemporary philosophical or theological heresies (from Swift's point of view) as the "optimism" of Shaftesbury or the "rationalism" of Descartes and the deists. It is surely, however, a much less far-fetched conjecture, especially in view of the familiar textbook Latin of the first letter, to see in "that definition" nothing other or more than the "sacred definition" of the logicians which had been inflicted on him, by thoroughly orthodox tutors, in his undergraduate days at Dublin.

I find this explanation, at any rate, much harder to disbelieve than any other that has been proposed; and all the more so because of another passage in the first letter which is almost certainly reminiscent of the Trinity logic course in the early 1680's. It is the famous sentence—just before the allusion to "that definition *animal rationale*" and leading on to it—in which Swift says: "But principally I hate and detest that animal called man, although I heartily love John, Peter, Thomas, and so forth." Now to any one at all widely read in the logic textbooks of Swift's time two things about this sentence are immediately evident: first, that the distinction it turns on is the distinction to be found in nearly all these books between a species of animals and individual members of that species; and second, that the names "John, Peter, Thomas, and so forth" are wholly in line with one of the two main traditions of names for individuals of the species man that had persisted side by side in innumerable manuals of logic since the Middle Ages: not, of course, the older tradition of classical names —Socrates, Plato, Alexander, Caesar—but the newer tradition (which I have noted first in Occam, although it doubtless antedates him) that drew upon the list of apostles—Peter, John, Paul, James, Thomas, in roughly that descending order of preference. (Other non-classical names, like Stephen, Catharine, Charles, Richard, also appear, but much less frequently.)

We can go further than this, however. For although all three of Swift's names occur separately in various texts (Thomas least often), the combination "John, Peter, Thomas, and so forth" was an extremely unusual one. I have met with it, in fact, in only one book before 1725; and I have examined nearly all the logics, both Latin and English, down to that date for which I can find any evidence that they had even a minor circulation in Britain. The exception, however, is a book which Swift could hardly have escaped knowing as an undergraduate, since it was composed expressly for the use of Trinity College students by the then Provost and had just recently come "on the course" when he entered the College in 1682—namely, the *Institutio logicae,* already referred to, of Narcissus Marsh (Dublin, 1679: reissued Dublin, 1681). Early in the book Marsh gives a full-page diagram of Porphyry's tree, with its inevitable opposition of *animal— rationale—homo* and *animal—irrationale—brutum;* and here, as *individua* under *homo,* we find "Joannes, Petrus, Thomas, &c." And a little later in the book the same names are repeated in the same order as individual specimens of *homo* in Marsh's analytical table for the category *substantia.*

Was this combination of names, then, Marsh's invention? There is one further circumstance which suggests that it may well have been. We know from his own testimony,[10] as well as from internal evidence,

---

[10] See his preface "Ad lectorem" in the 1681 issue (it is missing from some copies but can be found in the Cambridge University Library copy and in that belonging to Archbishop Marsh's Library, Dublin); also the entry for December 20, 1690, in his manuscript diary. I owe this latter reference to Mary Pollard, of Archbishop Marsh's Library. For the rather complicated bibliographical history of Marsh's *Institutio logicae* (the title was

that the source on which he based the greater part of his Dublin logic of 1679 was his own revision, published at Oxford in 1678, of the *Manuductio ad logicam* of the early seventeenth-century Jesuit logician Philippe Du Trieu. Now of the two passages in the Dublin book that contain Swift's three names, the first—the diagram of Porphyry's tree—has no counterpart in the Oxford book of 1678, although it has in Du Trieu's original text, where the names are "Petrus" and "Joannes." It seems likely, then, that Marsh first thought of the combination "John, Peter, Thomas, and so forth" when he revised his earlier revision of Du Trieu for his Trinity students in 1679; and this is borne out by what he did at the same time with the other passage— the table of substance. This he retained almost exactly as it had been in Du Trieu except for the names under *homo:* here, where in 1678 he had reprinted Du Trieu's "Stephanus, Johannes, Catharina, &c.," he now wrote "Johannes, Petrus, Thomas, &c." Which would seem to imply a certain sense of private property in these particular names in this particular combination.

It is somewhat hard, then, not to conclude that Swift was remembering Marsh's logic as he composed the sentence, in his letter to Pope, about "John, Peter, Thomas, and so forth." But if that is true, can there be much doubt, in view of the Porphyrian context in which these names appear in Marsh, about what tradition of ideas was in his mind when he went on to remark, immediately afterwards, that "the great foundation of misanthropy" on which "the whole building" of his *Travels* rested was his proof—against Marsh and the other logicians he had been made to study at Trinity—of "the falsity of that definition *animal rationale*"?[11]

---

altered to *Institutiones logicae* in the reissue of 1681), see her article, "The Printing of the Provost's Logic and the Supply of Text-books in the Late Seventeenth Century," in *Friends of the Library of Trinity College, Dublin: Annual Bulletin*, 1959–61.

11 I have discussed some further aspects of the subject in a brief article, "The Rationale of the Fourth Voyage," in *Gulliver's Travels: An Annotated Text with Critical Essays*, edited by Robert A. Greenberg (New York, 1961), pp. 300–307, and in a review of two papers on Swift and the deists, in *PQ*, 40 (1961): 427–30.

Jane Austen: "Persuasion"

HE ONE CONTINUOUS STORY Jane Austen tells in *Persuasion* is of a broken engagement finally restored, and with even deeper happiness for the heroine and hero, Anne Elliot and Captain Frederick Wentworth, than they had felt when the engagement was entered into eight years and a half before. It had not lasted long. Wentworth was then a young naval officer with no certain prospects, and Anne, a girl of nineteen, was soon persuaded by her friend Lady Russell, who stood to her as her dead mother, that the engagement would be an imprudent one for him no less than for herself. She therefore broke it off, though at the cost of much suffering and continued regret; she realized very quickly, in fact, that she would renew it at once if Wentworth asked her to. He, however, had left immediately for sea, greatly angered by her treatment of him and fully convinced that it showed "a feebleness of character . . . which his own decided, confident temper could not endure." This was still his state of mind when the two happened to meet again eight years later; he thought Anne's power with him was gone forever, and he was prepared to fall in love with almost any girl but her—any girl, at least, who possessed "a strong mind, with sweetness of manner." He did in fact become involved, half seriously, with one of Anne's friends, Louisa Musgrove, thinking her just the kind of woman Anne was not. Before long, however, he began to discover, on observing Anne more closely, that he had seriously misjudged her

An extract from a series of lectures on critical method given at the University of Notre Dame in 1957; not hitherto published.

character; and with this recognition of his error, his old affection for her, which had been latent throughout in spite of his "angry pride," began more and more to revive; her character, as he told her later, "was now fixed on his mind as perfection itself, maintaining the loveliest medium of fortitude and gentleness." He was unable to speak at once because of his involvement with Louisa, and then, when this difficulty was fortunately removed, he was held back for a time by his uncertainty about Anne's present feelings for him. She finally became aware, however, of his returning love and contrived to let him know how deeply welcome this was to her. Whereupon the engagement was restored, with a completer consciousness on both sides of one another's merits.

For a novel depicting such a simple series of events, there is a fairly large cast of characters. Leaving aside those who appear only once or twice in the narrative, these fall into two originally distinct groups: the family and friends of Anne and the family and friends of Wentworth. Anne is the daughter of Sir Walter Elliot, baronet, of Kellynch-hall in Somersetshire; she has an older sister, Elizabeth, a younger sister, Mary, and a cousin, William Walter Elliot, who is heir to the title and estate. Her closest friend is an older woman, Lady Russell of Kellynch-lodge, to whom her dead mother had committed her up-bringing. Her immediate circle at the time of Wentworth's return also includes Elizabeth's friend Mrs. Clay, the widowed daughter of the Elliots' estate agent, and, on a much more intimate footing, the Musgrove family of the neighboring village of Uppercross: Mr. and Mrs. Musgrove, their son Charles, who had married Mary Elliot after Anne had refused him, and their daughters Henrietta and Louisa; there is also Mrs. Musgrove's nephew Charles Hayter. And later on, Anne sees a good deal of an old schoolmate of hers, Miss Hamilton, now Mrs. Smith, whose late husband had been for a time a friend of William Elliot.

The other group is smaller and consists almost entirely of naval persons, without notable family connections, who have become prosperous or at least comfortable as a result of the recent war: Wentworth himself; his sister and her husband, Admiral Croft; and his close friends, Captain and Mrs. Harville, and Captain Benwick. Wentworth also has a clergyman brother, who had been a curate in the Kellynch neighborhood at the time of his first meeting with Anne.

It is in this world of country gentry and their connections and of naval officers just out of service that the action of *Persuasion* takes place. The narrative begins in the summer of 1814, eight years after Anne had broken her engagement, so that we learn of this earlier event only retrospectively. From that point until its climax in February of 1815, it passes through five stages, marked off chiefly until the last one by the doings and movements of the subordinate characters. The main happenings in the first stage are Sir Walter Elliot's discovery that he must live at a less extravagant rate than has been his habit, his decision that he can do this best by letting Kellynch-hall to a tenant and going to live in Bath, his finding of a satisfactory tenant in Admiral Croft, and his departure, with Elizabeth and Mrs. Clay; Anne is to rejoin the family after Christmas and in the meantime she is to stay first with Mary in Uppercross and then with Lady Russell.

The second stage presents what goes on in Uppercross and the neighborhood while Anne is there: the coming of Wentworth on a visit to his sister and brother-in-law; his meeting with the Musgroves and consequently with Anne; their other meetings at parties, on walks, and in Mary's cottage; his attempts to attach himself to Louisa, her apparent reciprocation of his interest, and Anne's awareness of all this; and finally an excursion of all the younger people to Lyme Regis, where the Harvilles and Captain Benwick are now living; Anne's meeting with them, her chance glimpse of her cousin Mr. Elliot, and the shocking culmination of the holiday in Louisa's fall and concussion while attempting to display to Wentworth her firmness of character; after which Anne, who has been the one resolute person in the group during the crisis, is obliged to return to Uppercross.

The third stage is a brief one: after a day or two at Uppercross (Wentworth and the Charles Musgroves remaining with Louisa in Lyme), Anne goes as she has promised to Lady Russell, visits the Crofts at Kellynch-hall, hears reassuring news of Louisa, becomes convinced that Louisa and Wentworth will now certainly marry, and then, at the beginning of the new year, accompanies Lady Russell to Bath.

The fourth stage is one of absorption on Anne's part in family and personal matters of an immediate sort quite removed from Wentworth and the happenings at Uppercross: the continued presence of Mrs. Clay; the constant visits of Mr. Elliot; the successful efforts of Sir Walter to become reconciled with some aristocratic relations of his; Anne's reunion with Mrs. Smith, who is now living as an invalid in Bath; and Lady Russell's unsuccessful attempt to persuade her that she ought to marry her cousin, who is apparently on the point of proposing to her.

This stage ends abruptly, and the final stage begins, with the news that Louisa has become engaged to Captain Benwick. Wentworth now comes to Bath; and except for one episode—Anne's discovery through Mrs. Smith of Mr. William Elliot's real character—all the happenings until the end are parts of the delayed resolution: a first embarrassed meeting with Wentworth by chance in a shop; a second meeting at a concert, where Anne becomes aware both of his returning love and of his jealousy of Mr. Eliot, to whom rumor in Bath has it that she is already engaged; and then the occasions provided by the surprise visit of Mrs. Musgrove, Charles and Mary, and Captain Harville, for undeceiving him on this point.

The essential story of *Persuasion*, thus, is to all appearances a very simple one; it is a story, as presented in the narrative, that really involves only the private thoughts and emotions of two persons. Given the constancy and the strength of Anne's feelings for Wentworth, the renewal of the engagement is inevitable once he comes to realize his mistake about her character and the inadequacy of the standard by which he has judged her; there are no external obstacles of any sort on either side. Why then so many incidental happenings, and especially why so many subordinate characters? One answer, true as far as it goes, is that they serve to give concrete body and life—surface life, at any rate—to a story that might otherwise seem too far abstracted from the ordinary daily circumstances in which private changes of opinion and feeling about other persons actually come about. And there is no doubt that in *Persuasion*, as in Jane Austen's other novels, an all-important cause of our pleasure in reading is her ability to invent and depict a great variety of persons who are alive and intrinsically interesting quite apart from any artistic functions they may have: consider Sir Walter Elliot and Mary Musgrove, for instance, or, at the opposite extreme, the Crofts. But neither this nor the other kind of value in happenings and characters is incompatible with the artist's use of them as necessary or desirable expedients in the working out of his governing conception. They may be good in themselves and at the same time be good for the plot and its effects. And so we need to

ask, as one of our main critical questions about *Persuasion,* what all
the minor characters and surface events I have listed are doing in the
novel in relation to its central story. To what extent are their presence and treatment determined, in one way or another, by Jane Austen's conception of the novel as a whole and the problems to which
this gave rise?

Now *Persuasion* is clearly conceived as a serious work—serious ethi-
cally no less than artistically. While it is pervaded with morality of
what seems to me a very fine sort, however, it has no moral and argues no thesis. It is a novel of personal relations: the relations of two
persons who had once been everything to one another, then apparently nothing, and finally everything again, but on a higher level of
affection and understanding. It is a love story, in short, which moves
us as all good love stories do, not because its hero and heroine are
embodiments of abstract values, ideological or social, larger than
themselves, but simply because they are particular human persons
who have fallen in love and suffer and are happy in the end. That is
the way, I am sure, that we all read *Persuasion* when we are not be-
mused by critical theory: not as a typical case of anything or an embodiment of a "theme," but as an individual history the course of
which is determined by circumstances peculiar to itself, and the moral
of which, if it can be called a moral, is merely that such things can
conceivably happen, and that when they happen in fiction they tend
to hold our interest as fellow human beings.

It is a love story but assuredly not a mere love story: not a love
story, that is, which depends for its emotional power solely or chiefly
on our general human sympathy with young lovers, whoever they may
be. For most love stories, undoubtedly, this basis of appeal is enough;
but not for *Persuasion* as Jane Austen conceived it. I think there can
be little doubt about the quality of the response she wanted her novel
to evoke at its climax. To perceive this, one has only to read the passage, in the next to the last chapter, that begins just after Charles
Musgrove has apologized for leaving Anne alone with Wentworth on
the streets of Bath:

> There could not be an objection. There could be only a most
> proper alacrity, a most obliging compliance for public view; and
> smiles reined in and spirits dancing in private rapture. In half a

minute, Charles was at the bottom of Union-Street again, and the other two proceeding together; and soon words enough had passed between them to decide their direction toward the comparatively quiet and retired gravel-walk, where the power of conversation would make the present hour a blessing indeed; and prepare for it all the immortality which the happiest recollections of their own future lives could bestow. There they exchanged again those feelings and those promises which had once before seemed to secure every thing, but which had been followed by so many, many years of division and estrangement. There they returned again into the past, more exquisitely happy, perhaps, in their re-union, than when it had been first projected; more tender, more tried, more fixed in a knowledge of each other's character, truth, and attachment; more equal to act, more justified in acting. And there, as they slowly paced the gradual ascent, heedless of every group around them, seeing neither sauntering politicians, bustling house-keepers, flirting girls, nor nursery-maids and children, they could indulge in those retrospections and acknowledgments, and especially in those explanations of what had directly preceded the present moment, which were so poignant and so ceaseless in interest.

How many other love stories are there in which the resolution is achieved in lovelier prose? But it would surely not be appropriate to write thus about the reunion of two persons whose only claim on our interest is that they are generally likeable people coming together again after a long separation. Or to write as Jane Austen did in her earlier version of the same episode, in which the scene was laid in the house of Admiral Croft: "There was time for all this to pass, with such interruptions only as enhanced the charm of the communication, and Bath could hardly contain any other two beings at once so rationally and so rapturously happy as during that evening occupied the sofa of Mrs. Croft's drawing-room in Gay Street." We are invited in both passages to share sympathetically in the lovers' new-found happiness. But the desired response is clearly more than one of sympathy merely. The happiness of Anne and Wentworth is "rational" as well as "rapturous," and it is "rational" because its basis is the fuller knowledge they have acquired since their first meeting many years before "of each other's character, truth, and attachment." It is the happiness, in short, not simply of lovers but of moral individuals—a happiness which can be achieved only by persons of superior minds and characters, and to which, consequently, when we are convinced that this is indeed the case, we tend to respond in a more complex way than to the merely "sentimental" resolutions of ordinary love tales. What we feel is an effect compounded of sympathy and moral approbation; it is not simply that a marriage is to take place, but a good marriage, of the kind we would wish all persons we particularly value to have.

Jane Austen, in short, conceived of *Persuasion* as a serious comedy: a comedy in the general sense that its plot moves from unhappiness to happiness; and a serious comedy in the sense that what makes its events interesting and moving for us is not so much their intrinsic painfulness and pleasurableness as the fact that they happen to persons for whom we have a special concern by reason of their merits as individuals. Consequently, her primary task in writing the novel was to do whatever was necessary with her materials to mold them effectively to this form, and more particularly to justify by all that she did before the climactic scene the peculiar kind and degree of emotion she clearly wished it to evoke.

But this was not all. For given her basic story as outlined above, there were obviously several ways in which she might have presented this to us. She might have begun with the original meeting of Anne and Wentworth and moved continuously from that point to the end (as she had done with the stories of *Pride and Prejudice* and *Mansfield Park*); and she might, again, have contrived a narrative that allowed us to enter as fully into Wentworth's thoughts and feelings, from the beginning on, as into Anne's. Actually, of course, she did neither of these things. We are introduced to the story only on the eve of Wentworth's return, eight years after the first engagement had been broken, so that we know of the earlier events only through the generalized narrative of chapter 4; and except in the opening exposition and in a relatively few scattered passages later on we are given no more of the events and of the thoughts of the other characters than Anne herself can know through direct observation and listening to conversations or through not always correct inference from what she sees or hears. We thus learn fully what has been going on in Wentworth's mind only after the resolution, in his long self-accusing narrative to Anne.

These were all technical decisions, but of a kind that were bound

to have a significant effect on Jane Austen's conception of her subject
and its emotional form, and hence bound to impose on her various
particular problems of invention and treatment. The plot proper of
a novel is not its story but the continuity of morally and emotionally
determinate acts, thoughts, feelings we are expected to respond to in
sequence as we read. And in *Persuasion*, by virtue of the manner in
which Jane Austen chose to shape her novel, this is the succession of
things which Anne Elliot undergoes and does with respect to Wentworth from the time of his return to the Kellynch country to her final
reunion with him in Bath. The plot, in short, centers in her rather
than in her and Wentworth conjointly: in what she does, unknow-
ingly until just before the end, merely by being herself, to draw
Wentworth gradually back to her; and in what she undergoes meanwhile in her private thoughts (there being no one to whom she can
speak of them) as she moves from the state of "desolate tranquillity"
in which we first see her, through painful agitation (when she and
Wentworth meet), more softened pain (when she thinks that he will
surely marry Louisa but remembers his growing kindness to herself),
then absorption in other interests (when she rejoins her family in
Bath), then sudden hope only half believed in (when she hears of
Louisa's engagement to Benwick), then full felicity (when she con-
vinces herself at the concert that Wentworth has "a heart returning
to her at least"), then worry (when she discovers his jealousy of Mr.
Elliot), to her final state when she enters her house after the reconciliation, "happier than any one in that house could have conceived."
The plot is bounded by these extremes of feeling in Anne; and its
emotional form is the pattern of pained suspense followed by ultimate gratification which her passage from the one extreme to the
other creates in our minds. The moving cause of her changing feelings is of course the succession of Wentworth's actions after his return, as she interprets these from time to time. But she is our primary
object of concern throughout; what Wentworth does or appears to be
doing matters to us only as it matters to her.

There is one more thing to be said about Jane Austen's subject as
thus narrowed down; namely, that Anne's breaking of the original
engagement and her reasons for doing this are not parts of the plot or
subject proper of *Persuasion:* they are necessary antecedent conditions only. The engagement had to be broken if it was to be restored,

and it had to be broken for reasons which would naturally lead Wentworth with his "decided, confident temper" to misconstrue Anne's character and in his young pride to resent what she had done. Hence Lady Russell and the nineteen-year-old Anne's sense of duty toward her. But the heroine of *Persuasion* is no longer a young girl but a mature woman approaching twenty-eight, who is both free to act and disposed to act as her own feelings and judgment dictate, independently of the friend whom she continues to love. Lady Russell is therefore the source of no suspense whatever (for the reader) in the plot: we know from the fourth chapter that Anne will surely marry Wentworth if he proposes again. The only source of suspense and delay is Wentworth himself—nothing else; certainly nothing in the respective social positions of the two or in any other external circumstance. For Wentworth, to be sure, Lady Russell and what happened eight years before *is* important, but only in his thoughts, as conditioning the state of mind in which he acts so coldly toward Anne on his return, a state of mind which pushes him into his entanglement with Louisa and which makes him fear, even toward the end, when he sees Lady Russell at the concert, that Anne may still be under her influence. But except thus subjectively for Wentworth (where it works as a "retarding weight" in the action), the whole matter of Lady Russell and of Anne's persuadability is not an issue in the plot. There are no signs, for instance, that Anne's unhappiness is in any way colored by regret for what she had done (she would have suffered more, she tells Wentworth at the end, if she had gone against her friend's advice) or by any mental conflict, such as has been attributed to her, between the claims of prudence and the claims of love.

Of the many problems of invention and treatment which Jane Austen had to face as a result of her commitment to this general view of her novel, I will touch here on only a few of the more obvious ones —enough to suggest some of the various reasons of art that appear to have governed, whether consciously or not, her detailed working out of her subject.

Like any other novelist, she faced the elementary task of giving to the happenings of her plot enough of an illusion of probability to justify, for the reader, the degree of serious concern in the action her conception of it called for. It is important to observe that, because of the nature of her plot, this was really a double problem for her. What is essential to the plot of *Persuasion,* as we have seen, is what goes on in the minds of Anne and Wentworth; that is to say, it is primarily a plot of internal action, the only strictly external actions being the final communications to one another of their mutual feelings. But before this can take place, they have to meet after their long separation and they have to see enough of each other, in different situations, to enable them either to confirm their former opinions and feelings, as with Anne, or to form new ones, as with Wentworth. Now this could be effected only through the invention of incidents, and of characters to initiate or take part in them, over and above anything that the plot itself made necessary; and in fact the greater part of what happens from chapter to chapter in *Persuasion* consists of incidents of this kind —let me call them "occasions" to distinguish them from the psychological "events" of the plot proper. Unlike the latter, they form no continuous sequence but come about independently of one another as a result of immediate and, so to speak, accidental causes: someone, for example, suggests a walking party on which Anne and Wentworth, being present, go along; or Anne goes shopping with her family in Bath and chances to meet Wentworth; or the two happen to meet, without prearrangement, at a concert. Not any occasion, however, that one might think of will do in any given novel; quite as much as the events, the occasional incidents in *Persuasion* had to be made to seem probable as happenings in that novel; but the problem they presented to Jane Austen was quite distinct from the problem of conferring "essential" probability, as it might be called, on Anne's persistence in her love for Wentworth and on Wentworth's reversal of opinion and feeling about Anne.

There are occasions of two kinds in *Persuasion.* One kind is illustrated by the examples I have just given—taking a walk, going shopping, attending the weekly concert. It is necessary that they should happen for reasons that go back to the nature of the plot and its representation; but their probability can in a sense be assumed, given the general definition of the social world in which the action takes place. We need no particularized preparation to make us accept the fact that people in the world of *Persuasion* do such things as I have mentioned—and that they also meet socially in the evening for conversation or cards, or pay visits to one another's houses, or sometimes at least, journey to places like Lyme Regis or Bath; and so on. The chief artistic problem with these ordinary occasions, I suppose, is one of variety—not inventing too many of the same kind, so that the reader fails to keep them distinct in his memory—and this was not a problem that gave Jane Austen much trouble in any of her novels.

But there are also occasional incidents in *Persuasion* of a rather more special kind. I am thinking of happenings such as Wentworth's return to Anne's neighborhood while Anne is there, Louisa's fall and concussion at Lyme Regis, and Anne's conversation with Captain Harville in the inn at Bath about constancy in men and women. These, again, are parts not of the novel's action properly speaking but merely of the external enabling circumstances in which it develops: the first is a necessary condition if this action is to begin where and when it does; the second and third help to precipitate changes in its course which would have come about in any case or might have been made to come about by other means. What distinguishes them from the other occasions I have spoken of is that they are all particular rather than customary happenings, which require, therefore, particular preparation if they are to seem to us artistically plausible.

I can consider only the first of the three. It has been objected that what brings about the new meeting of Anne and Wentworth is a series of quite shocking coincidences such as no good artist would indulge in: Sir Walter's extravagance; his acceptance of Wentworth's brother-in-law as his tenant; the sudden invitation to Anne to stay with Mary in Uppercross; Wentworth's choice of this moment to visit the Crofts, and so on. Coincidences, certainly; but are they really shocking? In any case, it is hard to see how Jane Austen could have managed the new meeting in any more tightly probable way. Given Wentworth's state of mind, she could not have made him seek the meeting deliberately; and given Anne's character and situation, she could not have made her invite him. But after all, there is nothing deeply sinful about such improbabilities in art provided our minds are diverted from dwelling on them as we read. And it seems to me that this condition is sufficiently met in the opening chapters of *Persuasion,* partly because of our ignorance until after the Crofts are introduced of what has happened in the past, partly because of the immediate interest we are made to take in Anne's relations with her father and Elizabeth and then with Mary and the Musgroves, and partly because of our hope that the coming of Wentworth may after all have happy results.

The problem of making sufficiently probable the essential internal action of the novel was inseparably bound up, for Jane Austen, with the problem of its emotional effect. What were the general conditions she had to fulfill if the reader was to respond with a maximum of appropriately serious pleasure to the happy reconciliation scenes at the end? And this in a novel of which the heroine was to be not merely the "central consciousness" but the primary object of interest?

It is clear that we will respond all the more fully in proportion, first of all, to the strength of our attachment to Anne as an individual and hence of our wishes for her happiness, and in proportion, secondly, to the completeness of our conviction that it was natural and right, in terms of both her character and Wentworth's, that she should continue to love and esteem him—in short, that a marriage with him will be a good marriage for her. And it is also clear so far as Wentworth himself is concerned, that we must be convinced that his early misunderstanding of Anne was compatible, again in terms of both her character and his, with the ultimate revival of his love in greater force than ever. To fulfill these conditions was perhaps Jane Austen's major task in the detailed making of *Persuasion,* a task partly of poetic invention and partly of rhetorical representation; and it will be worthwhile to consider by what means, and to what extent, she achieved it.

The problem of achieving it for Anne was not an easy one for two main reasons. In the first place, if Wentworth's mistake about her was not to seem wholly implausible, she had to be a woman whose virtues all lay on the quiet side: a woman with strength of character indeed, but with markedly gentle and self-effacing manners; sensible and intelligent, but not vivacious—almost the antithesis in temperament of Elizabeth Bennet in *Pride and Prejudice* and a considerably more difficult type of character to make vivid and appealing. And this difficulty was compounded, in the second place, by another and perhaps greater one. By virtue of her role in the plot, Anne had to be, until the last few chapters of the novel, a completely passive heroine and, more than that, for at least the first two-thirds of the narrative, a heroine in constantly low spirits, with nothing but cheerless prospects, as it seemed, before her; pained, without being able to do anything about it, by her family, still more deeply pained, of course, by Wentworth's real or apparent indifference. About this last, moreover, she was unable to speak to anyone, least of all to her only confidante Lady Russell; she was thus cut off from the possibility of consoling sympathy; and she had no such external outlet as the troubles of Marianne afforded Elinor Dashwood in *Sense and Sensibility*, when Elinor was in a situation similar to Anne's. A silent, solitary sufferer: how depict her so that she would not seem merely dreary and insipid to the reader? It was an exacting problem, which Jane Austen had only recently faced with Fanny Price in *Mansfield Park* and had solved with somewhat less than perfect success, I think.

That she succeeded brilliantly with Anne in overcoming both of these difficulties, there can be little question. We can surely agree with John Bailey that "there are few heroines in fiction whom we love so much, feel for so much, as we love and feel for Anne Elliot." The reason lies ultimately of course in the clarity and human warmth of Jane Austen's conception of her; but I think we can point to at least some of the devices through which she made this conception accessible and compelling for the reader. I shall speak of them under three heads, beginning with her handling of Anne's unspoken thought in the narrator's discourse. It is thus that we get all our direct insights into Anne's feelings until near the end, until, in fact, her conversation with Captain Harville at the White Hart inn. We are left in no doubt about the painfulness of these throughout the period of her estrangement from Wentworth; but the pain is, without becoming attenuated for us (which would be an error), kept from seeming excessive or monotonous by the manner of the rendering. The passages in which her suffering appears are all relatively brief; they recur at fairly long intervals only; and they represent her states of mind analytically rather than imitatively, in a fashion that suggests a certain amount of rational control and objectivity on her part, while keeping us aware that she is feeling as well as thinking. One example may serve—the summary of Anne's reflections as she is about to leave Uppercross after the episode at Lyme Regis: "Scenes had passed in Uppercross, which made it precious. It stood the record of many sensations of pain, once severe, but now softened;

and of some instances of relenting feeling, some breathings of friendship and reconciliation, which could never be looked for again, and which could never cease to be dear. She left it all behind her; all but the recollection that such things had been."

A second main device for impressing Anne on us as we need to see her is Jane Austen's invention of happenings and conversations, most of them peripheral to the main business of the novel, that define and vivify for us her positive traits of personality and character: her serious principles, her superior standards, her sound judgments of people, her ability to look at herself and others (including Wentworth) objectively, her sense of what needs to be done in an emergency, her readiness to be at the service of her friends, her capacity for happiness, her personal charm, her quiet sense of the ridiculous (notice the frequency with which, even in her days of low spirits and anxiety, she is made to smile). On some of these occasions—as notably that of Louisa's injury at Lyme, when Anne is the only one who knows what to do—Wentworth is also present and draws his own conclusions; but mostly the incidents and conversations I am thinking of are in the novel for the sake of the reader rather than of the action; they are parts not so much of the "subject" as of the "treatment," to use Henry James's distinction.

The third principal device in the depiction of Anne involves the juxtaposition of her with other characters. We form very definite and favorable judgments of her, for instance, when we see her in company with Mary or Louisa, or follow her relations with Mrs. Smith, or compare her reactions to the Christmas visit to the Musgroves or to the prospect of spending the winter in Bath or to the character of Mr. Elliot with the reactions of Lady Russell. But there are two sets of characters that the author uses as means of rendering her with particular vividness and conviction: her immediate family and the Crofts. Neither group plays any role in the central action after the very beginning, where they function merely as part of the mechanism that brings Wentworth back to Somersetshire. Yet both are given much space in the narrative, and both are delineated with considerable fullness and particularity and by a variety of means, including much direct dramatization. It would be incorrect to say that all of this is for the sake of building up and vivifying our image of Anne; but much of it clearly has this as its raison d'être. What is being impressed upon us as we read is a radical contrariety in character and personality between two worlds, in both of which we see Anne in the course of the novel.

The contrariety, it should be emphasized, is a moral rather than a social one. It is not at all a question of a decaying feudal class on the one hand and a rising middle class on the other, as several recent critics in love with such abstractions have wanted us to believe. The contrast is between people—Sir Walter, Elizabeth, Mary, Mr. Elliot, Mrs. Clay—who are cold, self-regarding, proud, calculating; and other people—Admiral and Mrs. Croft and the Harvilles—who are conspicuously pleasant, warm-hearted, self-reliant, unpretentious. We see Anne at different points through the novel first with one group and then with the other; and we see her comparing the two in her mind and being more and more strongly drawn to the second, in whom she comes to see "the frank, the open-hearted, the eager character," which she had prized beyond all others since her first meeting with Wentworth. When she goes with Lady Russell to call on the Crofts in her own home after her family have left it for Bath, she reflects that "however sorry and ashamed for the necessity of the removal, she could not but in conscience feel that they were gone who deserved not to stay, and that Kellynch-hall had passed into better hands than its owners'." Later on she sees the Crofts frequently on the streets of Bath, walking arm in arm and greeting their many friends. "Knowing their feelings as she did, it was a most attractive picture of happiness to her. She always watched them as long as she could; delighted to fancy she understood what they might be talking of, as they walked along in happy independence, or equally delighted to see the Admiral's hearty shake of the hand when he encountered an old friend, and observe their eagerness of conversation . . . , Mrs. Croft looking as intelligent and keen as any of the officers around her." And the one thing that pains her after her marriage with Wentworth is her "consciousness of having no relations to bestow on him which a man of sense could value . . . ; nothing of respectability, of harmony, of good-will to offer in return for all the worth and all the prompt welcome which met her in his brothers and sisters."

Now the function of all this in the novel, so far as Anne is concerned, is to constitute a kind of rhetorical argument from contraries, and a very effective one, I think, thanks to Jane Austen's success in convincing us artistically that the two sets of people do indeed have the qualities which Anne sees and estimates so contrastingly. We thus come to know more concretely than we otherwise could what kind of person she is, what standards she judges by, what ideal of happiness in life she cherishes, and, indirectly, what it is that has put Wentworth so high in her esteem. We are persuaded, moreover, in proportion as we are made to share her feelings about her family on the one hand and about the Crofts and Harvilles on the other, that it is with the latter rather than the former that she properly belongs. And this perception inevitably enhances our wishes for a reconciliation and our sympathetic pain so long as it seems not to be in prospect; as when, for instance, she first meets the Harvilles at Lyme. " 'These would have been all my friends,' was her thought; and she had to struggle against a great tendency to lowness."

These were some of the means—but only some—which Jane Austen brought to bear on the difficult problem of Anne. The problems she faced with Wentworth were of a rather different order, but perhaps equally great, given her evident desire to write a love story that called for something more positive than merely "sentimental" acquiescence in its dénouement. It was to be a novel the final effect of which, as we have seen, depended on our recognizing that the outcome was not merely happy but good, because of the value we set upon the lovers as moral individuals. Hence she had to convince us of the probability, in terms of Wentworth's intrinsic merits, that he should be loved as deeply and constantly as he is by a mature woman who is both discerning and strict in her judgments of characters. And the more she did to attach us to Anne, the more she had to do to vindicate Anne's attachment to Wentworth. There must at least be no obvious disproportion between the kind and degree of goodness Anne sees in him and the kind and degree of goodness we see in him. It will of course be to his favor, in our eyes, that Anne continues to feel about him as she does, for she is a person not given to illusions about others, whose affections must be grounded on esteem for intelligence and goodness of character; but we must be given some objective evidence that she is right.

The task of providing this was not an easy one on two accounts.

The story, for one thing, was to be Anne's; and this committed Jane
Austen, as she saw it, to giving us, with very few exceptions at any
point in the narrative, only what Anne herself could see, hear, conjecture, and feel. There was no possibility of taking us at all fully
within the mind of Wentworth as we are taken within Anne's mind,
and of so giving us the kind of sympathetic apprehension of *his*
thoughts and feelings, especially after these have turned decisively
back to Anne, that we get of Anne's thoughts and feelings throughout. We have to wait for this until he can finally speak, in the next
to the last chapter; which is a great limitation on what Jane Austen
could do to recommend him to us. And, for another thing, the plot
of the novel required that he should act, for some time after his
return in the seventh chapter, in a manner painfully contrary to
both Anne's wishes and ours: treating her coolly as a mere indifferent
acquaintance whom he is forced to see with the Musgroves, looking
about in a somewhat cynical spirit for a suitable girl to marry, accepting uncritically and irresponsibly the attentions of Henrietta
and Louisa, becoming entangled with the obviously inferior Louisa
without being really in love with her. The plot also required that,
after the great reversal in his judgment and feelings, he should remain away from Anne for a time and that, after his coming to Bath,
he should still, out of jealousy of Mr. Elliot, hold himself aloof until
he overhears her conversation with Captain Harville. All of which,
again, put difficulties in the way of so depicting him as to convince
us that he really possessed the high qualities of goodness and intelligence which Anne discerned in him.

How far Jane Austen overcame these difficulties, I will leave it
to others to decide; my own judgment is that Wentworth is one of
the best of her heroes: even better than Darcy; much better than
Edward Ferrars or Edmund Bertram; inferior, perhaps, only to
Knightley, who posed a much simpler problem. But whatever the
degree of her success, it is clear that she was aware of what had to
be done, and knew what kinds of devices of "treatment" would best
help her, in the circumstances of the novel, to do it. It is notable
that, except for one brief statement in the fourth chapter (where
Wentworth is said to have been, at the time of the first engagement,
"a remarkably fine young man, with a great deal of intelligence,
spirit and brilliancy"), she avoided falling back on the authority of

the narrator, possibly judging that the testimony of Anne's clear-sighted devotion would carry greater weight, as it undoubtedly does. But she obviously felt that something more was needed by way of proof; and in the novel as she finally constructed it, this something more took two main forms—the first a kind of proof by sign, the second a kind of proof by analogy.

It would clearly help to set Wentworth right for us, particularly in the earlier part of the narrative, if we could see him acting, on various occasions, in a fashion that signified not his "angry pride" but his innate kindness and intelligence. We are therefore given a series of little incidents, at Uppercross and Lyme, the main (though not always the only) function of which is to demonstrate dramatically his possession of these qualities. The first incident is the episode of the Musgroves' dead son, the worthless "poor Dick," who had been a midshipman under Wentworth some years before, and who comes back into his mother's mind when she hears of Wentworth's impending visit to the Crofts at Kellynch-hall; she is more upset by thoughts of him now than she had ever been before, and mentions him to Wentworth at the party the Musgroves give for him shortly after his arrival. The episode (in chapters 6 and 8) has been attacked as a gratuitous intrusion into the novel of Jane Austen's alleged hatred of people like Dick and his mother. Dick's worthlessness and Mrs. Musgrove's sentimentality are perhaps overplayed; but the artistic function of the incident is clear enough: it is a device for emphasizing Wentworth's intelligence and goodness of heart at the moment when we most need to perceive these virtues in him—just before and just after his painful first meeting with Anne. It is made plain that he has no illusions about "poor Dick" but has nevertheless treated him kindly at sea (before getting rid of him) and is now equally kind to Mrs. Musgrove, though he sees as clearly as Anne does the false pathos of her feelings: the boy and his mother had to be depreciated if the point about Wentworth was to come out. And much the same function of demonstrating the real Wentworth is served by other minor happenings in this early part of the novel: his conversation with the Crofts about women on shipboard (chapter 8); his quick intervention when Anne is beset by the little Musgrove boy (chapter 9); his silent rebuke of Mary's snobbishness about the

Hayters (chapter 10); his thoughtfulness in putting Anne into the Admiral's gig (chapter 10); his appreciation of her helpfulness after Louisa's accident (chapter 12). All these are examples of what we would expect from him if he is the kind of man Anne believes he is: we therefore infer that she is probably right.

The inference, of course, is immediate; it carries us at once from a felt impression to an attitude; it is, in short, artistic rather than intellectual demonstration. And the same thing is true of the other line of proof with respect to Wentworth's qualities of mind and character that runs through the whole novel. We are continually seeing him in analogical relations, both negative and positive, to other characters. Part of the function in *Persuasion* of Sir Walter Elliot, Charles Musgrove, and Mr. Elliot is to set off for us, negatively, as they explicitly do for Anne, Wentworth's superiority: we can feel as well as understand why she has rejected Charles, why she can think for only a moment of marrying Mr. Elliot (and this before she really knows about him), why she is depressed when thoughts of her father and of Wentworth come together in her mind. But the positive analogies, I think, are still more effective: how much less assurance we would have of the rightness of Anne's belief in him if the Crofts and the Harvilles had been left out of the novel or rendered less vividly and fully than they are! They are all made to seem to us not only pleasant but admirable people—sensible and intelligent, open, easy, and decided; and they are Wentworth's closest friends. We therefore insensibly argue from them to him, on the basis of what might be called the principle of goodness by association; and the argument is reinforced by the fact that they feel as warmly toward him as he does toward them. The analogy begins to work very early in the narrative. There is a clear likeness between the impression we get of the Crofts in chapter 3, before we have heard of Wentworth, and the narrator's statement about him in chapter 4. We then learn (in chapter 6) that the Crofts are looking forward to his visit and (in chapter 9) that he is coming "to Kellynch as to a home, to stay as long as he liked, being as thoroughly the object of the Admiral's fraternal kindness as of his wife's." And then we get (in chapter 12) Captain Harville's story to Anne of how Wentworth had behaved at the time of Fanny Harville's death: "You may think, Miss Elliot, whether he is dear to us!" Like can only feel thus for like; and hence we inevitably conclude that there must be something in Wentworth (which Anne has seen but which we so far cannot fully see)—some parity of good nature and good sense—that justifies these feelings for him. And so these characters—and more especially the Crofts—become stand-ins, so to speak, for Wentworth during all that long part of the novel in which he is unable to do justice to himself in our eyes, at the same time that they are continuing to attach us to Anne.

Ernest Hemingway: *"The Killers"*

Dₑₐᵣ B——:

Many thanks for your remarks on "The Killers." These have led me to think about the story again in the light both of what you say and of some notes I made several years ago after reading Brooks and Warren's "analysis" in *Understanding Fiction*. I send you the results in the hope that you will answer me if you think I am wrong.

The question I want to raise is one that has been overlooked or evaded in most of the discussions of Hemingway's tale I have read or heard. It is the technical question of how the characters, actions, and speeches of the boys in the lunchroom are related to the situation involving the killers and Ole Andreson. And it is best answered, I think, in terms of what Henry James says about the difference between "subject" and "treatment" in his Preface to *The Portrait of a Lady*. You will remember the passage: "It is a familiar truth to the novelist, at the strenuous hour, that, as certain elements in any work are of the essence, so others are only of the form; that as this or that character, this or that disposition of the material, belongs to the subject directly, so to speak, so this or that other belongs to it but indirectly—belongs intimately to the treatment."

A letter to a friend in reply to a letter from him in which he reported his experiences in discussing Hemingway's story with a class of undergraduates. Written in 1956 and not hitherto published.

303

Now the view I have taken all along, and would still take, is that Nick and his friends, and what they are made to do and say from first to last, are in "The Killers" primarily as not "of the essence" but "of the form." They belong to the "subject" of the story not directly but indirectly; they belong intimately to the "treatment," as devices of disclosure and commentary which enable Hemingway to bring his essential "subject" before us with a maximum of concentration and dramatic liveliness and a minimum of ambiguity as to its desired emotional effect. If it is hard to conceive of the story without them, that is merely a tribute to Hemingway's success in concealing the craft of its construction.

It is one thing to say this and another to prove it; and anything like full proof would require a much longer letter than I care to impose on you. But here is the general line of argument I would take.

1. To begin with, the story clearly has a "subject" (in James's sense) which is quite independent, in its structure of probabilities and events, of the boys in the lunchroom. You can forget about the occurrences in the lunchroom and still have a coherent situation that would have worked itself out precisely as it does had these occurrences never been invented—a situation of which the only necessary elements are the characters, motives, and intentions of the killers with respect to Ole, Ole's character and the state of mind in which he reacts to his present danger, and, given these two, his inevitable death. The killers are bent on murdering Ole, Ole will do nothing to prevent them, they will therefore succeed—these three facts are sufficient in themselves to constitute an intelligible story; and nothing that happens in the lunchroom and nothing the boys do or say as a result affects in any manner the course of its development. Ole escapes killing in the lunchroom merely because he has decided not to come; Nick's talk with him tells him nothing he is not already aware of and alters in no way the resolution he has already formed; and after Nick's return to his friends, there is no further thought on the part of the boys of doing anything that might change the outcome (surely, in spite of Ole, they might have called the police).

2. You get much the same result, moreover, when you consider not merely the constituents of this action but its peculiar moral and emotional quality. This is undoubtedly clarified and vivified for

us by the boys' reactions; but they in no sense create it, and it would remain, in kind if not in degree, the same quality in almost any other manner of rendering the situation between the killers and Ole that one might think of. It is plainly a situation which, however brought before us, is calculated to evoke in any reader the response expressed in George's "It's a hell of a thing" or Nick's "It's an awful thing." "The Killers" is not a merely sensational story (had this been Hemingway's conception of it he would surely have written the scene of Ole's death); it is a story, however, that exploits to the full, as its governing effect, the possibilities of shock contained in its basic materials.

It is faintly shocking that the action in prospect from the beginning is a gangster murder. It is more shocking that this is to take place in a quiet small town far removed from the normal sphere of such killings. It is still more shocking that it is being carried out, in a completely passionless and impersonal spirit ("Just to oblige a friend, bright boy"), by creatures as obnoxiously inhuman as Al and Max. And it is greatly more shocking still that the intended victim of this horrible "vaudeville team," whatever he may have done to get in wrong, is a big, friendly, and polite Swede, whom no one we meet in Summit thinks other than pleasantly of ("An awfully nice man. He was in the ring, you know").

All these are cumulatively shocking circumstances which, if there were nothing else, would go far toward justifying the boys' final reactions. But Hemingway's piling up of elements of shock goes one step farther still. Ole doesn't try to leave town or to do—or allow others to do for him—anything else that might possibly save him from Al and Max. You speak in your letter of his "courage," but is that a proper description of his state of mind? It would be if the only choice he had under the circumstances were between giving in to his physical fears and deciding to go out and face the killers. But this is not really his only choice: he could at least try to leave town, or he could encourage Nick to go and see the police. He is aware of these possibilities and has rejected them—not, I should say, because he is a courageous man, though he is that too ("After a while I'll make up my mind to go out"), but because he has fallen somehow into a state of passive despair which is not entirely beyond fear ("I just can't make up my mind to go out. I been in here all day"), but is beyond any capacity or desire to act on his own behalf as a normal man would.

"The plight of Andreson," you say, "is marvelously suggested by the repeated impressions of him turned to the wall of his bedroom, dead-end." And so it is; but his "plight" is something greatly in excess of the external danger that he knows threatens him; it is the moral "plight" of a once active man (isn't that partly the reason Hemingway makes him a one-time heavyweight prizefighter?) who has completely given up. "There isn't anything I can do about it"; "I don't want to know what they were like"; "No. There isn't anything to do"; "No . . . I'm through with all that running around"; "There ain't anything to do now"; "There ain't anything to do." There is surely something unnatural and in a high degree shocking in the state of mind which these thoughts signify—and all the more so because they are the thoughts of an otherwise normal, friendly, and "gentle" human being. Don't you feel a kind of nightmare quality in the situation, the quality of being fixed to the spot as a terrible danger we know all about rapidly approaches? It is not merely that of course; Ole's immobility also has a moral aspect: it is something he has deliberately chosen, knowing that there are other possibilities and what the outcome of his decision is bound to be and how imminent it is. And so I should say that the inevitable effect of this part of the action is not either admiration for Ole's courage or pity for his impending misfortune but rather the kind of emotion expressed in Nick's final speech: "I can't stand to think about him waiting in the room and knowing he's going to get it. It's too damned awful."

There is some further support for this view of the emotional form of "The Killers" in Hemingway's obviously deliberate vagueness about the events that must have preceded the parts of the action represented in the story. We learn from Max in the opening scene that he and Al are killing Ole just to oblige a friend; we learn from Ole that he has got in wrong and has been "running around" presumably to escape the consequences of whatever he has done; and we have George's speculations that he "must have got mixed up in something in Chicago" and probably "double-crossed somebody," because "that's what they kill them for." I suppose we can fairly conjecture that, since Ole has been a prizefighter, he very likely got in wrong by breaking an agreement with Max's "friend" to throw a fight, but we don't really know what the nature or degree of his offence was—merely that he had done something, out of good or treacherous motives, that is going to lead to his murder. These reticences, as I say, are surely part of Hemingway's design; and their function, I think, is to shift the main emphasis of the story away from causes and antecedents to the final situation resulting from these and, within this situation, to those aspects of it that are most directly provocative of the effect I have tried to define, namely, the horrifying quality of the two killers and their completely impersonal relation to Ole, and the even more "awful" quality of Ole's passive acquiescence in his fate. This is especially clear, I think, for Ole: since we don't know precisely what he has done in Chicago or exactly why he is "through with all that running around," we tend to take his final state of mind merely as a given fact and, therefore respond, all the more purely to its intrinsically shocking character; it could easily seem less shocking and more tragic or pitiable or admirable if we knew all the circumstances leading up to it. The image of Ole "waiting in the room and knowing he is going to get it" is all the more "damned awful," that is, because of the disproportion between this deliberate inactivity in the face of death and anything we know or can conjecture of its causes.

3. I come back now to the lunchroom and the boys, and to their artistic functions in relation to the killers-Ole situation. The extent to which the boys and the happenings they are directly involved in are parts of the "treatment" rather than of the "subject" will appear, I think, if we consider what takes place and what they are made to say and do in each of the four "scenes" that make up the story as Hemingway has chosen to tell it.

There is first the scene in the lunchroom—much the longest of the four—that begins with the coming of the killers and ends with their departure after Ole fails to walk into the ambush they have set for him. I should call it altogether a scene of disclosure rather than of essential action, the abortive ambush being no necessary part of the "plot" in the sense that without it the "plot" would take a different course, but a device for giving us dramatically certain requisite information. The main function of the scene is to provide us with all we need to know and feel about the killers before we learn anything about their victim except that he is "a big Swede" who sometimes comes to the lunchroom at six o'clock for his dinners and is being killed "just to oblige a friend." It is the only scene in which the killers appear, and it necessarily precedes any scene centered on Ole for the simple reason that otherwise the climactic cumulation of elements of "shock" which Hemingway apparently wanted to get would be impossible.

The course of the scene is determined wholly by the gunmen: coming in, ordering food, taking over, tying up Nick and Sam, arranging the details of the ambush, waiting, going away. It is a long scene, partly because the events cover a considerable span of time, but mainly because the impression we have to get of the killers for the sake of the effect of the story as a whole will be all the more vivid and horrifying if it is allowed to grow gradually on us. This impression is built up for the reader, in the first place, simply by the appearance and actions of the gunmen apart from anything that is said: a pantomime or silent movie would be sufficient to make us feel the sinister quality of the situation, with the killers ready, as you say, "to blow off a man's head at eight feet with a sawed-off shotgun while they eat, or just after they've eaten."

But more is required if we are to know and feel all we need to know and feel at this stage; and so we have all the talk that goes on throughout the scene between Al and Max and the boys. I say "the boys," but the scene is really, except for one or two exchanges at the start, between the two gunmen and George, Nick and Sam having very little to say before Al ties them up, gagged, in the kitchen while he prepares the ambush for Ole, after which they remain offstage and silent until the gunmen go. The role of George in the first part of the scene (as also, briefly, of Nick) is that of a butt for remarks by the gunmen that serve to vivify their peculiarly repulsive natures and arouse our curiosity as to what they are up to. George then becomes, during the middle part of the scene, primarily the asker of questions which draw gradually from Max all the information we need at this point about the intended killing, the identity of its victim, and its reasons. In the final part of the scene he serves simply to emphasize the suspense about Ole's coming and to bring the scene to a close: "Your friend, Ole Andreson, isn't going to come." He is, in short, in all parts of the scene, merely an instrument of disclosure, an eliciter of facts and impressions which we wouldn't get without someone to set the gunmen talking. He is in the scene, while Nick is not, by virtue only of the fact that he is in charge of the lunchroom and that the gunmen want to keep up normal appearances as long as possible. And if he appears to be a rather independent and insistently curious boy, and to keep his head, the reason is clearly that this is the character he has to have if he is to do for us what he does. He and the other boys are of course in danger; but this is not emphasized, and the dominant suspense of the scene, after the beginning, turns not on what may happen to them but on whether or not Ole will come.

The second short scene, involving the boys alone, reflects back chorically on the first in Nick's remarks when the towel is taken out of his mouth and especially in the frightened speeches of Sam; but what it chiefly does is to focus the suspense, and the reader's curiosity, still more clearly on Ole and to provide a probable means by which that curiosity may be satisfied. We must now have a scene in which we see Ole in the same direct manner as we have just seen the killers; and what more plausible way, in the circumstances, of giving us this than to make one of the boys in the lunchroom go to warn him? So George is made to suggest this to Nick, who is freer to go than George, and Nick, in spite of Sam's warnings and George's refusal to insist, is made to say quietly (his earlier "swagger" completely gone), "I'll go see him. . . . Where does he live?" There is no special character or feeling implied in this decision: Nick is here merely the willing messenger which the method of narration Hemingway has chosen demands at this point. Note how the extreme brevity of the passage in which he is carried from the lunchroom to the boardinghouse excludes any suspense about what may happen to him en route. The whole brief scene, apart from the retrospective choral remarks at the start, is simply a necessary mechanism for getting us as quickly as possible to Ole, while we have the killers still vividly in mind.

The third scene, in Ole's room, resembles the first in being a scene not of action or decision but of disclosure. Ole's decision has already been taken before Nick appears—he has apparently been anticipating all day the coming of the gunmen and has made up his mind what in the end he will do; and nothing in the scene suggests even the possibility of change. Hence the role of Nick here is not greatly different from that of George in the opening scene with the killers. He is no more than a necessary device for objectifying Ole's thought and feeling at this climactic stage of the situation; and he accomplishes this by putting to Ole a series of questions, such as any one might ask in the circumstances, the answers to which bring out for us with cumulative force what Ole's choice is and the state of mind in which it has been made. Nick does nothing else in this scene except to serve as an occasion for Mrs. Bell's characterizing remarks. (His mistake about her name, like his previous question to George about where Ole lives, I take to be merely a sign of his lack of personal involvement in the situation, except as a casual visitor in Summit; it is natural enough since George had said "at Hirsch's rooming-house.") The disclosure in this scene, as in the first, is also partly effected through pantomime: necessary as are Nick's questions and the short, unargued answers Ole gives to them, they would be inadequate to render the full intended effect without the objective descriptions, nine times repeated, of the big Swede lying on the bed, his face to the wall, and speaking in a "flat voice."

In the final brief scene in the lunchroom Nick is first of all a returned messenger answering the questions George naturally asks of him; and then he and George (Sam having shut the door after his one characteristic outburst) move into a short exchange of speeches on what has happened and is certain to happen and on how bad it is and how especially awful is the thought of Ole "waiting in the room and knowing he's going to get it." There is nothing in these speeches that goes beyond what any normal person would inevitably wonder and feel who had seen what the two boys have seen. The boys, in fact, are simply acting here as a two-part chorus; and the only differences I can detect between them are that Nick has actually watched Ole "waiting" whereas George has not, and that Nick *can* get out of town while George is tied to his job. They start, you will note, on exactly the same theme: George's "It's a hell of a thing" and Nick's "It's an awful thing"; and this unity of feeling is further suggested in the pause that immediately follows: "They did not say anything. George reached down for a towel and wiped the counter." And thereafter if any distinction has to be made between the two, it is one of technical function in relation to the final effect of the story. Nick's "I'm going to get out of this town" and his "I can't stand to think about him," accentuate the immediate shock we must all feel at what has happened. The last two speeches of George— "Yes, . . . that's a good thing to do" and "Well, . . . you better not think about it"—while reflecting the same shock, point to the only catharsis the story can have: get it out of your mind! But these are both good traditional choric functions.

The boys, then, and all that happens to them and all that they say and do on their own and all that we are given of their characters seem to me pretty completely explicable on the theory I started out with— that they belong directly to Hemingway's "treatment" and only indirectly to his "subject." The technical peculiarity of "The Killers" lies in the fact that the functions of disclosure and commentary usually embodied in a single narrator, in whose words and through whose thoughts the essential action is told, are here embodied in a secondary action (presented objectively, without any explicit narrator) which, though set in motion by the main action, has a certain continuity and direction of its own. The boys decide, that is, once the gunmen have left, to do what they can to save Ole, and so Nick goes to see him and then returns to report to George what he has learned. This is an action, and it is the only action in the story which we follow step by step from beginning to end; the events and crises of the essential "plot" all happen offstage, either before the beginning or after the end of the action involving the boys. We follow this action of theirs, however, with questions in our minds that focus our attention not on the boys but on the killers and Ole: What are the two men up to? Will Ole come? What will he do if Nick gets to him in time? And the resolutions of these questions in each of the successive scenes, though given us through the actions of the boys, are merely the necessary discoveries *we* must make if we are to grasp the situation between the killers and Ole and respond to it with the emotions it demands. The action involving the boys is thus primarily a sequence, expertly contrived, of expository and choric devices, in which the boys help to elicit for us the facts of the central situation and to define their human import. I have just indicated some of the ways in which they do this by their questions and comments in the successive scenes. But their usefulness to the story also depends rather importantly, I think, on the general character Hemingway gives them. We surely feel all the more vividly the horrible abnormality both of the killers themseves and of Ole's reaction to their coming because of the contrasting qualities ascribed to George and Nick as ordinary decent boys in an ordinary lunchroom in an ordinary small town. And the effect on us of Ole's decision is surely all the more startling because we have been prepared for something quite different by the boys' perfectly normal expectation that if he is warned in time he will at least try to save his life.

4. Whatever the limitations of the preceding hypothesis, it seems to me to account for the facts of "The Killers" more plausibly and to do greater justice to its technical merits than the view (stated most fully perhaps by Brooks and Warren) which makes Nick Adams the central character of the tale and defines its primary action as the sudden discovery by him, through his contact with the killers and Ole, of the "reality of evil." It is assumed, in this view, that Nick is a somewhat naive boy who has known about such things as gangster killings only at second hand from the newspapers or the movies, and who now undergoes the shock of seeing what they are like in actuality, with the result that the episode marks a crucial stage in his passage from adolescence to manhood, a kind of initiation into life as it is. And it is further assumed that the function of George and Sam, as persons presumably more mature from the beginning, is to highlight by contrast the change in Nick.

There are two objections to this theory. In the first place, I can't see that Nick makes any such discovery as Brooks and Warren suppose. He does indeed pass from ignorance to knowledge, but the knowledge he attains at the end is not at all of "the reality of evil" but simply of the much more particular fact, which inspires his final "It's too damned awful," that Ole is going to allow himself to be killed. The discovery, that is, is not of anything he didn't know before because he has had only a boy's experience of life but of something peculiar to the very special situation depicted in this story. What he learns we also learn, and it is as unexpected to us as to him —and just as "awful."

In the second place, I can find no evidence in the text that Nick is intended to impress us as the central character of the story. We are not allowed or compelled to focus our attention on him, in any special way, until he goes at George's suggestion to see Ole; in that scene he is merely an impersonal messenger asking questions that have the effect of vivifying not himself but Ole; and in the final scene he merely expresses the emotion which anyone would feel about what Ole was going to do. He is depicted, moreover—and this is true also of the other boys—with less particularity and sharpness of outline than either the killers or their victim.

So I come back to my view that Nick in this story—whatever may be true of some of the other stories in which he appears—is a utility character in Hemingway's rendering of an action with which Nick has nothing essential to do. He is in no sense a protagonist figure, and as a character in the "treatment" he is no more prominent or central than George. He is before us, in fact, much less of the time than George is; he says much less; and he is not any more vividly depicted. It is easy, too, to exaggerate the differences between the two boys. They react to the coming of the killers in the same way: " 'What's the idea?' Nick asked. . . . 'What's the idea?' George asked"; and their summing up at the end, as I have said, shows a similar parallelism of feeling. I don't mean that there are not differences, but they amount very largely, I think, to differences in expository function. Each boy, that is, has his own special job to do in disclosing to us Hemingway's "subject" in its two essential aspects: George to help us understand and feel the killers, Nick to give us Ole. This division of labor, how-ever, is not determined by any basic difference of character but sim-ply by the fact that George must stay in the lunchroom while Nick, as a visitor, is free to move about. It is commonly said that Nick's re-sponses are more naive than George's; but the only signs of this I can see are his exclamation after the towel is taken from his mouth (" 'What the hell?' He was trying to swagger it off") and his question to George at the end about what Ole had done. These are certainly not much to go on; and their effect is offset by the fact that in the scene with Ole the questions Nick asks reflect every bit as mature a grasp of the possibilities of the situation as anything said by George in the scene with the killers. (Can you think, in fact, of any sugges-tions that George or any one of us might have made to Ole in this situation which Nick does not make?) A striking thing about the be-havior of both boys in the story—Nick as well as George—is the rela-tive quickness with which they catch on to what is happening and the good sense with which, once the facts are clear, they act on their knowledge. Both have precisely that degree of knowingness at any moment—no more or no less—that is required to disclose the facts to us with appropriate suspense and to determine our reactions to them: you can see this by tracing step by step the behavior of George in the opening scene and that of Nick in the scene with Ole. Therefore I can see no reason for thinking that Nick is more central to the narrative and its effect than George. The narrative that gives us the story is the joint result of what two boys say, do, and think (plus the recurrent choric exclamations of Sam), just as the story they give us is the joint result of the killers' deadly impersonal mission and of Ole's "waiting and knowing he's going to get it."

Ernest Hemingway: "The Short Happy Life of Francis Macomber"

MY DEAR M——:

I am very grateful to you for sending me the three papers on "The Short Happy Life of Francis Macomber." I have read them with much interest, and with only two major reservations.

One of these has to do with your attempt to interpret Macomber as an "Aristotelian" tragic hero. This came as a surprise after your earlier statements about the plot. With these I largely agree. Like you, I think that the action begins with Macomber "in his lowest condition" and proceeds to his achievement, for a brief moment before his death, of a "happiness" greater than he had ever known before; as you put it, he is transformed from an *object* into a *man*. The essential change is thus not one of fortune but of moral character. For such a change the appropriate response of the reader is obviously a pleasurable rather than a painful one, that is, some degree of rejoicing dependent on the depth of "unhappiness" from which the man has risen, and on the suddenness of the change. That something like this is what we are intended to feel for Macomber is suggested by the reactions of Wilson

---

Written in 1949 as a letter to a former student who had sent me, for comment, essays on Hemingway's story by himself and two of his colleagues in the Freshman English staff of his university; published in the third edition of *Readings for Liberal Education*, edited by Louis G. Locke, William M. Gibson, and George Arms (New York: Rinehart & Company), © 1957 by the editors; reprinted here with some modifications by permission of the editors and publisher.

315

in the paragraph beginning, "He was very embarrassed" and in his remark at the end to Margot, "I'd begun to like your husband."

All this you say or imply in the concluding paragraphs of your first section, and here at least you don't treat Macomber's death as a tragic catastrophe, although I think you fail to make sufficiently clear what its relation is to the "emotional satisfaction" of which you correctly say that the "change in Macomber's life is . . . a principal cause." Plainly the answer turns in part on how we construe the act of Margot which brings her husband's "short happy life" to a sudden end; and I am puzzled by W——'s contention, with which you appear to agree, that Hemingway meant to leave us in doubt whether the killing was accident or murder and that this very uncertainty constitutes "the finest artistic touch in the story." I should say, on the contrary, that if "suspension of judgment" about the cause of Macomber's death is the intended final state of mind of the reader, then Hemingway has bungled his job. For the climactic emotion in that case becomes a species of wonder, much as in trick stories like "The Lady or the Tiger"; our attention, moreover, is shifted away from Macomber, who up to this point has been the major object of our feelings, and concentrated on Margot, who is suddenly turned into a lady of mystery, with the result that all the reiterated signs of her emotions and intentions during the buffalo hunt become retrospectively ambiguous; and, finally, the doubt about Margot is extended to Wilson, who certainly gives every appearance of being certain about the facts—and what then becomes of our confidence in him as a trustworthy chorus which has been built up through the story? Can we suppose that now, and for the first time, he is wrong in his judgment of Margot? But the whole idea is untenable except on the supposition that Hemingway was no artist or a deliberately irresponsible one.

In spite of the narrator's statement that "Mrs. Macomber . . . had shot at the buffalo" and so on, I think we can no less easily rule out the possibility of accident. To begin with, the theory of accident implies an intention on Margot's part to save Macomber's life, and such an intention doesn't accord either with what we have been led to believe about her character from the beginning or with the clear indications of her growing hatred for her husband in the immediately preceding scene; and, for another thing, it implies that the outcome of her act was determined merely by chance, and there are no previous instances of this sort of probability in the story. (The last objection can also be brought against E————'s suggestion of "unconscious motivation." Where in the narrative up to this point are the motives of the agents ever presented except as conscious ones deriving from relatively simple states of passion?) But there is also a further and more important objection, which will appear when you ask how our feelings would be affected if we really thought that the killing of Macomber was accidental. Wouldn't the inevitable effect be to arouse some degree of pity for Margot at least at the moment when we see her "crying hysterically" over her husband's body, and hence to make us resent the rough handling of her by Wilson? But I can't think that any reader ever reacted in this way; and we don't so react because, as we are reading the story, we never seriously entertain the notion of accident.

We must suppose, then, either that Hemingway didn't know his business or that Macomber was murdered by his wife. But if he was murdered, why do we continue to feel toward him at the end of the story the "emotional satisfaction" which I agree with you is the effect on us of his final achievement of courage? Or why is it that, although we experience a painful shock when we come abruptly, at the end of the sentence telling us of his victorious stand against the buffalo, to the clause "and he felt . . . ," the shock we then feel is momentary only and the pain never becomes the pity which we normally feel for victims of murder when they are good men whom we know vividly? I think the reason is partly to be found in certain tricks of technique by which, in the first place, our attention is centered so wholly on Macomber and the buffalo during the last stages of the hunt that we don't think of danger from any other source, and by which, in the second place, as soon as Macomber has fallen, our thoughts are turned away from him to Wilson and Margot. But the causes lie also in the plot itself. We tend to feel pity at the murder of anyone whose destruction seems to involve waste or who appears to have unexhausted possibilities of "happiness" or possibilities of greater "happiness" in the future. But Macomber is clearly not so conceived. Within the story he is only (a) the ineffective husband of a "predatory" wife and (b) such a man engaged in an African safari—in short, one who satisfies completely all our expectations and hopes when he finally dominates Margot and acts without fear as a hunter. Once this climax is reached he has done the best that is in him, and we have no active desire that he should live on; or rather, as you shrewdly suggest, we take his death as in some sense necessary to our full appreciation of his victory over himself—he is so ordinary a creature that had he survived, the perfection of the moment might well have been spoiled. Again, no matter how nobly a man acts on the eve of his death, we still pity him as long as we think of his courageous act as something done in spite of a natural human aversion to dying. But this is ruled out for Macomber by the very nature of his victory over his previous fear, and here once more, as you point out, Wilson serves as chorus (note his words in the passage beginning " 'You know, I'd like to try another lion,' Macomber said"). Finally, not only is Macomber's death part of his moral triumph, it marks also the complete and deserved defeat of his wife; she has got rid of her husband only to fall under the power of Wilson; and our satisfaction at this, aroused in the concluding dialogue, effectively counteracts our momentary shock at the murder.

But if all this is true, isn't it quite misleading to analogize Macomber to the "Aristotelian" tragic hero? I should think that you would have been more struck by the essential differences between the two than by their superficial likenesses as protagonists who suffer death in serious actions. "Tragedy," as Aristotle defines it in *Poetics* 13 and 14, is a very special plot form, which has been fully achieved, I think, only by a few of the Greeks and by Shakespeare in some of his major works, notably *Hamlet, King Lear,* and *Othello.* Its distinguishing pleasure is a catharsis of fear and pity, the peculiar "tragic" quality of which is determined by the other causes which Aristotle specifies in these two chapters. The formal cause is a change of fortune rather than of character (though this may also be involved) from good to bad, resulting from an unjust deed, productive of great pain and suffering, committed by the protagonist on a friend or friends, as a consequence of which the protagonist himself is ruined; the material cause is a hero of the intermediate type, not bad but not "preeminently virtuous and just," though within these limits better rather than worse, and also preferably (for then the change will seem all the more impressive) one who enjoys at the beginning great "reputation and prosperity"; and the efficient cause, located in the moral choices of the protagonist, is a course of action motivated not by evil intent but by *hamartia,* that is, a fundamental error with respect to the circumstances of the situation which is yet compatible with goodness of character, so that though the hero acts voluntarily, the evil results of his acts are non-voluntary and he himself suffers more deeply than any of his victims. When all these conditions are fulfilled in the construction of a plot, the effect for the normally sensitive spectator is tragic fear and pity; and this effect will be enhanced if the change of fortune comes about suddenly and unexpectedly and is accompanied or followed by a change from ignorance to knowledge that reverses the attitudes of the major characters to one another and also, in the best tragedies, to themselves.

But how completely different from this is the plot form of "The Short Happy Life"! The change upon which the effect depends is not a change of fortune from good to bad but of character from bad to good. It comes about as a result of action by the hero (in the buffalo hunt) which involves no injustice, has no destructive effects on anyone who is dear to him, and proceeds not from error concerning the circumstances but from a wholly praiseworthy cause, his conquest of fear. The decision to go on the hunting trip may have been, as you suggest, a mistake; but it is merely one of the given conditions of the plot, not a primary factor in its development or in the determination of our emotions before and at the climax, as is always the case with tragic *hamartia.* Macomber's suffering before the buffalo hunt, moreover, has its source not in any sense of erroneous or misdirected action (as in Oedipus or Hamlet) but in shame at his own bad conduct in the face of the lion. The only mistake that functions in the plot is that of Margot, for which she pays in the end; but this is not "tragic" either in its motivation or in its results for Macomber; and Margot, in any case, is not the protagonist. (If she had been, a very different plot form would have resulted, but it would not have been "tragic" either.) The only thing, in short, that Hemingway's tale has in common with tragedy, in Aristotle's sense, is that issues of life and death are involved in the change it depicts. But they are involved in such a way that we do not experience fear for Macomber as he proceeds to assert his new-found courage or pity for him when he falls.

Parenthetically, I think that the antecedents and circumstances of the lion hunt are also "conditions"; the action proper begins with the immediate consequences of the hunt in Margot's act of kissing Wilson and in Macomber's shame. Therefore, it seems to me, there is only one formal peripety—Macomber's unexpected coming of age; the murder is a peripety only in a material sense, its formal significance, as I said before, being inseparable from that of Macomber's final act. Because of the nature of the action the only possible kind of discovery is self-discovery, and this occurs when Macomber recognizes that he no longer fears death. There are plenty of "discoveries" to the reader besides the one you mention, but these are not discoveries in a poetic sense, since they proceed not from the events of the plot but from Hemingway's decisions about what he must disclose to the reader and when.

My second reservation about the essays concerns the adequacy of their analytical apparatus. A critic among other things ought to be able to say how successful artistically—as a constructed whole—"The Short Happy Life" really is and to give relevant reasons for his judgment. This necessitates his finding answers to three main questions: How good is Hemingway's plot in producing the kind of pleasure intended? How effectively is it brought before the reader in the words of the story? and How well adjusted to the specific requirements of the plot are the subordinate parts of characterization, thought, and language?

Of these three questions only the first is touched upon in the essays, and it is dealt with for the most part in a fashion that doesn't permit of a critical appraisal of the story. Except for one place in your paper, the three of you are more concerned with the underlying matter of Hemingway's plot than with the plot itself considered as an artistic construction. It is true that you all look for the form of this matter, that is, what holds its successive parts together. But the direction in which you look for it takes you away from the story viewed as a sequential whole with a particularized system of suspense and surprise, and leads to the discovery not of a plot, in the strict sense of the principle that organizes the action and gives to it its peculiar emotional quality, but of some general "pattern" of human conduct in terms of which the things done and thought by Hemingway's characters can be made abstractly intelligible. For E—— the pattern is given by his conception of Macomber as a neurotic egoist who finally frees himself "from the incubus of his heroic self-portrait"; and he has some difficulty in adjusting to this what he calls "the most complicated dilemma of the story," the question whether the Macomber marriage is or is not "spiritually dead." For W—— the story is essentially an instance of the behavior of "predatory" creatures seeking "advantages" over one another in a "predatory" world. For you the dominant pattern is one which you take to be central in many or most of Hemingway's writings: the problem of how different kinds of men face death. The three of you come out, in other words, in spite of your protests of mutual agreement, with three perceptibly different "plots"! I don't doubt that the story rests on a material substrate of ideas and unconscious associations that can be interpreted, without doing complete violence to the text, in some or perhaps all of these ways. A plot, however, is more than its substrate of ideas or beliefs; it is the form that actually synthesizes the materials and successive incidents of an individual story and hence, as we infer it progressively from the writer's words, determines the sequence of our emotions with respect to the characters and the changes they undergo.

The difficulty is that the essays tend to approach the story in terms of preestablished formulas applicable to many stories rather than by way of close attention to the successive effects which Hemingway, in this story, is engaged in producing. You are something of an exception, as I have said, and as a result you come nearer to seeing what the form of the story is (in the sense of the working on us of its particularized action) than do your colleagues, who seem to me to be talking about the plot in more or less complete separation from the special sequence of emotions which is at once its artistic end and the principal source of the criteria whereby, at least as a constructed whole, it ought to be judged. I wish, however, that you had elaborated your insight in relation to the peculiar correlation of character and event that produces the effect you recognize and had then gone on to say something about how successful, in the light of its form, you think Hemingway's construction is.

On the first point something might be made of an aspect of the story that struck me when I reread it the other day. Part of the effect depends, I think, on the fact that there has been a long literary tradition of characters like Macomber, cuckolds in subjection to their wives who are also, in moments of physical danger, cowards. Until the middle of the nineteenth century such characters for the most part were comic butts. Then, in various novels and plays, their traits and actions were employed to produce "naturalistic" effects of sordidness or the like. In the twentieth century they (and other similar characters, like alcoholics and ineffectives generally) have often been given the status of protagonists in serious plots, in which a certain impression of nobility is sought by making them unexpectedly act or speak like heroes. I think this is Hemingway's central idea in "The Short Happy Life," as something not greatly different is Eliot's idea in "Prufrock" and Graham Greene's in *The Confidential Agent*. On this view of the story, the function of Wilson in the plot, as distinguished from his technical function as chorus, becomes evident: part of Macomber's triumph is the admiration his action elicits from his latest cuckolder! And so too with Margot. The state of her marriage is not a problem in the sense of being material to the unifying suspense —it is merely one of the preconditions of the action; and Margot's role in the plot is threefold: she is a sign of her husband's initial degradation, the immediate occasion of the hate which frees him from fear, and finally the instrument that makes his heroism complete.

As for the virtues and weaknesses of the plot, I should like to have had your opinion on two points. One is the manner in which Margot's shooting of her husband is related to the previous events. The moral probability is strong enough, but what about the probability that she will have the gun? Is it good enough to support the intended seriousness of the final effect? The other point is more important. I have often thought that the power of the story is considerably attenuated by the fact that the change in Macomber, which ought to have something of the quality of a miracle (it surprises and embarrasses Wilson), is rather too easily foreseeable from the beginning. Macomber has begun as an abject coward and a slave to Margot: what else can he now do except what he does—namely, get over his fear and in so doing emancipate himself from his wife? I grant that there is plenty of suspense during the buffalo hunt, but it turns only on the physical danger, not at all on the complexity of the central action. The plots of the best short stories are not as obvious as this. And there is finally the question of how seriously, in the moral sense, we can take the action as a whole in spite of its fatal ending. Macomber himself, I can't help thinking, is too commonplace a creature to excite in us any strong wishes, on his own account as an individual, that he should rise from the low state in which we first see him. I agree with you that we feel a certain "emotional satisfaction" when he does, but I wonder if this is not to be accounted for by a combination of two things that have little to do with the particularity of his character: our general disposition to take pleasure in any sudden access of virtue in human beings even when, as persons, they are indifferent to us; and our detestation of Margot and consequent desire that whatever would most frustrate and displease her should happen in the story. The effect produced by the change in Macomber is thus of the relatively inferior order which we properly call "sentimental"; it is certainly, for me at least, less "serious" than is (say) the generically similar effect aroused by the emergence of good sense in Jane Austen's Emma.

For an adequate judgment of Hemingway's success, however, it is necessary to go beyond the plot and, holding this constant, to ask about how the story is told. This, you will see, is our old problem of representation as distinct from what is represented, or, in James's words, of "treatment" as distinct from "subject." It concerns all the devices a writer employs, vis-à-vis his audience, for the sake of inducing a proper judgment of the emotional quality, the probability, or the importance of the things going on in his plot when this would not be evident from a simple and direct presentation of them. The sources from which the devices derive are common to rhetoric and poetics, but since the final end to be served is a certain poetic pleasure determined primarily by the construction of the plot, the criteria for judging the success of any representational device must be drawn from a prior consideration of what the plot and its peculiar "power" are intended to be. You were right therefore to center your first discussion of Hemingway's tale on its action; what I regret is that you did not then proceed to the further question of how well the plot form, as you conceive it, is clarified and sustained by the narrative.

Looked at from this point of view, "The Short Happy Life" is not, it seems to me, one of Hemingway's most expert jobs. Consider the manner in which Macomber's behavior during the lion hunt is made clear to us. We see it first in terms of the effects of his cowardice on himself, his wife, and Wilson (to say nothing of the servants), and then, in a "flashback" that takes off from Macomber's thoughts that night, we are given the incident itself in full and vivid detail. As an expedient for forcing us to attend closely to what has happened before the story proper begins, this inverted order of narration is effective enough, though a bit shopworn. But think of what the result is for our opinion of the hero. If the story is indeed one in which Macomber passes suddenly (in your phrase) "from *object* to *man*" and if the function of Wilson, in relation to this, is to provide the "norm" by which we are intended to evaluate the change, then clearly nothing should be done in the narrative that will obscure this view of the case. Now I think we do become more or less convinced during the opening scene that Macomber is "less of a man and more of an object than ever before" and that Wilson, if not Margot, is probably right in judging him as severely as he does. But then we learn for ourselves what has actually happened earlier in the day, and I think he would be a rather exceptional reader who could feel quite sure that, if he were put into the same fearsome circumstances as Macomber, and with no more previous experience with African lions, he would not, like Macomber, suddenly find himself "running wildly, in panic in the open, running toward the stream." It may be, as you suggest, that Hemingway wishes us to think of Macomber, in this situation, as "less . . . even as an *object,* than the lion itself"; and this may be the reason for the otherwise somewhat arbitrary glimpses he gives us into the lion's thoughts. But if so, the device surely misses the mark, with the result that so far from thinking that Wilson's previously indicated contempt has been warranted by the facts, we now tend to feel that he and his professional code are below humanity in a sense in which Macomber's regrettable but wholly natural "cowardice" is not. I repeat that I don't think this is a part of the plot as Hemingway conceived it; about that you seem to me to be right. But certainly to the extent that you are right, Hemingway is wrong! Either he should not have told the story of the lion hunt at all or he should have told it in such a way as to confirm rather than contradict the impression of Macomber's initial moral state which he had been careful to fix in our minds at the start.

It seems to me also that in several parts of his narrative Hemingway has resorted too much to inferior and makeshift devices for keeping the reader aware of what is going on. What we are led to expect from the opening pages is an objective and dramatic rendering of events in the manner, for instance, of "The Killers," and I can see no reason why the whole story could not have been told in this way. The device is modified, however, in the course of the first scene, by the singling out of Wilson as a kind of observer-chorus whose inferences and judgments about Macomber and Margot are given to us in brief asides. This has some obvious advantages, and entails no great sacrifice of that economy of representation on which Hemingway always prided himself; and if he had been content to do the later scenes in a technique consistent with this beginning, there would be nothing more to say. But then comes the scene of the lion hunt as recollected by Macomber lying on his cot, and here the crudities begin. Observe the flat narrative statements about how Macomber felt as he listened to the night noises; the shift to the lion's perceptions when the motor car reached the place and the later return to these as the beast is about to spring; the amateurish "He could not know that Wilson was furious because he had not noticed . . ."; and lastly the two paragraphs on the marriage, in which Macomber's reflections are allowed to merge, not imperceptibly, into mere historical report.

And what is done in the final scene of the buffalo hunt is even worse, except that we are spared a look into the buffalo's mind. The scene starts in the manner of the first, with Wilson as chorus in an otherwise dramatic rendering. But this method presently breaks down, and we get many direct statements of thought and feeling not only for Macomber but, in one or two places toward the end, even for Margot, who has hitherto been merely heard and seen (note "but her contempt was not secure. She was very afraid of something" and "Because she had done the best she could for many years back and the way they were together was no one person's fault"). Most of these statements seem to me superfluous in view of what is obviously going on, or, when they serve a purpose, to be clumsy explicit notations of things that could be better shown dramatically. The worst are the reiterated assertions, in the narrator's flat prose, of Macomber's "happiness": "he had no fear, only hatred of Wilson"; "Macomber felt a drunken elation"; "In his life he had never felt so good"; "For the first time in his life he really felt wholly without fear. Instead of fear he had a feeling of definite elation"; and so on. Hemingway at his best would have left all this to the reader's inference, as he does similar things in "The Killers," and he would never have printed a passage like the following:

Macomber felt a wild unreasonable happiness that he had never known before.

"By God, that was a chase," he said. "I've never felt any such feeling. Wasn't it marvellous, Margot?"

There is in all this little of the concision we appreciate in Hemingway's better work, and the result is a watering down of the effect proper to this crucial part of the story; there is a certain jarring incongruity, too, between the commonplace flavor of Macomber's thoughts as the narrator states them and the relatively heroic quality of his actions. I can explain these lapses only by supposing that, having begun to write like himself in the opening section, Hemingway then suddenly became conscious of the limited intelligence, in matters of art, of his prospective readers in the *Cosmopolitan* magazine!

Index

Index